SCIENCE ENCOUNTERS THE INDIAN, 1820–1880

Science Encounters the Indian, 1820–1880

The Early Years of American Ethnology

BY ROBERT E. BIEDER

THE UNIVERSITY OF OKLAHOMA PRESS
NORMAN AND LONDON

This book has been published with the aid of a grant from the
Andrew W. Mellon Foundation.

Library of Congress Cataloging-in-Publication Data

Bieder, Robert E. (Robert Eugene), 1938–
    Science encounters the Indian, 1820–1880.

    Bibliography: p. 253
    Includes index.
    I. Indians of North America—Study and teaching—
United States—History. 2. Ethnology—United States—
History. I. Title.
E76.6.B54   1986   973'.0497'0072073   86–40068
ISBN 0–8061–1995–0 (alk. paper)

For
my mother
and to
the memory of my father

Contents

List of Illustrations

Preface

I cannot bring the world quite round,
Although I patch it as I can.

I sing a hero's head, large eye
And bearded bronze, but not a man,

Although I patch him as I can
And reach through him almost to man.

—Wallace Stevens, "The Man with the Blue Guitar"

ONCE, in an essay on nineteenth-century anthropology, George W. Stocking bemoaned the rather narrow scope of studies on the historical concept of classical evolution as it affected anthropological theory. Too often, he pointed out, such studies confined themselves merely to major figures in the pantheon of anthropology. He also identified another problem. These studies did not adequately consider the larger historical context in which ethnological and anthropological thought developed.

As a historian interested in the history of anthropology, I was intrigued with exploring this larger context. I chose to study the early and middle years of the nineteenth century partly because of my own fascination with the intellectual currents of the period and partly because these years constitute a period that Stocking has termed the "Dark Ages" of American anthropology. I wanted to discover what had happened to the concept of progress (sometimes referred to as developmentalism) that was so much a feature of eighteenth-century studies of man and society and that again assumed importance in the late nineteenth century under the term *evolution*. This study explores evolutionary concepts in the works of several prominent students of ethnology and in the writings of several others less conversant with the field. Since race and environment proved popular topics for speculation in the early nineteenth century, they were widely discussed in both the scientific and the popular press of the day. In each chapter I have attempted to employ these popular accounts along with those of lesser-known students of ethnology as a setting against which the works of more prominent figures in the science can be measured. Although some may disagree with my sampling of the popular literature and feel that I have not brought a "world quite round," I believe that I have expanded the universe about which Stocking was concerned.

Because I see the influence of American Indians as a force in the development of American ethnology and anthropology, I realize that no adequate history of these fields can be written apart from a consideration of their role. During my youth in upstate New York and time spent among the Iroquois, I early learned of the contribution of Lewis Henry Morgan to Iroquois studies. It was my experiences among Seneca and Mohawk friends and especially with John Fadden, with whom I walked on cold winter nights in Rochester and talked of Iroquois culture and history, that served, subliminally at least, to direct this study. And so I first thank these friends.

Footnotes do not adequately convey my full indebtedness to those to whom I owe so much. Many scholars, some uncited, have shared freely with me their ideas and provided stimulation and encouragement. Many will undoubtedly recognize their contribution. To these friends—Robert F. erkhofer, Jr.; E. Adamson Hoebel; David W. Noble; eorge W. Stocking, Jr.; Raymond D. Fogelson; Regna Darnell; Peter Powell; and Sherene Baugher—who have ead all or part of this work in one draft or another and whose perspicacious comments were generously given, I am indeed grateful. Their contributions expanded and clarified my original thesis and have improved this work.

Others have aided immeasurably through their backing

and support. Three years at the Newberry Library's Center for the History of the American Indian and discussion with the center's fellows, especially Martin Zanger, Peter Iverson, R. David Edmunds, and Bea Medicine, were most helpful. A Fulbright lectureship in Germany in 1980–81 and subsequent lectures in Europe allowed me the opportunity to present chapters and discuss my ideas with friends at the University of Mainz, the University of Frankfurt, the University of Exeter, the University of Paris, the University of Provence, and the University of Basel. These occasions proved most enjoyable and helpful. An opportunity to test some of my ideas with the students of Frederick Churchill's graduate seminar on biological and anthropological conceptions of race proved both pleasurable and beneficial.

No study of this kind can be done without the assistance of numerous librarians. Besides the staffs of those many libraries and archives listed in my notes, I extend special thanks to Lawrence W. Towner, John Aubrey, and Michael Kaplan, of the Newberry Library; Murphy Smith, of the American Philosophical Society; and Karl Kabelac, of the Rush Rhees Library, University of Rochester.

I also appreciate the financial support that aided the research for this project. Generous support from the Ford Foundation, the American Philosophical Society, and a Newberry Library postdoctoral fellowship are gratefully acknowledged.

Finally, I would like to thank Sandra Herzog, who typed the manuscript, the editorial staff of the University of Oklahoma Press, and my wife, who heard much more about this subject than she ever wished to hear.

Bloomington, Indiana   ROBERT E. BIEDER

SCIENCE ENCOUNTERS THE INDIAN, 1820–1880

Abbreviations Used in the Notes

APS   American Philosophical Society
BHC   Burton Historical Collection, Detroit Public Library
BLY   Beinecke Library, Yale University
BPL   Boston Public Library
HEH   Henry E. Huntington Library
LCP   Library Company of Philadelphia
MHS   Massachusetts Historical Society
NA   National Archives
NLS   National Library of Scotland, Edinburgh
NL   Newberry Library
NYHS   New York Historical Society
SI   Smithsonian Institution Archives
UR   Rush Rhees Library, University of Rochester
WCL   William Clement Library, University of Michigan

1

Introduction

THE STORY of five blind men describing an elephant delighted generations of children. Although one may smile at the paradoxical nature of the tale—all the blind men were partly correct, but all were wrong—there are aspects of the story that correspond to the way nineteenth-century ethnologists contemplated American Indians. Most of the ethnologists, like the blind men, generalized from particulars. Few recognized differences between tribes or disagreed with the popular notion that having seen one Indian you had seen them all. Likewise, as each blind man defined the elephant in terms of previous experience and hence according to familiar objects, so also did ethnologists allow their descriptions of Indians and their cultures to be colored by a priori theories and assumptions.

These assumptions on man, on races of man, on theories of origins, and on concepts of progress and degeneration inherited from Europe greatly affected the development of American ethnology. Americans, however, did not accept European theories uncritically. Indeed, in many ways ethnology in the United States originated as a patriotic reflex in sharp disagreement with certain European thinkers.[1]

[1] The defense of American environment and inhabitants is clearly seen in Thomas Jefferson, *Notes on the State of Virginia* (1787); Samuel Stanhope Smith, *An Essay on the Causes of the Variety of Complexion and Figure in the Human Species* (1810), ed. Winthrop Jordan. [Smith published a briefer edition of this essay in 1787]; Benjamin Smith Barton, "Essay Toward a Natural History of the North American Indian," *Dissertations of the Royal Medical Society of Edinburgh* 23 (1788–89): 1–17; Benjamin Rush, *An Inquiry into the Natural History of Medicine Among the Indians of North America: and A Comparative View of Their Diseases and Remedies With Those of Civilized Nations* [read before the American Philosophical Society, February 4, 1774]; Thomas Jefferson, *The Papers of Thomas Jefferson*, ed. Julian P. Boyd, 8:

Americans objected to the disparaging comments of Europeans claiming the existence of degenerate life-forms in America and especially the inferiority of American Indians and their cultures. Although European images of Indians often proved ambivalent, these images were rooted in the belief that the environment affected the organism.[2] Thus to many Europeans it followed that, since Indians were clearly inferior, that inferiority must stem from the environment. The implications of such reasoning were not missed by Americans.

If the theory was correct, in time transplanted Europeans would also degenerate. Incensed by the credulity of some European thinkers on this subject, Thomas Jefferson was the first to react. He directed his criticism at several writers, in particular Georges Louis Leclerc, count de Buffon, a famed French naturalist; Abbé Guillaume Thomas François Raynal; Cornelius De Pauw, a cleric turned philosopher; and William Robertson, the Scottish

---

184–85. See also Daniel J. Boorstin, *The Lost World of Thomas Jefferson*, p. 83; William L. Joyce, "Antiquarians and Archaeologists: The American Antiquarian Society, 1812–1912," *Proceedings of the American Antiquarian Society* 91 (1982): 306–307.

[2] For the ambivalent view of Indians in European thought, see Margaret T. Hodgen, *Early Anthropology in the Sixteenth and Seventeenth Centuries*, esp. chaps. 9, 10; Anthony Pagden, *The Fall of Natural Man: The American Indian and the Origins of Comparative Ethnology*; Lewis Hanke, *Aristotle and the American Indians: A Study in Race Prejudice in the Modern World*; Henri Baudet, *Paradise on Earth: Some Thoughts on European Images of Non-European Man*, trans. Elizabeth Wentholt; Clarence J. Glacken, *Traces on the Rhodian Shore: Nature and Culture in Western Thought from Ancient Times to the End of the Eighteenth Century*, pp. 681–85; Bernard Sheehan, *Savagism and Civility: Indians and Englishmen in Colonial Virginia*, pp. 2–3; Robert F. Berkhofer, Jr., *The White Man's Indian: Images of the American Indian from Columbus to the Present*; Gilbert Chinard, "Eighteenth Century Theories on America as a Human Habitat," *Proceedings of the American Philosophical Society* 91 (February, 1947): 27–55; Joseph François Lafitau, *Customs of the American Indians Compared with the Customs of Primitive Times*, ed. and trans. William N. Fenton and Elizabeth L. Moore, 2 vols.; Cornelius J. Jaenen, *Friend and Foe: Aspects of French-Amerindian Cultural Contact in the Sixteenth and Seventeenth Centuries*; Ray Allen Billington, *Land of Savagery, Land of Promise: The European Image of the American Frontier*; Eugene E. Reed, "The Ignoble Savage," *Modern Language Review* 59 (1964): 53–64.

cleric and historian.[3] In a general way the ideas of these Enlightenment figures, and to a lesser extent, the Scottish philosopher Lord Kames, constituted a broad range of thinking on American Indians that included notions about environmentalism, progress, degeneration, polygenism, and monogenism.[4]

Enlightenment philosophers assumed no fixed position or consensus in their thinking regarding American Indians but rather tended to employ them, or their way of life, metaphorically in praise or condemnation of European civilization. Depicted as children of nature, imbued with stoic nobility, rustic innocence, courage, and physiques able to withstand harsh climates that might cause death in Europeans, Indians were also viewed as cunning and cruel, dirty and ignorant, and prone to lewdness, cannibalism, and torture.[5]

The pejorative views propounded by Buffon incited the severest American criticism directed against any Enlightenment philosopher.[6] Buffon, a member of the Royal Academy of Science at twenty-six and later appointed Intendant of the Royal Garden and Keeper of the Royal Cabinet of Natural History, did not intentionally set forth to disparage plant and animal life in the Americas—and especially Indians—yet his descriptions painted a depressing picture. He perceived the Americas to be literally a newer world on

[3] Jefferson, *Notes*, pp. 55–66.

[4] Count de Buffon, *Natural History, General and Particular*, trans. William Smellie; Phillip R. Sloan, "The Idea of Racial Degeneracy in Buffon's *Histoire Naturelle*," in *Racism in the Eighteenth Century: Studies in Eighteenth-Century Culture*, ed. Harold E. Pagliaro, pp. 293–321. For the views of Cornelius de Pauw on Indians, see Cornelius de Pauw, *Selections from M. Pauw, with additions by Daniel Webb*, pp. 1–7. On de Pauw and other Enlightenment figures, see Antonello Gerbi, *The Dispute of the New World: The History of a Polemic, 1750–1900*, ed. and trans. Jeremy Moyle; Fredi Chiapelli, Michael J. B. Allen and Robert L. Benson, eds., *First Images of America: The Impact of the New World on the Old*, 2 vols.; Ernst Cassirer, *The Philosophy of the Enlightenment*, trans. Fritz C. A. Koelln and James P. Pettegrove, pp. 77–80; Bernard Sheehan, *Seeds of Extinction: Jeffersonian Philanthropy and the American Indian*, pp. 66–88.

[5] Berkhofer, pp. 76–80; Sheehan, *Savagism and Civility*, pp. 1–8.

[6] Jefferson, *Notes*, pp. 183–86; Boorstin, pp. 83, 101–103.

the scale of geological time, only recently emerged from the sea and still covered with lakes, swamps, and jungles that produced humid and noxious airs. These conditions stunted animal life and caused the American Indians to be, in Buffon's view, miserable specimens of humanity. As a physical type, the Indian approximated the European in stature and was more agile and swift of foot, but he was not as strong, nor were his senses as acute. His "organs of reproduction" were "small and feeble," tending to make him impotent. Furthermore, he lacked abundant hair and beard—signs of masculinity to Europeans—and was reported to have no "ardour for the female," the absence of which made him indifferent to sex and thus a disgrace to Nature. According to Buffon, Indians were "estranged from society": they were devoid of the requisite bonds for true families, for society, for republics, for a social state. He also added: "Their heart is frozen, their society is cold, their empire cruel."[7]

Buffon's view represents a synthesis of late Enlightenment thought on American Indians. Those who followed Buffon—Abbé Raynal and Cornelius De Pauw, for example—although even more pessimistic than Buffon in their assessment of Indians, still reflected his basic ambivalence. Indians as children of nature mirrored a certain innocence, but basically their physiques and cultures were the products of degeneration caused by an adverse environment.[8] The Scottish historian William Robertson, although not as harsh in his view of Indians as Raynal and De Pauw, still saw Indians as children or childlike. They were capable of improving, but their passion for a hunting life limited their intelligence and made impossible not only society, agriculture, and the idea of private property but also law, government, and civilization.[9]

[7] Buffon quoted in Chinard, p. 31.

[8] Gerbi, pp. 45–58; de Pauw, pp. 7–9; Benjamin Keen, *The Aztec Image in Western Thought*, pp. 263–65.

[9] William Robertson, *The History of the Discovery and Settlement of America* (1777; reprint, 1785), 1: 293; 2: 1–150. Also see E. Adamson Hoebel, "William Robertson: An 18th Century Anthropologist-Historian," *American Anthropologist* 62 (1960): 648–55 for a discussion of Robertson's ethnology.

After the debates of the sixteenth century, in which the Indians' humanity was decided in the affirmative, few Europeans believed that American Indians were not part of the family of man.[10] Questions, however, continued to plague scholars regarding who the Indians were and how they had arrived in the Americas. Enlightenment thinkers added to the speculations, but few cast Indians beyond the pale of common humanity. One who tentatively broached an alternative view was the Scottish philosopher Lord Kames.[11] From what he knew of Indians, Kames believed they could be a different species of man. The work of Bernard Romans, a traveler who observed Indians in Florida,

[10]The debate over this question proved a lengthy one. See Don Cameron Allen, *The Legend of Noah: Renaissance Rationalism in Art, Science, and Letters*, pp. 113–32; John Block Friedman, *The Monstrous Races in Medieval Art and Thought*; Robert Wauchope, *Lost Tribes and Sunken Continents: Myth and Method in the Study of American Indians*; Lee Eldridge Huddleston, *Origins of the American Indian: European Concepts, 1492–1729*; Stanley L. Robe, "Wild Men and Spain's Brave New World," in *The Wild Man Within: An Image in Western Thought from the Renaissance to Romanticism*, eds. Edward Dudley and Maximillian E. Novak, pp. 39–53; Gary B. Nash, "The Image of the Indian in the Southern Colonial Mind," *William and Mary Quarterly* 29 (April, 1972): 197–230; John C. Greene, "Some Early Speculations on the Origin of Human Races," *American Anthropologist* 56 (1954): 31–41; John C. Greene, *The Death of Adam: Evolution and Its Impact on Western Thought*; Conway Zirkle, "Father Adam and the Races of Man: Some Notes on Medieval Anthropology," *Journal of Heredity* 45 (January–February, 1954): 29–34; Pagden, *The Fall of Natural Man*; Hanke, *Aristotle and the American Indian*; Lewis Hanke, *The Spanish Struggle for Justice in the Conquest of America*; Hodgen, *Early Anthropology*, especially chap. 10; J. S. Slotkin, ed. *Readings in Early Anthropology*. The advent of the printing press and publication of drawings purported to represent non-Europeans often determined sixteenth-century views as to whether Indians and Africans were similar to Europeans or even if they were human, or so argues Richard G. Cole in "Sixteenth-Century Travel Books as a Source of European Attitudes Toward Non-White and Non-Western Culture," *Proceedings of the American Philosophical Society* 116 (February, 1972): 59–67. Regarding Africans, Nancy Stepan writes, "Racial sterotypes became fixed by the printing press, restricting the way Europeans 'saw' and understood real Africans." See Stepan, *The Idea of Race in Science: Great Britain 1800–1900*, p. 8.
[11]For an excellent discussion of the development of Kames's thinking on American Indians, see George W. Stocking, Jr., "Scotland as the Model of Mankind: Lord Kames' Philosophical View of Civilization," in *Toward a Science of Man: Essays in the History of Anthropology*, ed. Timothy H. H. Thoresen, pp. 67–89.

stated as much.[12] Yet by the late eighteenth century this was the minority view.

Far more common was associating Indians with the American wilderness in terms of objects to be subdued and domesticated. John Locke, in proclaiming that in the beginning all the world was America, implied a teleological concept of progress. In the eighteenth century America represented a new world, both primitive and innocent, one that waited to be tamed and civilized.[13] With the temporalizing of the Great Chain of Being in the eighteenth century, man discovered a world of change and possibilities.[14] In natural history, attention to change focused on man's physical characteristics and on the varied forms of his societies. The belief in stages of social progress beginning with savagism continuing through barbarism and eventually culminating in civilization found a wide acceptance throughout western Europe and indeed proved fundamental to a school of historical writing in Scotland.[15] Although reports depicted the Indians as savages, cruel in their ways and without society, this placed them not outside history

[12] Bernard Romans, *Concise Natural History of East and West Florida* (1775; reprint, 1962).

[13] Among the many works that play with this imagery are Howard Mumford Jones, *O Strange New World. American Culture: The Formative Years*; Roderick Nash, *Wilderness and the American Mind*; Wilcomb E. Washburn, "The Moral and Legal Justification for Dispossessing the Indians," in *17th-Century America: Essays in Colonial History*, ed. James Morton Smith, pp. 22–25; Billington, chaps. 1, 3; Berkhofer, pp. 129–31.

[14] The classic presentation of this idea is Arthur O. Lovejoy, *The Great Chain of Being: A Study of the History of an Idea.*

[15] Characteristic of Scottish thinking was the fundamental belief that mankind was all one species and, more pointedly, that mankind was "so much the same in all times and places that history informs us of nothing new or strange in this particular." David Hume quoted in Louis Schneider, ed. *The Scottish Moralists on Human Nature and Society*, pp. 44–45. A full discussion of the Scottish school of comparative history is presented in Gladys Bryson, *Man and Society: The Scottish Inquiry of the Eighteenth Century.* See also Ronald Meek, *Social Science and the Ignoble Savage*, p. 41. According to Frederick J. Teggart, comparative history grew out of the debate between the ancients and the moderns. See his *Theory of History*, pp. 87–90. An excellent survey of this debate and its importance for both history and anthropology can be found in Frank E. Manuel, *The Eighteenth Century Confronts the Gods.*

but rather at its very beginning. That the Indian possessed a certain amount of reason had long been documented. Many Europeans believed that that very characteristic would allow the Indian to improve and to progress beyond his rudimentary state of existence, just as European man had marched forward from a similar stage of existence to civilization. Left to themselves, however, Indians would progress slowly.[16]

Only through an altered environment would their improvement in nineteenth-century terms be possible. Climate, food, living conditions, and state of social organization were held to be factors that determined man's physical characteristics and level of civilization. Following Jean Lamarck, most eighteenth-century thinkers believed that acquired characteristics were passed on to succeeding generations. Thus man's moral and social progress depended on education and alteration of the physical environment. Committed to this belief in environmentalism, many fully believed that Indians could progress rapidly through the three stages of society from savagism to barbarism to civilization—if the conditions under which they lived were changed. Such thinking underscored philanthropic efforts to lift the Indians from their lowly state.[17]

Naturally there were those who objected to the whole concept of progress. Some believed that man had degenerated—that the accomplishments of the Greeks and Romans far surpassed those of modern man. Others, although ac-

[16]Pagden, pp. 94–106; Robertson, 1: 189; C. F. Volney, *View of the Climate and Soil of the United States of America*, pp. 406–12.

[17]On Lamarck, see Greene, *The Death of Adam*, pp. 159–60. For the philanthropic impulse, see *The First Annual Report of the American Society for the Promoting the Civilization and General Improvement of the Indian Tribes in the United States*, pp. 3–4; Roy Harvey Pearce, *Savagism and Civilization: A Study of the Indian and the American Mind*, pp. 61–63; Sheehan, *Seeds of Extinction*, pp. 119–81; Berkhofer, pp. 149 and passim. See also Robert F. Berkhofer, Jr., *Salvation and the Savage: An Analysis of Protestant Missions and American Indian Response, 1787–1862*; R. Pierce Beaver, *Church, State and the American Indian: Two and a Half Centuries of Partnership in Missions Between Protestant Churches and Government*; R. Pierce Beaver, ed., *To Advance the Gospel: Selections From the Writings of Rufus Anderson*, pp. 22–27, 73–75.

cepting the concept of progress, limited it to Europeans and hesitated to grant it to nonwhites. They believed instead that nonwhites represented a degeneration from a superior original type.[18] Yet not all who subscribed to degeneration theory doomed the Indians. If the environment had caused decline in the Indians, changing that environment could reverse the process and lift them to civilization.[19]

The environmental explanation of change appealed to many who saw Indians as the descendants of the lost tribes of Israel. Some believed that sin had reduced Indians to savagery, but others attributed the decline of the Indians to environmental factors. Many perceived Indian life as one of hardship. Wandering in a harsh wilderness, plagued by want, and constantly beset by danger, Indians had lost the

[18]The concept of degeneration was expressed not only in scientific thinking, but also in the political and religious thinking of the eighteenth and nineteenth centuries. The following works explore one or more aspects of the "concept of degeneration." Hayden White, "The Forms of Wildness: Archaeology of an Idea," in *The Wild Man Within*, eds. Edward Dudley and Maximillian E. Novak, pp. 3–38; Margaret T. Hodgen, *The Doctrine of Survival: A Chapter in the History of Scientific Method in the Study of Man*; Richard Bernheimer, *Wild Men in the Middle Ages: A Study in Art, Sentiment, and Demonology*; Edmund S. Carpenter, "The Role of Archaeology in the 19th Century Controversy between Developmentalism and Degeneration," *Pennsylvania Archaeologist* 20 (January–June, 1950): 5–18; Winthrop Jordan, *White Over Black: American Attitudes Toward the Negro, 1550–1812*; Katherine George, "The Civilized West Looks at Primitive Africa 1400–1800: A Study in Ethnoscience," *Isis* 49 (1958): 62–72; George W. Stocking, Jr., "Some Problems in the Understanding of Nineteenth-Century Cultural Evolution," in *Readings in the History of Anthropology*, ed. Regna Darnell, pp. 407–25; Greene, *Death of Adam*.

[19]Benjamin Rush, who believed in the degeneration of both nations and people, saw environment as the prime source for change. He claimed that "human nature is the same in all ages and countries, and all the differences we perceive in its characters in respect to virtue and vice, knowledge and ignorance, may be accounted for from climate, country, degree of civilization, forms of government, or other accidental causes." Quoted in Jordan, p. 287. Other examples of the use of environmentalism in explaining Indian culture and physical characteristics can be found in Smith, *An Essay*, pp. 233–34; Benjamin Rush, *An Inquiry*, pp. 108–11; Hugh Williamson, *Observations on the Climate in Different Parts of America, Compared with the Climate in Corresponding Parts of the Other Continents*, pp. 172–73; Samuel Williams, *The Natural and Civil History of Vermont*, pp. 163–86, 386–96.

knowledge of letters, of religion, and of society that they once had possessed. Only in a few words and legends could rudiments of a prior knowledge of civilization, of God, and of their ancient languages be found. The hope for the civilization of the Indians fed upon the assumption that Indians, having attained civilization in the past, could— through altering their environment—do so again.[20]

By the end of the first two decades of the nineteenth century, when philanthropy and the churches could show few positive results from their efforts to lift the Indians, doubts were raised about whether they could really be civilized. Critics increasingly saw such attempts as futile. They felt that Indians did not respond to these efforts because they were different from other human beings; indeed, they might be an entirely different species of man. Many such critics began to question the monogenetic assumption, set

[20]The belief that Indians were descendants of lost Israeli tribes was popular both in Europe and America. One of the earliest American expressions of the belief is found in Roger Williams, *A Key into the Language of America*, eds. John Teunissen and Evelyn J. Hinz (1643; reprint, 1973). Some later accounts are John Adair, *The History of the American Indians* (1775; reprint, 1930); Elias C. Boudinot, *A Star in the West; or a Humble Attempt to Discover the Long Lost Ten Tribes of Israel, Preparatory to Their Return to Their Beloved City, Jerusalem*; John Haywood, *The Natural and Aboriginal History of Tennessee, Up to the First Settlements Therein By the White People in the Year 1768*; Constantine S. Rafinesque, "Ancient Annals of Kentucky; or Introduction to the History and Antiquities of the State of Kentucky," in H. Marshall, *The History of Kentucky*, 1; Charles Crawford, *An Essay on the Propagation of the Gospel . . . to prove that the Indians in America are descendants from the Ten Tribes*; Ethan Smith, *View of the Hebrews*; Charles Beatty, *The Journal of a Two Month Tour; With A View of Promoting Religion Among the Frontier Inhabitants of Pennsylvania, and of Introducing Christianity Among the Indians to the Westward of the Aleghgeny Mountains*. See also Samuel F. Haven, "Archaeology of the United States or Sketches, Historical and Bibliographical, of the Progress of Information and Opinion Respecting Vestiges of Antiquity in the United States," *Smithsonian Contribution to Knowledge* 8 (1856): 5–6, for other authors who believed that Indians were remnants of the lost tribe of Israel. The Moravian missionary John Heckewelder, although believing that Indians were descendants of the ten lost tribes, did not mention this in his *History, Manners, and Customs of the Indian Nations* (1819) because he thought insufficient proof existed for this theory. See John G. E. Heckewelder to Peter S. Du Ponceau, August 6, 1818, Peter Du Ponceau Papers, APS.

forth in the Bible, that all mankind shared the same origin. Increasingly they began to explain Indians' recalcitrant nature in terms of polygenism. To polygenists Indians were separately created and were an inferior species of man. But if the Indian were an inferior species of man, what then was his fate? Would the effect of the environment be the same on the Indian as it had been on European man? Were Indians capable of further progress, or had they reached the limits of their potential?[21]

Thus the eighteenth century provided early-nineteenth-century ethnologists with a collection of intellectual arguments—a kit bag, so to speak—to rummage through and rework. Just how these arguments were combined and re-combined,—how they were tailored to meet contemporary needs and how they were applied to the study of American Indians and their cultures—is the subject of this book. Early ethnologists often presented, or misrepresented, Indians in ethnocentric terms. Not surprisingly Indians were judged by the criterion of how they measured against a particular scientific theory rather than how effectively their

[21]Benjamin Smith Barton, "Observations and Conjectures Concerning certain Articles which were taken out of an ancient Tumulus, or Grave, at Cincinnati, in the County of Hamilton, and Territory of the United States, North-West of the River Ohio. . . ." *Transactions of the American Philosophical Society* 4 (1799): 190–98; Timothy Flint, in his *Recollections of the Last Ten Years in the Valley of the Mississippi*, ed. George R. Brooks (1826; reprint, 1964) saw Indians as one of two extremes of human nature, the other being the African. According to Flint, exposure to a harsh environment had reduced them to brutes. "Their continual converse with woods, rocks, and sterile deserts, with the roar of the winds, and the solitude and gloom of the wilderness, their alternations of satiety and hunger, their continual exposure to danger, their uncertain existence, which seems to them a forced and un-natural state, the little hold which their affections seem to have upon life, the wild and savage nature that always surrounds them—these circumstances seem to have impressed a steady and unalterable gloom upon their countenance. . . . It has been told me, with how much truth I know not, but I believe it, that in amputation, and other surgical operations, their nerves do not shrink, do not show the same tendency to spasm, with those of the whites. . . . This increasing insensibility, transmitted from generation to generation, finally becomes inwrought with the whole web of animal nature, and the body of the savage seems to have little more sensibility than the hoof of horses." See Flint, pp. 101–102.

societies functioned in a changing environment. For many ethnologists theoretical models describing the mechanics of social change, intelligence, and progress all too often assumed the rigidity of truth; and when ethnographic data contradicted theory, neither the evidence nor the theory was questioned. Rather the fault rested with the Indians, and they were harshly condemned for lacking intelligence or for having a mind-set that rejected progress.

Other ethnologists sought to adjust theory in response to new evidence and changing social views. This is particularly true of the evolutionists.[22] The way theories of social evolution changed is a major theme of this book. During the early nineteenth century there was a constant tinkering with eighteenth-century theories of progress. That which was common to all of these theories—movement from savagery to civilization—remained. Particulars of why and how change occurred and how long such change would take were sharply debated. Trying to bring ethnological theory into accord with ethnographic evidence concerned several Americans at the turn of the century, but the major effort to accomplish those ends took place between 1830 and 1870.

In the chapters that follow, the ideas of five ethnologists will be explored along with the ethnological writings of their contemporaries. The five men selected not only represent five different areas within ethnological research but also were recognized at the time as the major figures in their field. All five were either acquainted with each other or familiar with one another's works. Through the auspices of the American Ethnological Society—of which all but one were members—a network of communication existed.

Despite the emphasis on these men, this book does not constitute a biographical approach to early-nineteenth-century ethnology. Although such an approach is often useful for exploring theoretical developments in science,

---

[22] For the sake of concision and clarity, I frequently employ the term *evolution* in its post-Darwinian sense. Most nineteenth-century writers used several terms, including *developmentalism* and *progress*, to denote this phenomenon.

it is rejected here in favor of one I believe better able to explicate the many influences affecting the development of early-nineteenth-century ethnology. Accordingly, the chapters are structured by fields within nineteenth-century ethnology. The subject of each chapter, like a fugue, is presented with various ethnologists' ideas as a counter subject and, finally, considered juxtaposed in free counterpoint.

The structure of the book emphasizes this development and especially the important role of evolutionary thinking. But evolution, or the progressive development of society, is not the only theme. Lesser themes are also presented here, although not as sharply delineated, that contributed to the evolution of ethnology in early America. The debate between monogenists and polygenists is, of course, extensively covered, along with arguments over evolution and degeneration. Chapter 3 on Samuel G. Morton and physical anthropology discusses the issue of biology versus culture. Likewise in the pronouncements of Lewis Cass, Henry Rowe Schoolcraft, and others the merits of frontier ethnology (fieldwork) as against an "armchair approach" to ethnology are seen. Although most of the ethnologists made cases for the application of ethnology to the problems encountered by the government in dealing with Indians, only Schoolcraft and Lewis Henry Morgan (and to a lesser extent Albert Gallatin) attempted to develop what might be called an applied ethnology. Others, like Morton and Ephraim G. Squier, were more content to see their contributions to ethnology as pure science. Thus this book, while presenting two major debates, also includes a skein of interwoven issues or concerns that affected early American ethnology and the ways ethnologists viewed American Indians.

The book begins with Albert Gallatin, the foremost representative of evolutionary Enlightenment thought in ethnology in the early decades of the nineteenth century. The next two chapters consider the ethnological investigations of several scholars who, although they subscribed in some measure to elements of Enlightenment thinking about man, in one way or another offered opposing views to evolutionary and monogenetic thinking. The last two chapters present thinkers who, though firm in their conviction that mankind is one species and that both Indian mentalities and cultures had evolved, nevertheless were not left untouched by the theories proposed by those who countered such thinking. Since the ethnological careers of Albert Gallatin, Samuel G. Morton, Ephraim George Squier, Henry Rowe Schoolcraft, and Lewis Henry Morgan only slightly overlap, the order of the chapters reflects to a degree the rise in reputations of these men and the periods of their relative activity in the field of ethnology.

2

Albert Gallatin and
Enlightenment Ethnology

IN HIS *Seventh Annual Report* for the Bureau of Ethnology
prepared in 1891, John Wesley Powell stated that a parallel
existed between Linnaeus, who brought order to biology
through classification, and Albert Gallatin (1761–1849),
who did the same for North American Indian languages.
Before Gallatin there were, of course, other American philologists—Benjamin Smith Barton, Peter Stephen Du Ponceau, and John Pickering—but Powell concluded that the
work of Gallatin "marks an era in American linguistic science, from the fact that he so thoroughly introduced comparative methods, and because he circumscribed the boundaries of many [language] families, so that a large part of his
work remains and is still considered sound."[1]

Although Powell's claim has been deflated in recent analy-
ses,[2] Gallatin's legacy should not be diminished. His importance for American ethnology rests on his labors in founding the American Ethnological Society and on the thoughts
he expressed in his essays "Synopsis of Indian Tribes"
(1836) and "Notes on the Semi-Civilized Nations of Mexico,
Yucatan, and Central America" (1845) and in his "Introduction" to "Hale's Indians of North-west America, and Vocabularies of North America" (1848).[3] Considered together,

---

[1] John W. Powell, "Indian Linguistic Families of America North of Mexico,"
Seventh Annual Report of the Bureau of American Ethnology (1885–86): 9.
[2] See for example Mary Haas, "Grammar or Lexicon? The American Indian Side of the Question from Du Ponceau to Powell," *International Journal
of American Linguistics* 35 (July, 1969): 239–55.
[3] Albert Gallatin, "A synopsis of the Indian Tribes of North America,"
Transactions and Collections of the American Antiquarian Society 2 (1836):
1–422; Albert Gallatin, "Notes on the Semi-civilized Nations of Mexico, Yu-

these works carry into the nineteenth century assumptions prevalent during the Enlightenment that emphasized a comparative approach to the study of man and that perceived man as one species with a basically progressive culture. Since Gallatin belonged to the era of the Enlightenment, the parallel between him and Linnaeus is greater than is first imagined. Yet Gallatin did not seriously undertake ethnological studies until the 1820s, a time when Enlightenment assumptions about man were under attack.

Albert Gallatin was born in 1761 in Geneva, Switzerland, into one of the town's important propertied families, one connected with minor nobility.[4] As a member of the governing oligarchy, the family became acquainted with the many distinguished visitors the city received from northern Europe and England. Voltaire, one of Geneva's distinguished citizens and a particular friend of the Gallatin family, often received Gallatin's grandmother with young Albert in tow. Gallatin passed his childhood in this intellectually charged atmosphere and received an excellent education first at home and later at the renowned Geneva academy. At the latter he acquired a solid background in classical and modern languages, geography, and mathematics.

Upon completion of his course of studies, his family obtained for him a commission in the army of Frederic, the Landgrave of Hesse, then preparing to fight in the Ameri-

----

catan, and Central America," *Transactions of the American Ethnological Society* 1 (1845): 1–352; Albert Gallatin, "Introduction" to "Hale's Indians of North-west America, and Vocabularies of North America," *Transactions of the American Ethnological Society* 2 (1848): xxiii–clxxxviii.

[4]The biographical information is drawn from the following works: Raymond Walters, Jr., *Albert Gallatin: Jeffersonian Financier and Diplomat*, pp. 1–25, passim; [Edward E. Hale,] "Memoirs," *Proceedings of the American Antiquarian Society* (1850): pp. 16–31; David S. Muzzey, "Gallatin, Abraham Alfonse Albert," in *Dictionary of American Biography*, ed. Allen Johnson and Dumas Malone (1960), 103–09, "Albert Gallatin," in *Cyclopedia of American Literature*, ed. Evart A. Duyckinck and L. George, 1: 492–95; "Albert Gallatin: Autobiography, 1798," *Collections of the Maine Historical Society* 6 (1859): 93–103; Henry Adams, *The Life of Albert Gallatin*, pp. 1–75.

Albert Gallatin. Secretary of the Treasury in the administrations of
Thomas Jefferson and James Madison, Gallatin also was one of the
founders of the American Ethnological Society.

can Revolution on behalf of England. Gallatin refused the
commission. Instead he left Geneva and with a friend sought
out the American wilderness on his own. Why Gallatin
elected this course is uncertain. His biographers attribute
his departure to romantic notions of a wild, free land full
of opportunity, but to this motivation must be added his

growing disenchantment with the increasingly oppressive and conservative nature of Geneva politics and his search for personal independence.

Gallatin arrived in America in 1780 and spent his first winter on the Maine frontier near an Indian village. According to one biographer, Gallatin visited these Indians in his spare time, investigating their customs and attending their feasts.[5] Although it is unlikely that these observations inspired later studies in ethnology, they do pinpoint an early interest, if only romantic, in Indian "culture."

Maine and its Indians, however, did not hold Gallatin's attention for long. After this brief frontier experience he traveled to Boston and succeeded in obtaining a tutorial position in French at Harvard College. But Boston's atmosphere proved too chilly for young Gallatin. After two years, he moved briefly to Philadelphia and then to Virginia before settling on the western frontier of Pennsylvania, where he engaged in land buying with the fond hope of founding a Swiss colony. Gallatin's political fortunes, however, fared more brightly than his speculative ventures. In 1790 western Pennsylvania sent him as representative to the first of three successive terms in the state legislature.[6]

An expansive frontier society at the time, western Pennsylvania was becoming radically anti-Federalist, and, as the area drifted toward the Republican Party of Jefferson, so did Gallatin. Elected to the United States Senate in 1793, Gallatin lost his seat as a result of a dispute over his citizenship. But in 1795, Pennsylvania sent him back into national politics as a congressman. After six years in the House of Representatives, Gallatin became Jefferson's secretary of the treasury. In this position he continued an apparent affinity for financial matters first manifested in the Pennsylvania legislature. Although secretary of the treasury in both the Jefferson and the Madison administrations, Gallatin did not always follow orthodox Republican financial thinking. Indeed, apparently following Hamiltonian economic philosophy, he gravitated toward a more

[5] John Austin Stevens, *Albert Gallatin*, p. 16.
[6] Walters, p. 16.

conservative viewpoint that accepted banks and supported commercial interests.[7]

As secretary of the treasury under Jefferson, Gallatin assumed an influence in government beyond the confines of his own department. Jefferson's great respect for Gallatin's intellect led him not only to consult Gallatin on economic and diplomatic matters but also to value him as a confidant. Gallatin's superb knowledge of geography proved indispensable to Jefferson in assuring the success of the Lewis and Clark Expedition and also in delineating the boundaries of the newly acquired Louisiana Territory. Jefferson often sought Gallatin's advice on other matters as well, often sending him drafts of speeches and even inaugural addresses for comments and suggestions. Indeed, Gallatin offered advice not only on financial matters but also on delicate international concerns and Indian affairs.

In Indian affairs Gallatin strongly advocated education to prepare the Indians for a future in American society.[8] Perhaps it was in such an advisory capacity that Gallatin discovered the value of ethnology. As a staunch nationalist, he looked forward to the opening up of the West, but he also felt an obligation first to learn about the Indians and the scope and location of their territorial claims. In memoranda to Jefferson, Gallatin cited the need for correct surveys of Indian land, and he even went so far as to map the location of some Indian tribes himself. In a letter to Jefferson in 1805, he states:

> I have taken notes of the situation of the Indian tribes in Lower Louisiana as given by Sibley, and, having compared them with Humboldt's and Nolan's sketches, think that I can lo-

[7]The best account of Gallatin's economic theories is Alexander Balinsky, *Albert Gallatin: Fiscal Theories and Policies*. But see also Raymond Walters, "The Making of a Financier: Albert Gallatin in the Pennsylvania Assembly," *Pennsylvania Magazine of History and Biography* 70 (1946): 258–69.

[8]Albert Gallatin, *The Writings of Albert Gallatin*, ed. Henry Adams, 1: 227, 233, 426, 638, 640; John Logan Allen, *Passage Through the Garden: Lewis and Clark and the Image of the American Northwest*, pp. 73–98, 102–06; John F. Freeman, "The American Philosophical Society in American Anthropology," in *The Philadelphia Anthropological Society*, ed. Jacob W. Gruber, pp. 32–46.

cate them all with sufficient correctness for present purposes. But the great desideratum is a map, not good, but at least tolerable. The documents we have are not merely imperfect, but altogether contradictory, principally for the Attacapa and part of the Opelousas districts.

This passage reflects the close attention to detail that characterized Gallatin's work. A later passage in the same letter is significant for Gallatin's later ethnography, which was heavily weighted with a geographical component, and for Gallatin's utilization of ethnography in governmental affairs.

I am now preparing at leisure moments a rough sketch, in which the ascertained points will be fixed, and an attempt made to reconcile the clashing authorities. This, till we have better information, will at least do better than any of our existing maps, and I will locate the Indian tribes in it.[9]

In 1813, Gallatin resigned from the cabinet and accepted a diplomatic mission to Russia. The United States and England were at war. According to some accounts, Gallatin's compulsion to balance the national budget left both the army and the navy ill prepared to withstand British encroachments. Gallatin accepted the Republican premise that the debt with its corresponding interest bore heaviest upon the small landowner and benefited the wealthy commercial class. The army and especially the navy constituted major drains upon the treasury and were, Gallatin believed, instruments of the commercial class; therefore, he decreased their budgets accordingly.

More than merely reflecting a Republican agrarian bias against the commercial class, Gallatin's actions mirrored his attitudes about war. War, he believed, was the barbaric luxury of the European commercial class instigated to deprive farmers of their money and their freedom. He maintained that the United States as an agricultural nation could avoid war if the president so desired. Perhaps with Europe in mind, Gallatin held that the army and navy served only to increase a nation's desire to use force for its own aggrandize-

[9]Gallatin, *The Writings of Albert Gallatin*, 1: 233.

ment, a practice contrary not only to Republican ideals, as Gallatin understood them, but to Enlightenment ideals on liberty as well.[10] Regardless of the president's actions, war enveloped the nation in 1812. Russia offered to mediate the conflict, and Gallatin undertook his mission to Russia to pursue the offer. Although Russian aid evaporated, Gallatin remained in Europe from 1815 to 1823 as minister to France. Twice approached to return to the treasury, he declined, feeling that changes in American politics made his economic views obsolete.[11]

Apparently Gallatin began to think himself somewhat out of place in American society. A certain ambiguity colored his feelings about his adopted country. Western Pennsylvania, which exerted a sentimental attraction upon his sympathies, was his home. Furthermore, he had held positions of importance at the federal level, and many government officials in Washington still accorded him due respect. Offsetting this was Gallatin's belief that the country had changed for the worse. Jeffersonian Republicanism with its emphasis on the yeoman farmer appeared to be dead or dying. Cities and their attendant, deplorable brand of commercialism prevailed. To Gallatin the country seemed to be in the grip of inept leaders, a view he would hold even more firmly when Andrew Jackson, whom he detested, assumed the presidency. Leaders no longer held the public interest paramount, and the people themselves also had changed. Their priorities no longer were placed on the improvement of man but were now placed on the acquisition of wealth. In short, after enjoying eight years of the stimulating and intellectual atmosphere of Paris, Gallatin felt that changes in the United States made return to America less desirable.[12]

But ties with America prevailed. In 1823, Gallatin retired to his western Pennsylvania farm. That year he reluctantly accepted the Republican nomination for the vice-

[10] Balinsky, pp. 215–460.
[11] Albert Gallatin, *Selected Writings of Albert Gallatin*, ed. E. James Ferguson, p. xxxii; James Gallatin, *The Diary of James Gallatin, Secretary to Albert Gallatin a Great Peace Maker 1813–1827*, ed. Count Gallatin, pp. 19–93.
[12] J. Gallatin, p. 193.

presidency. Happily for Gallatin, the party later chose another for the office. But retirement in Pennsylvania did not suit Gallatin, and he moved to Baltimore. In a letter to his close boyhood friend Hector Badollet, Gallatin claimed that although he was content to spend the rest of his days on the farm, his family could not suffer such a prospect. Candidly, however, he admitted that even for him the farm provided little intellectual stimulation.[13]

Shortage of funds clouded Gallatin's retirement in Baltimore, so when offered a diplomatic mission to England in 1826, he accepted government employ for the last time. Although his year abroad perhaps made him more contemptuous of the world in general, his return dispelled any lingering enthusiasm for the United States, and he retained a marked preference for Europe.[14] An acerbic Gallatin confided to Badollet in 1829, "I am not pleased with the present aspect of public affairs, still less with that of the public mind." Politics seemed to focus not upon any one "system of public measures over another, but solely in relation to persons, or at best to sectional feelings. . . . But we are going off the scene; I think that we have discharged our duties honestly, and the next generation must provide for itself."[15] One of Gallatin's biographers sensed his dismay with the country in the late 1820s and commented, "The election of 1828 terminated the long sway of the old Republican party, and if what he [Gallatin] saw about him had not convinced Mr. Gallatin that his opinions and methods belonged to a past era, instinct must have taught him that his career and that of his party had best close together."[16]

Gallatin eagerly sought the anonymity of private life and retreated to New York, where he found solace in science during his declining years. From the wreckage of the old

[13] Ibid., p. 219; Gayle Thornbrough, ed., *The Correspondence of John Badollet and Albert Gallatin, 1804–1836*, Indiana Historical Society Publications, no. 22 (1963): 309.

[14] J. Gallatin, pp. 174, 181, 268; Henry Adams, *Albert Gallatin*, p. 598. For a further account of Adams's view of Gallatin, see William H. Jordy, *Henry Adams: Scientific Historian*, p. 47.

[15] Adams, p. 631.

[16] Ibid., p. 629.

order and his party a liberated Gallatin pursued a fresh endeavor. But he found that debates in the arena of science could be as ticklish as those in the arena of diplomacy.

That Gallatin should choose the science of philology was consistent with his Enlightenment temperament and growing conservatism. In few other sciences did Enlightenment theories retain explanatory force. Since Gallatin's contributions to ethnology are seen predominately as philological contributions, a brief survey of early-nineteenth-century philology is useful in order to see more clearly Gallatin's special contribution.

The Enlightenment belief that language was the product of reason, and reflected reason, endured in America. In Europe, however, especially among German philologists Johann Georg Hamann, Johann Herder, and others, support for this view had eroded. The search for a universal grammar and the collecting of languages were rooted in the Enlightenment belief in universal consciousness and faculties of perception: "Beneath the diverse forms which historic languages display, there could be discovered a 'universal' language, one which would ideally represent the concepts of mind." Comparative study of "primitive" languages, it was believed, would hold clues not only to the origin of language but also to reason itself, since "primitive" languages were considered simpler and thus older than historic languages and hence closer to the first language of mankind. Viewed as ancient artifacts, Indian languages could disclose the early history of man. Americans, however, sought to push this reasoning further. They believed that the study of a people's language would reveal the origin and history of that people; the study of Indian languages thus would shed light on the Indians' clouded past.[17]

[17]Robert L. Miller, *The Linguistic Relativity Principle and Humboldtian Ethnolinguistics: A History and Appraisal*, pp. 14–33; James N. Ryding, "Alternatives in Nineteenth-Century German Ethnology: A Case Study in the Sociology of Science," *Sociologus* 25 (1975): 1–4; Wilhelm E. Mühlmann, *Geschichte der Anthropologie*, pp. 52–84.

Benjamin Smith Barton, a Philadelphia physician, and DeWitt Clinton, governor of New York, were among the American advocates of these views. Both believed that the secret of the Indians' past lay hidden in their languages.[18] Lawyer-philologist John Pickering also subscribed to this view and encouraged the study of such languages. Pickering, who had spent years in Europe pursuing his interest in philology, wrote in *An Essay on a Uniform Orthography for the Indian Languages of North America*:

> For, if the origin of the population of this Continent is, as all admit, a most interesting and important question; and if we can more successfully arrive at the solution of it, by tracing the progress of the various nations of men over different regions of the globe, through the medium of their languages, than in any other manner (which every day experience renders more and more probable); then it is undeniable, that a careful inquiry into the languages of a people, who were formerly the possessors of one entire hemisphere, is a subject of great moment to the inhabitants of the old as well as the new world.[19]

Although some of Pickering's views on Indian language were sneered at by scholars on the frontier, the opinion that philology could be useful in tracing origins found ready acceptance by Lewis Cass, territorial governor of Michigan. According to Cass, through the study of Indian languages "we may therefore be enabled, by diligent investigation and comparison, to ascertain the connexion, which exists between the languages spoken of [sic] our different aborig-

---

[18] Benjamin Smith Barton, *New Views of the Origin of the Tribes and Nations of America*; DeWitt Clinton, "A Discourse Delivered Before the New-York Historical Society, 6 December 1811," *Collections of the New-York Historical Society* 2 (1814): 78–79; DeWitt Clinton, *Memoir on the Antiquities of the Western Parts of the State of New York*, pp. 3–4.

[19] John Pickering, *An Essay on a Uniform Orthography for the Indian Languages of North America*, pp. 7–9; John Pickering, "Remarks on the Indian Languages of North America," *Encyclopedia Americana* 6 (1831): 581–600. See Franklin Edgerton, "Notes on Early American Work in Linguistics," *Proceedings of the American Philosophical Society* 87 (July, 1943): 27–28 and Raoul N. Smith, "The Interest in Language and Languages in Colonial and Federal America," *Proceedings of the American Philosophical Society* 123 (February, 1979): 31–33 for useful surveys on early American work on American Indian languages.

inal tribes, and thus ascend by regular gradation through the various degrees of relationship to the parent stock." This being so, "It is probable, that this process will reflect more light upon the long contested and doubtful question of the first settlement of this continent, than any other means within our power."[20]

Cass, however, could not accept the refined opinions of eastern philologists who discovered "wonderful structures" in Indian languages and held that they truly reflected the Indians' power to reason. Since Cass believed Indians reasoned poorly, he was convinced that their languages could not possess those attributes which eastern philologists were so ready to bestow. To Cass,

> The range of thought of our Indian neighbors is extremely limited. Of abstract ideas they are wholly destitute. They have no sciences, and their religious notions are confused and circumscribed. They have but little property, less law, and no public office. They soon forget the past, improvidently disregard the future, and waste their thoughts, when they do think, upon the present. The character of all original languages must depend, more or less, upon the wants, means, and occupations, mental and physical, of the people who speak them, and we ought not to expect to find the complicated refinements of polished tongues, among those of our Indians.[21]

Two years later Cass underscored these comments and presented a succinct rendering of the Enlightenment theory that man's mind is reflected in his language: "There is an intimate connexion between the powers and process of the mind, and the means by which its operations are disclosed." This, Cass believed, certainly proved true with the Indian:

[20] Lewis Cass, *Additional Inquiries respecting the Indian Languages,* p. 13; for Cass's earlier inquiries, see *Inquiries, respecting the history, traditions, languages, manners, customs, religion, etc. of the Indians living within the United States.*

[21] [Lewis Cass], Rev. *Manners and Customs of several Indian Tribes* [and] *Historical Notes respecting the Indians of North America . . .* , in *The North American Review* 22 (January, 1826): 79. See also Amos Stoddard, *Sketches, Historical and Descriptive, of Louisiana,* p. 432. Stoddard presented the same argument as Cass but arrived at different conclusions.

After all the laudatory remarks, which have been made on the subject of the Indian languages, it will be found that they partake essentially of the character of the people, who use them. They are generally harsh in the utterance, inartificial in their construction, indeterminant in their application, and incapable of expressing a vast variety of ideas, particularly those which relate to invisible objects.[22]

Cass particularly disagreed with eastern philologist Peter S. Du Ponceau, president of the prestigious American Philosophical Society. As a boy in France, Du Ponceau became interested in the study of languages, and as a youth he served as secretary to the French philologist Count de Gebelin. Like Gallatin, Du Ponceau arrived in the United States during the American Revolution. At its conclusion he settled in Philadelphia, where he practiced law. He maintained an interest in languages and in the Enlightenment dream of a universal grammar. In 1816, when the American Philosophical Society set up its Historical and Literary Committee to collect material on the American Indian, Du Ponceau became the committee chairman.[23] In this capacity he corresponded with the venerable Moravian missionary to the Delaware Indians, Rev. John Heckewelder, who became Du Ponceau's tutor in the Delaware language. Through Heckewelder, Du Ponceau acquired the works of other Moravian missionaries, including those of Rev. David Zeisberger on the Iroquois. The beauty of Indian languages appealed to Du Ponceau, and as he progressed in his studies he made a startling discovery: Indians joined many words together to form one large, inflected

[22][Lewis Cass], "Rev. *Travels in the Central Portions of the Mississippi Valley* . . . [and] *A Vindication of the Rev. Mr. Heckewelder's History of the Indian Nations* . . .," in *The North American Review* 26 (April, 1828): 387.
[23]Freeman, p. 36. Du Ponceau was president of the American Philosophical Society from 1828 to 1844. See Edgerton, p. 28. The Historical and Literary Committee was also called the Standing Committee on Antiquities of the American Philosophical Society. See A. Irving Hallowell, "Anthropology in Philadelphia," in *The Philadelphia Anthropological Society*, ed. Jacob W. Gruber, p. 6; Gilbert Chinard, "Jefferson and the American Philosophical Society," *Proceedings of the American Philosophical Society* 87 (1943): 263–76.

word. Thus a word could have numerous prefixes and suffixes to render it descriptive powers of great precision, a process Du Ponceau termed *polysynthetic*. In addition, Du Ponceau discovered that all Indian languages to which he had access from Tierra del Fuego to the Arctic possessed this characteristic.

In their inflection, Indian languages seemed to compare favorably with Greek and Latin, languages highly esteemed by scholars.[24] The classical vogue emphasizing the beauty and mystery of antiquity prevailed in American art, architecture, and literature, and if Indian and classical languages were similar it followed naturally that Indian languages should merit greater respect than previously given.[25] Furthermore, that a "primitive" people conversed in seemingly advanced and sophisticated tongues implied that Indians at some time possessed a civilization more advanced, commensurate at least with the relatively advanced level of their languages.

Opponents countered that Indian languages were not polysynthetic, that a poverty of words compelled Indians to gesture to make themselves understood and that a paucity of abstract terms prohibited expression of metaphysical concepts. The methodology employed in philology also became a subject of debate. Critics pointed out that few if any philologists actually had listened to Indians but instead had gleaned their vocabularies from travel accounts, many of which were unreliable. Even if the accounts were accurate,

[24]The view that the languages of the North American Indians were comparable in complexity and beauty to the classical languages of Greek and Latin was shared by several linguists, to whom it suggested that although the Indians had degenerated in the "cultural sphere," they had maintained sophisticated language structures. This view led linguists to place great emphasis on the immutability of language and to advocate its importance in tracing the history of the Indians. See J. Pickering, p. 582; Peter S. Du Ponceau "Correspondence between Mr. Heckewelder and Mr. Du Ponceau on the Language of the American Indian," *Transactions of the American Philosophical Society* 1 (1819): 351–448.

[25]For a discussion of American interests in the classical world, see Howard Mumford Jones, *O Strange New World. American Culture: The Formative Years*, pp. 227–72. Carl Bode in *Antebellum Culture*, does not totally agree on the strength of classical influences, but see pp. 38–44.

they argued, vocabularies, having no set orthography to apply, differed depending on the ear and nationality of the recorder. In addition tribal language was polluted through intermarriage, trading, and intertribal adoptions. Finally, some critics doubted the main thrust of American philological research, calling into question the reliability of philology to determine whether language could even be used to trace Indian origins.[26] At this juncture in the state of the art, Gallatin entered seriously into philological pursuits, particularly into the study of Indian languages.

When Gallatin returned to the United States in 1823, he devoted his spare time to a classification of Indian tribes by language. He enlisted the aid of the government in this endeavor. In 1826, Secretary of War James Barbour agreed to send a circular to all Indian agents, superintendents, and missionaries. The circular, which Gallatin had prepared, contained a vocabulary and inquiries about Indian grammar. Gallatin wrote, but Barbour signed, the circular's prefatory statement of purpose, which pointed to the practical aspects of Gallatin's circular. It was anticipated that the circular would not only help the War Department learn more about various tribes and tribal affinities, but that it would also assist the government in determining tribal land claims by identifying Indian terms for local geographical features.[27] Returns, however, proved scanty. Gallatin attrib-

---

[26]Cass, Rev. of *Travels* . . . , pp. 387–400; Caleb Atwater, *Remarks Made on a Tour to Prairie du Chien; Thence to Washington City, in 1829*, pp. 75–80; James H. McCulloh, *Researches on America: Being an Attempt to Settle Some Points Relative to the Aborigines of America, etc.*, pp. vii–xi; James H. McCulloh, *Researches, Philosophical and Antiquarian, Concerning the Aboriginal History of America*, pp. 33–34.

[27]See the printed questionnaire prepared by Gallatin with a cover by Secretary of War James Barbour and sent under government auspices and dated May 15, 1815. See also Albert Gallatin's letter to James Rochelle, (June 1826?), microfilm edition of *The Papers of Albert Gallatin*, New York University, reel no. 1, next to frames 361–62; James Barbour to Albert Gallatin, April 4, 1826, Gallatin Papers, NYHS; Albert Gallatin to Thomas L. McKenny, April 29, 1826, Bureau of Indian Affairs, Letters Received, Record Group 75, National Archives (NA).

uted the project's failure to Barbour's insufficient support.[28]

Gallatin also appealed to governor Lewis Cass and to Thomas L. McKenney of the Bureau of Indian Affairs. Both men sought diligently to provide Gallatin with the vocabularies he needed. Their labors were fruitful. Through McKenney, Gallatin procured from John Ridge, a Cherokee, an extensive description of his people's customs and current condition.[29] Governor Cass sent Gallatin Sioux vocabularies. William Clark, of the Lewis and Clark Expedition, proved another important source, for he forwarded descriptions of tribal customs in both the mid- and far west.[30] Gallatin also added to his vocabulary collection during his periodic trips to Washington to interview visiting Indian delegations.[31]

During the 1820s, Peter S. Du Ponceau proved Gallatin's greatest source of encouragement and stimulation as well as his most perceptive critic. Gallatin drew not only on Du Ponceau's great knowledge of Indian languages but also on the philological resources of the American Philosophical Society library, which Du Ponceau made available to him. A bond developed between these two men. Both were Europeans transplanted to America; both were native French speakers and versed in classical languages; both were well acquainted with the philological work being done in Eu-

[28]Albert Gallatin to W. Medill, July 21, 1846, copy, Gallatin Papers, NYHS; Albert Gallatin to John R. Bartlett, March 18, 1846, Bartlett Papers, JCBL. See also Edgerton, p. 30.

[29]Albert Gallatin to Thomas L. McKenney, March 4, 1826, Bureau of Indian Affairs, Letters Received, Record Group 75, NA; John Ridge to Albert Gallatin, Feb. 27, 1826, in "Letters From Missionaries, 1828. John Ridge Sketch of the Conditions of the Cherokee Nation," John Howard Payne Papers, vol. 8, NL. See also William C. Sturtevant, ed., "John Ridge on Cherokee Civilization in 1826," *Journal of Cherokee Studies* 6 (Fall, 1981): 79–91.

[30]Lewis Cass to Albert Gallatin, Oct. 3, 1826; William Clark to Albert Gallatin, March 31, 1826, Gallatin Papers, NYHS.

[31]Walters, *Albert Gallatin*, p. 329; Thomas L. McKenney to Albert Gallatin, April 1, 1825; Albert Gallatin to George Folsom, Nov. 27, 1835, copy, Gallatin Papers, NYHS; Albert Gallatin to unknown, March 31, 1826, Letters Received by the Office of Indian Affairs, Letter book 1, Record Group 75 NA.

rope; and each viewed the other as a compatriot expanding the frontiers of knowledge in philology.

In 1826, Gallatin published *A Table of Indian Languages of the United States*, complete with a colored map designating tribal locations.[32] The product of two years of intermittent labor, the work was significant not only because it contained the first tribal language map ever prepared for America, but also because it marked the first attempt to designate language groups by comparative methods. Although its brevity called for fuller explanation, Gallatin's mission to England that year precluded further research and writing. Du Ponceau congratulated Gallatin on this philological contribution, noting that maps of language distribution were much in vogue in Europe. He hoped Gallatin would be in a position while abroad to influence bodies such as the French Academy to support the mapping of more language areas, although he feared Gallatin's government mission would end his philological career.[33] Gallatin himself expressed distaste with his pending government employ and replied to Du Ponceau that it held prospects for neither pleasure nor profit and that he preferred to stay home engaged in his "historical pursuits."[34]

Du Ponceau's fears proved groundless, for when Gallatin returned the following year he plunged into his philological studies. He hoped to expand on his language chart of 1826, which had raised certain questions. For those who expected philology to provide clues to Indian origins, Gallatin's work held little comfort.[35] Others doubted that scholars who were poorly acquainted with Indians or who had never attempted to learn their languages and had never

[32] Albert Gallatin, *A Table of Indian Languages of the United States, East of the Stony Mountains, arranged according to languages and dialects.*

[33] Stephen Du Ponceau to Albert Gallatin, May 13, 1826, Gallatin Papers, NYHS.

[34] Albert Gallatin to Stephen Du Ponecau, May 16, 1826, Du Ponceau Papers, APS.

[35] Edward Everett to Albert Gallatin, June 27, 1826, Gallatin Papers, NYHS.

dealt with them at treaty or trade negotiations could offer any insight on their languages. Gallatin moved to prove such criticism wrong.

His chance came in 1834 when the American Antiquarian Society asked to publish Gallatin's essay on Indian languages, which he had written in 1823 for a volume Alexander von Humboldt was preparing. Gallatin's article was never published in von Humboldt's book. Instead it was given to Adriano Balbi, who praised it highly in the introduction to his *Atlas ethnographique du globe*.[36] Balbi's mention came to the attention of the American Antiquarian Society, which asked to publish the essay. Gallatin had not kept a copy of the essay and therefore offered to write a new article.

Gallatin's "Synopsis of the Indian Tribes of North America" was published by the American Antiquarian Society in 1836. According to one of Gallatin's biographers, it was his most "elaborate literary work."[37] In this essay Gallatin accepted several givens: all mankind constituted a single species; man progressed from savagery through barbarism to civilization; and the Indians of both South America and North America were one people. To Gallatin, the grammatical similarities found by Du Ponceau in the languages of Indians on both continents conclusively proved Indian affinity. Gallatin also firmly believed that through the comparative study of vocabularies tribes could be grouped into linguistic families.

"Synopsis" is actually an extension of the chart Gallatin published in 1826, although in essay form. Here he elaborated upon his methodology and sources. Gallatin drew primarily on early historical, travel, and missionary accounts, vocabulary lists, and material gathered through his own contacts with Indians in Washington. Four initial sections delineate the geographical and linguistic groupings of Indian tribes, an approach Gallatin employed to comment on

[36]George Folsom to Albert Gallatin, May 20, 1834; Nov. 13, 1834; Dec. 12, 1834; Albert Gallatin to George Folsom, Dec. 5, 1834, Gallatin Papers, NYHS; Walters, *Albert Gallatin*, p. 329.
[37]Hale, p. 29.

aspects of Indian behavior and culture.[38] In section 5, titled "General Observations," in an examination of the effect of climate and environment on subsistence patterns, Gallatin probed Indians' seeming inability to move toward civilization, commented on their origins, and conjectured about their future. Section 6 is an extended discussion of Indian languages, followed by appendices of grammatical patterns of various tribes, comparative vocabularies, and sentence lists.

Gallatin found through an analysis of the vocabularies of eighty-one tribes that they could be grouped into twenty-eight families. A "family" was considered broadly to include all languages "which contained a number of similar primitive words, sufficient to show that they must, at some remote epoch have had a common origin."[39] Not willing to proceed further to trace the twenty-eight groups to a single language or back to Asia as other philologists had attempted, Gallatin remained true to an older ethnological tradition concerned less with origins than with mustering evidence of universal reason and stages of development. Gallatin gathered data on Indian languages in order to better understand the formation and development of language. He reassured those to whom origins were important that the number of distinct language families did not disprove the possibility of Indian Old World origins, nor were they inconsistent with "Mosaic chronology."[40]

Although Gallatin lacked interest in searching for origins, he aggressively confronted the theory that the polysynthetic nature of Indian languages suggested a more advanced and sophisticated civilization than Indians currently maintained. By the 1830s the view that Indians had degenerated from a more advanced state of civilization had received wide acceptance. It was a theory seemingly supported by evidence from mound archaeology in the Ohio and Mississippi valleys and by the discovery of the poly-

[38] Gallatin, "Synopsis." See his prefatory letter to George Folsom, pp. 1–8.
[39] Ibid., p. 4.
[40] Ibid., p. 5.

synthetic nature of Indian languages. The theory of Indian cultural degeneration countered Enlightenment concepts of social progress or the slow evolution of societies out of savagery. Gallatin believed that many people associated the "vague notion of inflected languages with an advanced state of civilization. . . . [and that the] admiration felt for the great writers of Rome and Greece . . . have given us the habit of associating inflected languages with knowledge and civilization, and those destitute of those forms with barbarism and ignorance."[41] Gallatin's study of the formation of language suggested that the reverse was true. Inflected or polysynthetic languages actually revealed a primitive rather than an advanced level, an indication that Indians were more primitive than the ancient Greeks and Romans.

"Synopsis" has merited greatest attention as a study of the linguistic groupings of Indian tribes.[42] Given the proportion of text devoted to extended linguistic analysis and theories of language formation, studying these linguistic groupings also was Gallatin's main objective in writing the essay. Yet "Synopsis" was more than a philological study; it was also an essay on the interaction between environments and Indian cultures. Gallatin was interested in presenting "some peculiarities which appeared to deserve attention, and more especially to the means of subsistence of the Indians, to the causes of their gradual extinction, and to the only means by which, as it seems to me, the residue can be preserved," and the subject was important enough for him

[41] Ibid., p. 202.

[42] As one twentieth-century linguist has pointed out, "Considering the small amount of material at the time available, Mr. Gallatin's conclusions are sound and accurate." Pliny Earle Goddard, "The Present Condition of Our Knowledge of North American Languages," *American Anthropologist* 16 (1914): 558; Powell, "Indian Linguists," pp. 12–18, 25–26; Raymond Walters, *Albert Gallatin*, pp. 353–54; Edgerton, p. 30; Samuel F. Haven, *Archaeology of the United States, or Sketches, Historical and Bibliographical, of the Progress of Information and Opinion Respecting Vestiges of Antiquity in the United States*, Smithsonian Contributions to Knowledge 8; John Russell Bartlett, *The Progress of Ethnology*. Earlier editions of this work appeared in the *Proceedings of the New-York Historical Society* (1846) and *Transactions of the American Ethnological Society* 2 (1845).

to give it a central place in his essay.[43] It is in this section of "Synopsis" that one sees most clearly those concerns regarding the Indians' advance toward "civilization" that preoccupied Gallatin when he was secretary of the treasury. In 1805 he had written to Jefferson that the Indians' failure to improve rested on their licentiousness. This licentiousness Gallatin attributed to a "want of the social institutions which establish and secure *property* and *marriage*." Lack of these institutions was "the greatest obstacle to [their] civilization."[44] In "Synopsis," Gallatin would expand upon these assumptions.

By the 1830s there was an increasing tendency to judge progress in racial terms and to measure it on an individual rather than a social basis. Gallatin's emphasis on environment and its effect on man and society reveals his continuing affinity to Enlightenment thought. According to Gallatin, environmental, not racial, factors were the catalytic agents that propelled societies toward civilization. Gallatin demonstrated little concern over such physical attributes as skin color or physiognomy, but where he did he saw them as manifestations of the environment. Comparing Eskimos with Indians, he found that "the color and features are essentially the same; and the differences which may exist, particularly that in stature, may be easily accounted for by the rigor of the climate, and partly perhaps by the nature of their food."[45] Even the Indians' mental faculties, which he considered paralyzed, and their "moral feelings," which he thought debased, were "the result of the circumstances under which they were placed" and not the result of innate racial inferiority.[46] But this aspect of environmentalism, or ecological adaptation, was not Gallatin's real concern.

[43]Gallatin went on to point out that, "Notwithstanding the reckless cruelty and ravages of the first Spanish conquerors, the descendants of the native Mexicans are at present probably as numerous as their ancestors at the time of conquest. For this no other cause seems assignable than the fact, that they had then already emerged from the hunter state, and had acquired the habits of agricultural and mechanic labor." See "Synopsis," p. 7.

[44]Gallatin, *The Writings of Albert Gallatin*, p. 227.

[45]Gallatin, "Synopsis," p. 14.

[46]Ibid., pp. 155–56.

Gallatin was primarily interested in viewing environmentalism in terms of human subsistence patterns and how
such patterns explained differing degrees of social advancement. Thus his short essay at the beginning of section 5 on
"General Observations," on the geography and climate and
their effects on agriculture, is appropriate. For Gallatin,
the long march toward civilization began in agriculture; no
nation could ever be civilized without it.

The people in the western hemisphere who had progressed furthest along the road to civilization were agriculturalists. The Aztecs, Mayas, and Incas were so advanced that they seemed anomalies to many Americans
who believed their civilizations resulted from transoceanic
influence. Gallatin could not accept this theory. Asserting
that a similarity in climate existed between New and Old
World founts of civilization, he reasoned that centers of New
World advancement were found "precisely in those places,
where we might have expected to find them, if that civilization was of domestic origin." [47] New World civilization therefore was a product of Indian genius and an environment favorable to agriculture, not of foreign influence. [48]

Gallatin asserted the inevitability of agricultural development, given time and correct environmental conditions.
But a proper environment required more than appropriate
climate. Critical conditions such as scarcity of game, limited territory, and increased population must combine to
force nomadic tribes to become agriculturalists. To illustrate this point Gallatin pointed to three habitats. Tribes on
the plains suffered no food shortage because there the

[47] Ibid., p. 145.
[48] This does not mean that Gallatin regarded American Indians as autochthonous, for he endorsed their probable migration from Asia at a date
preceding the rise of civilization there. He deemed it ludicrous to seek proof
of an Asian migration from vocabulary lists, although he believed that coinci-
dental similarities would occur. According to Gallatin, "similarity of the
structure and grammatical forms of those of America indicate a common origin, and renders it probable that the great diversity of their vocabularies
took place in America." In addition Gallatin believed that the time required
for evolution of numerous languages from a common stock would be immense. See "Synopsis," pp. 143–44.

abundance of game could support a large population. The tribes north of the Great Lakes, however, although often enduring food shortages, were prevented from engaging in agriculture because of the severity of their climate. Where favorable climate and limited game resources combined, as in the area south of the Great Lakes and east of the Mississippi River, agriculture had taken hold.[49]

Not only did Gallatin believe that such factors affected agricultural development, he also discovered inextricable links between environment and social organization and behavior. Gallatin found Plains Indians gentle and honorable in war, especially tribes, such as the Pawnees, who were not "erratic" but instead lived in permanent villages along the river bottoms and practiced agriculture.[50] Those tribes on the plains that lived as hunters and ranged over vast tracts of land were characterized by extreme independence and often by indolence and improvidence.[51] Gallatin found that Indians living in the game-scarce woodlands, more hunters than farmers, had to jealously guard their limited territories and be constantly vigilant against intruders. They were ferocious in warfare and vicious in torture. The environment, specifically the scarcity of game, created conditions for the development of a more violent culture. Gallatin noted that as long as Indians retained their hunting ways, they required all the territory they possessed.[52] "We may also understand, how the affection of the Indian became so exclusively concentrated in his own tribe, the intensity of that natural feeling, how it degenerated into deadly hatred of hostile nations, and the excesses of more than savage ferocity in which he indulged under the influence of his unrestrained vindictive passions."[53] Gallatin claimed that the Iroquois had conquered only to destroy and had killed more Indians than the Europeans.[54]

[49] Ibid., pp. 151–53.
[50] Ibid., p. 129.
[51] Ibid., pp. 120–35.
[52] Ibid., p. 154.
[53] Ibid., p. 151.
[54] Ibid., pp. 79–80.

According to Gallatin, most tribes could not depend on hunting alone for survival, and they thus were forced to resort to agriculture to supplement their food resources. Women became the farmers while men continued as hunters and warriors, a practice Gallatin believed not only reduced women to slavery but also kept many tribes dependent upon a hunting economy that often failed and brought starvation. Yet even the limited farming performed by women often produced enough surplus food to allow village populations to increase. Population growth led, in turn, to the development of elaborate religions, well-defined measures of social control, and other features comprising a civilized society. But the conditions compelling the change to agricultural habits, Gallatin believed, had to be severe. Unlike the "culture hero" Manco Capac, reputed to have taught the Incas agriculture, "necessity and compulsion were the deities that made men submit to the fatigue of agricultural labor."[55]

Gallatin cited the southern tribes, especially the Choctaws, as interesting examples of people who, because of environmental restrictions, appeared to have advanced further than most. He based his opinion on Bernard Romans's claim that the Choctaws were more civilized, less prone to warfare, and less cruel toward prisoners than were neighboring tribes. Their men spent more time cultivating than hunting; fewer than half had killed a deer. They were an industrious people, doing what "'no other uncompelled savage will do, that is, work in the field to raise grain'" and helping "'their wives in the labor of the fields and many other works.'"[56] Gallatin's explanation of this anomaly rested on geographical and environmental factors. The Choctaws were confined on three sides by water in a territory of lim-

[55] Ibid., p. 156. Gallatin seemed impressed with the function of clans and moieties in defining marriage rules that prevented "degeneration into distinct tribes, and checked the natural tendency towards a subdivision of the nation into independent communities." According to Gallatin, they also functioned as integral parts of tribal political life and helped maintain village cohesiveness by "softening the effects of private revenge." Ibid., p. 112.

[56] Ibid., pp. 100–108.

ited game, but they were also favored with an environment that promised agricultural production with a minimum of labor. Conditions proved favorable to compel the southern tribes toward limited cultivation. Their choice of cultivate or starve was clear.[57]

Historically, in addition to environmental factors, slavery had enabled some societies to move from the hunter stage to an agriculture-based subsistence. This social condition played an important role in the Cherokees' advance toward civilization in the nineteenth century. Gallatin states: "The only well ascertained instance, amongst our own Indians, of their having, at least in part, become an agricultural nation, meaning thereby that state of society; in which the men themselves do actually perform agricultural labor, is that of the Cherokee. And it is in proof, that, in this case also, cultivation, was at first introduced through the means of slavery."[58] This historic fact may have proved ironic for the abolitionist Gallatin, especially at a time of increased agitation over the "peculiar institution." If slavery engendered civilization, did Gallatin advocate that slaves be provided to the Indians? Gallatin replied an emphatic no: "Example and persuasion can alone be resorted to."[59] His rationale lay in the Enlightenment belief that all men were rational and could improve through instruction. Therefore, instruction ought to be made the most conspicuous element in the Indians' environment.

But many in America questioned Gallatin's reasoning. If Indians responded to altered environments, why had so few changed when confronted by "superior" Euro-American civilization? Offered its advantages for more than two hundred years, Indians proved recalcitrant, turning away and retreating deeper into the woods. Those who could retreat no further merely disappeared, seeming to prefer death to change. The tragic history of the New England tribes

[57] Ibid., p. 108.
[58] Ibid., p. 157. See also John Ridge to Albert Gallatin, Feb. 27, 1826, Payne Papers, NL; and Sturtevant, "John Ridge."
[59] Gallatin, "Synopsis," p. 158.

seemed to offer proof, if not of Indian inferiority, at least of their inability to accept civilization. Indeed, some Americans who held this opinion seriously believed Indians so constituted as to be incapable of any change. Crossing the abyss from savagery to civilization was inherently impossible for them. The fault, some believed, lay not in the environment but in Indian biology.

Gallatin sharply denied the validity of these arguments. Agreeing that contact with whites may have "enlarged the sphere of ideas of the Indians and of late softened their manners," he felt changes were not extensive because of the very nature of the contact. In their relations with Indians, whites had altered the environment, but the result "has rather been to perpetuate than to change . . . [Indian] . . . habits."[60] In trade, "the fur and skin of wild animals were the only articles they could offer in exchange of European commodities; and commerce, which by increasing their wants might be considered as beneficial to them, has thus stimulated them to apply still more exclusively their time and faculties to the chase."[61]

Gallatin indicted the government as well as the fur trader: "Even the benevolent intentions of the government of the United States have not always taken the most proper direction. The larger compensation allowed for their lands, and the annuities bestowed upon them, have promoted the habit of being supported otherwise than by labor."[62] To subsist on the largesse of government rather than depending on their own toil for survival produced a debilitating effect upon the Indians, thus reinforcing what Gallatin believed to be their indolent nature. To treat Indians as beggars and yet expect them to change seemed unreasonable to Gallatin, who felt Indians often were treated unfairly. Yet he acknowledged that "if a scrupulous regard had always been paid to the rights of the Indians, this nation would not have sprung into existence." But assuring its own survival did

[60] Ibid., p. 155.
[61] Ibid.
[62] Ibid.

not absolve the nation from the responsibility of attempting the "converting [of] a purely hunting into an agricultural nation . . . one of the most difficult undertakings within the power of man."[63]

Gallatin assigned the government the task of creating a new environment and defining new conditions that would compel Indians to surrender old habits and embrace agriculture and civilization. Progress would then result; the abyss would then be bridged through education and example. Gallatin recommended that the government's program seize upon the Indians' attributes. Gallatin proclaimed that Indians were not without intelligence: "They have exhibited repeated proofs of intellectual powers apparently very superior to those of the African, and not very inferior to those of the European race." Neither were they insensible, for they displayed natural affection not only among themselves but often to total strangers.[64] Gallatin suggested that instruction be directed at the youth rather than at the population as a whole, for he believed the older generation too set in its habits to change, except perhaps to learn English. Although others accepted Indians as transitory figures on the landscape, Gallatin could not. Hope for their future lay with their youth, who must be made to understand that hunting and indolence were detrimental to their survival, and that their continued existence depended only upon acceptance of the "habit of manual labor."[65]

Overall, "Synopsis" reflected Enlightenment optimism. Indian languages were shown to be primitive. The large number of inflections indicated they were probably closer to mankind's original language than they were to Greek or Latin. If Indian languages were primitive, as believed, it followed that the people themselves were primitive and, contrary to speculation, had not degenerated from a more advanced civilization. Rather, the progress of some tribes toward civilization strongly indicated that further progress

[63] Ibid., pp. 155–56.
[64] Ibid., p. 156.
[65] Ibid., p. 159.

was possible. Faced with environments of limited resources, the Aztecs, Mayas, Incas, and to a limited extent, the American Indians living in the eastern woodlands of North America had acquired agriculture and had begun the momentous advance toward civilization. Gallatin underscored the points that environment was the significant factor in bringing about this movement and the requisite change in institutions, and that failure to progress lay with the environment and not in the Indian.

Gallatin felt that the Indians need not be exterminated to facilitate the advance of American civilization. His deep-seated conviction that war was wasteful both in money and in lives prompted him to suggest other ways to handle the impediment the Indians posed to the expanding nation. He recommended that the government foster an austere environment for Indians through its Indian policy. Large sums should no longer be paid Indians for their lands, and they should not receive annuities once they were placed on a reservation. Gallatin firmly believed that Indians faced with diminished game resources and limited funds with which to buy food would demonstrate their intelligence and turn to agriculture. In Gallatin's opinion, government aid ought to be calculated to advance that end. "It is not by treating them as paupers, that a favorable change can be expected."[66]

Gallatin's remarks echoed previously voiced sentiments and demands. For years supporters of the Indians had vociferously urged similar measures on the government.[67] Gallatin's "Synopsis" supported these demands with "scientific" rationale.

[66] Ibid., p. 155.
[67] Jedidiah Morse, *A Report to the Secretary of War of the United States on Indian Affairs*; Isaac McCoy, *History of Baptist Indian Missions: Embracing Remarks on the Former and Present Condition of the Aboriginal Tribes, and Their Settlement within the Indian Territory, and Their Future Prospects*; Isaac McCoy, *Remarks on the Practicability of Indian Reform, Embracing Their Colonization, with an Appendix*; Atwater, *Remarks*; McCulloh, *Researches, Philosophical and Antiquarian*; Cass, Rev. of *Travels*. . . .

To have a real influence on government policy, ethnology needed to speak with an authoritative voice. By 1840 the number of people involved in ethnological pursuits had increased markedly since the turn of the century. The lack of consensus among ethnologists on goals, however, resulted in chaos in the science. Although philology remained esoteric and the pursuit of gentleman scholars, archaeology and artifact collecting appealed to many as interesting and sometimes profitable enterprises. Those who envisioned the creation of a professional ethnology lamented that in the age of Jacksonian science anyone could be an ethnologist, a term that then included the archaeologist, merely by digging in Indian mounds or by collecting bones from Indian graves. Added to the concern about who ought to be considered an ethnologist was the problem of the use of ethnology in the growing racial controversy of the day. Given the debate between monogenists and polygenists in ethnology, it was inevitable that both sides in the slavery controversy should exploit the pronouncements of ethnology on the matter of race. An organization that could sift through and critically appraise the proliferation of racial theories was a welcomed desideratum.

Except for official governmental surveys that produced ethnological information, there was no organized body to which the government could turn for research and opinions on ethnological issues. Although organizations such as the American Philosophical Society, the American Antiquarian Society, the Academy of Natural Sciences of Philadelphia, and the New-York Historical Society supported ethnological research, no organization existed that was devoted especially to the promotion of ethnology. In response to this need, Gallatin assumed a leading role in helping to found the American Ethnological Society in 1842. He became its first president and subsidized the publication of the first two volumes of its *Transactions*. Because of Gallatin's poor health, most meetings were held at his house, where members enjoyed his conviviality and remembrances. Although there are no records of these early meetings, some of them were described in *The Literary World*.[68] After dinner the members would adjourn to another room where books, maps, and artifacts were presented and discussed. Sometimes a paper was read, as were communications from foreign ethnologists and missionaries. Two of the charter members, John R. Bartlett and Charles E. Welford, owned a bookstore and were a constant source of information on new ethnological publications. In the day before large research libraries, access to a bookstore in which the proprietors shared a devotion to the field proved invaluable.[69]

Gallatin gathered around him ethnologists who generally shared his monogenetic views and his belief in progress (only after his death did the polygenists launch an unsuccessful attempt to take over the society). His age, reputation, and accomplishments in ethnology made Gallatin the nation's foremost ethnologist. His presidency of the American Ethnological Society lent stature to the organization, and it was to this society that the Smithsonian Institution turned when it sought a panel of experts to provide critical appraisal of manuscripts in the field of ethnology. Yet not all members subscribed to Gallatin's ethnological theories and Enlightenment philosophy.

Society member Alexander Bradford is a case in point. In 1841 he published a book in which he argued that Indians did not demonstrate progressive tendencies but exemplified a people at different levels of degeneration from a higher civilization.[70]

> If the examination of the architectural monuments, and other remains of these three families of civilized nations, appears in

---

[68]"Reports of Societies," *Literary World* 8 (1851):371–74; see also other issues of *Literary World* and its column "Reports of Societies" between the years 1847 and 1853.

[69]For the founding of the American Ethnological Society, see John R. Bartlett, "Autobiography," Mss. pp. 30–33, Bartlett Papers, JCBL. A more extensive account is found in Robert E. Bieder and Thomas G. Tax, "From Ethnologists to Anthropologists: A Brief History of the American Ethnological Society," in *American Anthropology: The Early Years, 1974 Proceedings of the American Ethnological Society*, ed. John V. Murra, pp. 11–21.

[70]Alexander W. Bradford, *American Antiquities and Researches into the Origin and History of the Red Race*, pp. 171–74.

a measure, to identify their origin,—or at least to justify the inference, that they were constructed by members of the same primitive branch of the human race, separated after their arrival on this continent; whither are we to look for the origin of the other, and less civilized class of American aborigines? Whence came the tribes of barbarous Indians?

Perhaps in a veiled reference to Gallatin, Bradford posed rhetorically:

It may, possibly, be considered somewhat extraordinary, and unphilosophical, to search for any traces of their derivation from an ancient and civilized race, among the arts, customs, and traditions, of rude and ignorant savages. But although many of the Indian tribes, as well at the period of the discovery as at present, might be estimated as rude, and some of them nearly at the lowest grade of humanity, there exists reason for asserting of them, in common with other families of men, a descent from a more enlightened ancestry.[71]

Bradford claimed that the Indians had lost much of their cultural baggage during their wanderings and that consequently they had degenerated into that state of society in which the Europeans first found them. Contrary to those who felt philology held the key to Indian history, Bradford claimed that "similarity of language is not sufficient to indicate the common origin of nations, for by conquest and other causes, native languages have sometimes been adopted by the conquerors, and at others been eradicated and supplanted."[72]

An even greater threat to Gallatin's Enlightenment progressivism appeared in a long essay by W. F. Van Amringe submitted to the American Ethnological Society, probably for publishing consideration. According to Van Amringe, "all men possess, radically, the same principles, or elements of intellectual power; and although there are evidently specific modifications of them, which have, to this day, prevented some of the species from improving them beyond certain limits, and have caused others to retrograde

[71] Ibid., p. 172.
[72] Ibid., p. 246.

below the original standard, yet we know that all of the attributes may be highly improved by various means, the chief of which is exercise."[73] Van Amringe, however, did not confine his explanation of differences in man to degeneration. He pointed to other causes: "The anatomical and physiological differences between the races of men, constitute them distinct species. . . . All the historical facts of the human species, and all the scientific principles of classification, support and confirm these conclusions."[74]

By the 1840s the theories of degeneration and polygenism increasingly threatened Gallatin's firm belief in the validity of Enlightenment ideals concerning the unity and progressive nature of mankind. It is within that framework that Gallatin wrote his "Notes on the Semi-Civilized Nations of Mexico, Yucatan and Central America" and his "Introduction" to "Hale's Indians of North-west America." In "Synopsis," Gallatin wrote a more utilitarian address concerning public policy and its relation to the "civilization" of the Indians. It reflected the kinds of issues that had preoccupied Gallatin when he was secretary of the treasury: territorial expansion and payments to the Indians for land and annuities. In "Synopsis," Gallatin advocated even greater purchases of land from the Indians, so that they would be forced to abandon hunting; an austerity program of relief that would compel Indians to farm; and an expansion of educational programs especially for Indian children. Considered in this light, "Synopsis" fit well within the Enlightenment tradition that emphasized the gathering of useful knowledge. In his last two ethnological works, Gallatin moved from utilitarian concerns to address more theoretical issues. The focus then was on the question of parallel, or independent, development of Indian civilization.

[73] William Frederick Van Amringe, *An Investigation of the Theories of the Natural History of Man, By Lawrence, Prichard, and Others*, p. 491. This work was originally submitted to the American Ethnological Society for publication but was then withdrawn by Van Amringe and sold on subscription. See William Van Amringe to John R. Bartlett, Feb. 6, 1847; May 20, 1848, Bartlett Papers, JCBL; William Van Amringe to Albert Gallatin, Aug. 9, 1847, Gallatin Papers, NYHS.

[74] Van Amringe, *An Investigation*, pp. 419–21.

This he considered the "most interesting problem" in the field of American ethnology: the question whether Indian civilizations had grown and developed slowly or were the result of knowledge from foreign sources. This question, in turn, presupposed two further questions of equal significance: "that of the presumed inferiority of some races; and whether savage tribes can, of themselves, and without foreign assistance, emerge from the rudest and lowest social state, and gradually attain even the highest degree of civilization known to us."[75]

In these last two works, Gallatin reiterated his belief in the instrumentality of the environment to spur agriculture and progress. An agricultural state led to development of cities, arts, and science. Gallatin asserted that advances in mathematics and astronomy by Indian civilizations of both South and Central America confirmed his position. For those who claimed that these advances originated in Europe or Asia, Gallatin drew upon Mexican calendars to prove that the astronomical discoveries could have been made only in the tropics. Furthermore, he stated that the evidence relating to the astronomical knowledge of the Incas, Aztecs, and Mayas revealed radically different approaches to calendrical computation and indicated independent development between these peoples. "If both the Peruvian and Mexican calendars were not the result of their own independent observations, we must suppose a double importation of astronomical knowledge, one to Peru and another to Mexico, coming from two different quarters, and by people possessed of different degrees of knowledge."[76]

If this proof still did not silence the criticism, Gallatin was prepared to turn the question on his critics. Gallatin did not believe that primitive astronomers—probably of a "priestly order"—who held such esoteric knowledge would be allowed to emigrate. But if it were acknowledged that such men existed who "have communicated that astronomical knowledge which the Mexicans were found to possess,

[75] Gallatin, "Notes," p. 181.
[76] Ibid., p. 185.

why did they not bring also an alphabet, the art of working iron, mills, wheel-barrows, a multitude of other common arts, which remained unknown to the Mexicans, and at least the seeds of rice, millet, wheat, or of some other grain cultivated in the countries whence they came? If coming from one where agriculture was unknown, it is not probable that they were much advanced in science."[77] Gallatin chided his opponents on this matter. In what is now an axiom for scholarly investigation, Gallatin asserted, "in order to form a correct opinion, it is necessary to take into consideration, not only what the Mexicans knew, but also that which they did not know."[78]

Gallatin remained reluctant to explore the questions of polygenism and Indian migration to the Americas, yet he affirmed that "all probabilities" suggested Asian migration, a conclusion based on the Indians' physical characteristics and on the proximity of Asia to North America. Gallatin reasoned that unless one accepted the premise of special creation, "it is far more probable that they should be the descendants of people, whose physical type is the most similar to theirs, than of nations in that respect of a totally different character."[79] Furthermore, although this argument seemed to Gallatin to be common sense, he recognized its limitations when he stated that, "in the total absence of positive facts, this is a question of probability; and all that is contended for is, that the migration from Asia is much more probable" than from northern Europe or North Africa.[80] Admitting that philology could not prove conclusively that Indians emigrated from Asia and that vocabularies alone could not provide much help, Gallatin nonetheless affirmed that similarities between languages could be discovered in their grammatical framework or

[77] Ibid., pp. 186–87.

[78] Ibid., p. 187. In another context, Stephen Jay Gould points out that "nonevents" can be just as important as "events" in the history of science. See "Nasty Little Facts," *Natural History* 94 (February 1985): 14–25.

[79] Gallatin, "Notes," pp. 174–75.

[80] Ibid., p. 175.

"general structure," which was less subject to alteration in time.[81]

Gallatin surmised correctly that the drift toward degeneration and polygenism had at bottom a belief in the innate inferiority of the Indian and of nonwhite races in general. Such beliefs shaped the thinking of many in nineteenth-century America and found expression in calls for the removal of Indians beyond the sphere of American economic interest. People wrote openly of the Indians' ultimate demise and urged that "as a distinct nation or nations, they must vanish from the North American continent. . . ."[82] For many, Indians would always be anomalies in America, for their way of life and limited capacity for "improvement" precluded their ever achieving a place in American civilization. Gallatin firmly believed it a dangerous trend to indulge in such thinking. In a different context, but demonstrating the same concern, he asked, "Is it compatible with the principle of democracy, which rejects every hereditary claim of individuals, to admit an hereditary superiority of races?" Gallatin rejected as a "shallow attempt to disguise unbounded cupidity and ambition" the increasingly popular assumption that Anglo-Saxons possessed "an hereditary superiority of race" over other races.[83] Although Gallatin recognized that different levels of social complexity prevailed among races, he believed that positions of superiority were not dependent upon race "but to a variety of causes. . . . In the progressive improvement of mankind much more has been due to religious and political institutions than to races."[84] According to Gallatin, the institutions of a civilization were rooted in environments, as were, to a limited extent, the very personalities and habits of a people.

[81] Ibid., p. 177.
[82] Review of George Catlin's *Letters and Notes on the Manners, Customs and Conditions of the North American Indians* and Alexander W. Bradford's *American Antiquities and Researches . . .* , in *New York Review* 10 (April, 1842): 419–48.
[83] Gallatin, *Writings* 3: 585–86.
[84] Ibid., p. 585.

In his last years, poring over reports from government exploring expeditions to the Southwest, Gallatin became increasingly interested in the Indians of that region, who manifested a relatively high level of civilization. The eighty-seven-year-old ethnologist regretted that he did not have time to investigate the environment and languages of the Indians of New Mexico and Arizona, as they posed a pleasant anomaly. Writing in his "Introduction" to "Hale's Indians of North-west America," Gallatin acknowledged:

> The examination of the social state of the aborigines of America is an important leaf in the history of Man. It is undoubtedly interesting to ascertain the progress which a people may make, when almost altogether insulated, and unaided by more enlightened nations. But the result of the inquiry is almost universally afflicting; and if I have dwelt longer on the history of these people [of New Mexico and Arizona] than consistent with the limits of this essay, it is because it has been almost the only refreshing episode in the course of my researches.[85]

His letters to W. H. Emory and James W. Abert, two young army officers on General Stephen W. Kearny's exploring expedition to the Southwest, reflect a growing fascination with these Indians. The earliest correspondence suggests that Gallatin initially was interested merely in confirming these Indians' geographical location and in obtaining samples of their vocabularies, which "would at once settle the question of the identity with any of the Mexican nations." He quickly realized, however, that "the phenomenon of this insulated semicivilized population is in itself remarkable and difficult to explain." Here was a North American people living, like earlier-known examples of Central American peoples, in villages with well-constructed houses and practicing agriculture.[86] Within the context of Gallatin's theoretical model, these people either must have come from the south or from Mexico, or must have had contact with the southern civilizations where agriculture

---

[85] Gallatin, "Introduction" to Hale, p. xcvii.
[86] Albert Gallatin to W. H. E. [Emory], Oct. 1, 1847, copy; see also W. H. Emory to Albert Gallatin, Sept. 20, 1847, Gallatin Papers, NYHS.

began. What interested him was the selective borrowing of cultural traits.

Gallatin questioned Emory about the crops, warfare, and vocabularies of the Pima and Maricopa Indians, two tribes located near the mouth of the Colorado River. He also asked for more information about the Pueblo Indians. According to Emory, the Pimas and Maricopas were peace-loving, industrious farmers who tilled squares of earth; practiced irrigation; grew cotton, wheat, maize, and other crops; raised cattle, horses, ducks, chickens, and pigs; and constructed thatched houses. Polygamy was unknown, and adultery, like other crimes, was punished severely by public opinion, since these Indians maintained a "high regard for morality."[87]

Letters from James W. Abert informed Gallatin of the similar customs and level of advancement among the Pueblos. After describing various Pueblo villages, Abert mentioned that he had heard stories that the country surrounding Quivira was rich in "beasts and fruits," domestic cattle, and aquaducts.[88] Although Gallatin was skeptical about some of this information, especially that portion based on hearsay, the reports indicated a more advanced civilization than he had expected to discover. Considering earlier reports written by Abert and Emory, Gallatin wondered whether even the "seven towns (from Chiloli to Abo and Quivira) [were] actually Indian villages or [perhaps Spanish] pueblos now inhabited by Indians."[89] Behind Gallatin's thoughts lay his idea that wandering tribes had found these villages in ruins and had taken them for themselves. Certainly such a succession corresponded more with his theoretical view of the North American Indians. Contrary to Gallatin's conjecture, Abert felt the present tribes had built the houses in which they lived. Abert also accepted the

[87] W. H. Emory to Albert Gallatin, Oct. 8, 1847, Gallatin Papers, NYHS.

[88] John J. Abert to Albert Gallatin [with copy of J. W. Abert's letter], Nov. 18, 1847, Gallatin Papers, NYHS.

[89] Albert Gallatin to W. H. Emory, Oct. 1, 1847, copy; Albert Gallatin to John J. Abert, Oct. 23, 1847 (copy), Gallatin Papers, NYHS.

[90] J. W. Abert to Albert Gallatin, Nov. 13, 1847, Gallatin Papers, NYHS.

stories that the tribe had emigrated from Mexico sometime in the past.[90]

Gallatin tended to agree with Abert regarding emigration. Recognizing that Pueblo crops and agricultural techniques derived from Mexico, Gallatin felt that a study of their language would provide the best guide to their origin. Unfortunately, Abert's short letter provided insufficient data from which "to draw legitimate inferences," since he mainly included words borrowed from Spanish.[91] Yet despite the lack of good vocabularies, Gallatin was excited about the data he had received, for it seemed to provide further proof that the practice of agriculture and civilization were intricately related.

A major concern of Gallatin's centered on how these people, separated by seven hundred miles of "wild" Indian tribes, attained "a degree of civilization, inferior indeed in most respects to that of Mexico and Guatimala, but very superior to that of any other native tribe of North America." Gallatin considered that "this singular phenomenon deserves particular attention."[92] These people grew maize, a plant that Gallatin believed had been domesticated in the tropics. Somehow maize cultivation had spread northward while other traits of Central American cultures had not. This selectivity in borrowing traits posed a fascinating problem, one Gallatin realized he had not the time to answer.

Gallatin wrote that the southwestern tribes had no kings or nobility and thus no "serf of degraded caste"; no clique comprised of despot, favored caste, and priests "of a most execrable worship"; but rather a government in the hands of a council of old men. Knowing neither cannibalism nor human sacrifice, the Indians lived at peace and engaged only in defensive wars. In Gallatin's opinion, their emphasis on chastity and "conjugal fidelity of both sexes," their respect for property and great "integrity" in all their relationships, as well as their enforcement of social norms through

[91] Albert Gallatin to J. W. Abert, March 13, 1848, copy, Gallatin Papers, NYHS.

[92] Gallatin, "Introduction" to Hale, p. liv.

the rule of public opinion, "bespeak a far higher standard of morality than that of any other American nation." Furthermore, "if inferior to the Mexicans in the expansion of the intellectual, they were far superior in the exercise of the moral faculties."[93]

These indices of cultural advancement reveal much concerning the nature of Gallatin's values regarding property, integrity, and morality. A government of old men sitting in council perhaps even struck Gallatin as similar to the city council of Geneva, his birthplace. Perhaps Gallatin could say he had found his "noble savage," but then the "savage" was not very savage at all.

In many ways Gallatin was more European than American. He placed much emphasis upon education, claiming that during his youth in Geneva he had learned that "to all those who were ambitious of reknown [sic], fame, [and] consideration, scientific pursuits were the only road that could lead to distinction, and to these, or other literary branches, all those who had talent and energy devoted themselves."[94] Thus it was not modesty that prompted him to write to a friend that although his public writings on government and economics were of little account, his works in science, philology, and ethnology would cause his name to be remembered.[95] Although he embarked upon a scientific career late in life, Gallatin entered an arena of science much respected in Europe. That philology had scant recognition in America little concerned him.

If Gallatin identified with Europe, he also associated

[93] Ibid., pp. xcvi–xcvii.

[94] Albert Gallatin to Eben Dodge, January 21, 1847, quoted in Gallatin, *Selected Writings*, p. 5.

[95] Hall, "Gallatin," p. 109. For a slightly different view, see Albert Gallatin's letter to J. C. L. Sismondi in 1842: "All my writings . . . adhere to my political career and have only a local and transitory importance. I had not the talents to cultivate letters and science successfully; and my abililties have probably been more usefully employed in the active life into which I was thrown and for which I was better suited." Quoted in Walters, *Albert Gallatin*, p. 352. Gallatin was perhaps a bit modest in this letter to his friend and famed Swiss historian.

with an earlier America, that of Thomas Jefferson. The bold dream of the founding fathers had disintegrated for Gallatin, and late in life he seriously considered returning to Switzerland. In both temperament and lifestyle he belonged to another generation. Even his theories on man seemed outdated to many. Yet Gallatin resented theories that countermanded the Enlightenment optimism he held so close to his heart, and he defended his fundamental belief in man's rationality. His emphasis upon environmentalism and his attacks upon a racial interpretation of history were rooted in these concerns.

To Gallatin the abyss between savagism and civilization need not be swept away through the elimination of one side by extermination or war. "The people of the United States may rightfully . . . exercise a most beneficial moral influence over . . . less enlightened nations of America." And, in what may have sounded queer in a jingoistic and expansion-crazed America distracted by a "glorious" war with Mexico, Gallatin admonished, "truth never was or can be propagated by fire and sword, or by any other than moral means." The validity of this edict entailed some assumptions about human beings, and Gallatin, firm in his Enlightenment philosophy, reminded his readers that "our Creator has implanted in the hearts of men the moral sense of right and wrong."[96]

To Gallatin ethnology was a humanistic science, a science of man and for man. In ethnology lay the potential not only for human beings to retrieve their past but also to shape a better future. But Gallatin was out of step with his time; his ethnology drew upon an older tradition and expressed the optimism of another age. In an America increasingly raucous in its concern with questions of race, Gallatin's voice proved too quiet to be heeded.

[96]Gallatin, "Peace with Mexico," in *Writings* 3: 586.

3

Samuel G. Morton and the Calculations of Inferiority

GALLATIN'S ATTACK on racial thinking opposed a growing trend in ethnology. Attitudes and events in early nineteenth-century America inexorably channeled ethnological research into the service of racial causes. This new focus in ethnology stood in contrast to Gallatin's views and eighteenth-century ethnological concerns, which stressed environmental cause for change in man and saw man's history as a series of progressive stages. The new focus stressed the immutability of racial types and perceived race in deterministic terms and as the source of civilization.[1] Gallatin believed in monogenism, and the emerging trend moved toward an acceptance of polygenism. Thus while Gallatin's ethnology headed in one direction, this new focus veered off in another. If Gallatin's work reflected an earlier tradition, the work of Philadelphia physician Samuel G. Morton (1799–1851) competed with that tradition and seemed more in tune with the growing racial concerns of the day.

At the age of fourteen, having read Dr. Benjamin Rush's *Introductory Lectures on Medicine*, Samuel G. Morton decided to become a doctor. This was not an unusual choice. Because he was a Quaker, two popular eighteenth-century occupations—the pulpit and the bar—were closed to Morton, and he disliked the countinghouse to which he was apprenticed. Medicine represented an opportunity to improve his status and also appealed to his shy, studious nature.

[1]George W. Stocking, Jr., "Some Problems in the Understanding of Nineteenth Century Cultural Evolution," in *Readings in the History of Anthropology*, ed. Regna Darnell, p. 413.

Born in 1799 in Philadelphia and educated in Quaker schools in New York and New Jersey, Morton early retreated into the world of books and developed a fondness for poetry and history. Unfortunately, as he later recognized, his early schooling demanded little, and he acquired only a lackluster education. Medicine, however, did challenge Morton. He acquired his early medical instruction and experience in Philadelphia under the guidance of the strict Quaker physician Dr. Joseph Parrish, then at the height of his fame. Morton supplemented his apprenticeship with courses in anatomy, physiology, therapeutics, materia medica, physics, and surgery at the University of Pennsylvania, where in 1820 he was awarded the degree of Doctor of Medicine. In the same year the Academy of Natural Sciences elected him a member.[2]

With his degree in medicine and recognition as a scientist, Morton decided to see a bit of the world beyond the confines of Philadelphia. In 1820 he visited his uncle, James Morton, Esq., of Clomel, Ireland, a man of "affluent circumstances." The elder Morton soon convinced his nephew that an American degree in medicine was of little value and that "he should possess himself of one . . . more authoritative and distinguishing." James Morton suggested the University of Edinburgh, which, although past its prime, still maintained a distinguished medical school. Thus, in the autumn of 1820, Samuel Morton found himself again in medical school, where, in addition to medicine, he

[2] Henry S. Patterson, "Memoir of the Life and Scientific Labors of Samuel George Morton," in *Types of Mankind: Ethnological Researches* . . . , ed. J. C. Nott and George Gliddon, pp. xvii–xxii; Charles D. Meigs, *A Memoir of Samuel George Morton, M.D., Late President of the Academy of Natural Sciences of Philadelphia*, pp. 9–14; Sanford B. Hunt, "Samuel G. Morton," in *Lives of Eminent American Surgeons of the Nineteenth Century*, ed. Samuel D. Gross, pp. 597–603. Despite Morton's disparagement of his Quaker education, such an education may have had a greater influence than he realized. Quakers advocated an empirical approach to knowledge and emphasized things rather than words. See Brooke Hindle, "The Quaker Background and Science in Colonial Philadelphia," in *Early American Science*, ed. Brooke Hindle, p. 173; Frederick B. Tolles, *Meeting House and Counting House: The Quaker Merchants of Colonial Philadelphia, 1682–1763*, pp. 205–13.

found time to study both classical and modern languages and to attend the then famous lectures of Robert Jameson on geology and those of Professor John Gregory, an early advocate of phrenology.[3]

In 1821, Morton traveled to Paris, "then looked upon as the chief radiating point of medical science," and spent the year studying clinical medicine, probably under Pierre Louis, the great clinical scientist. The following year Morton returned to Edinburgh, and, after presenting his dissertation on the causes, diagnostic value, and effects of body pains, he received his medical degree from Edinburgh in 1823.[4]

Upon his return to Philadelphia, Morton took up the practice of medicine and renewed his affiliation with the Academy of Natural Sciences. He also was elected to the American Philosophical Society. One writer later expressed surprise that Morton had elected to enter the field of descriptive rather than comparative anatomy, the latter being a more popular field at the time.[5] Morton's decision, however, was consistent with his training in Paris, where he had come into contact with the "'school of observation' and the numerical method," which were then in their ascendency. Indeed, a statistical approach to medicine was growing in popularity in America at that time.[6] His work in Paris made him a valuable instructor, and he assisted Joseph Parrish, his former teacher, in his lectures. Morton also lectured at the Philadelphia Hospital, Pennsylvania College, and the Alms-House Hospital. Besides maintaining a practice, he found time to write articles and books on medical subjects

[3] Meigs, pp. 14–15.
[4] Patterson, pp. xvii–xxii; Meigs, pp. 14–17; Richard H. Shryock, *Medicine and Society in America: 1660–1860*, pp. 123–25; Richard H. Shryock, *The Development of Modern Medicine: An Interpretation of the Social and Scientific Factors Involved*, pp. 167–68; Erwin H. Ackerknecht, *Medicine at the Paris Hospital, 1794–1848*, pp. 102–103, 192–93.
[5] Hunt in Gross, pp. 586–87.
[6] Erwin H. Ackerknecht, "Elisha Bartlett and the Philosophy of the Paris Clinical School," *Bulletin of the History of Medicine* 24 (1950): 55–57; James H. Cassedy, *American Medicine and Statistical Thinking, 1800–1860*, pp. 3–4, 152–53.

and in 1839 was selected to fill the chair of anatomy in the Medical Department of Pennsylvania College.[7]

But medicine did not absorb all of Morton's time. Between 1823 and 1835 he explored another interest, geology. With friends, Morton tramped the New Jersey and eastern Pennsylvania countryside, poking around marlpits and stream and canal beds in search of fossils and mineral deposits. He reported his findings and research before the Academy of Natural Sciences. Morton proved especially interested in taxonomy and the discovery and classification of new species.[8]

In 1830 a new field of inquiry engaged Morton's attention and clearly competed with his continuing preoccupation with geology. Morton was to derive most of his fame from his new interest, the collection and classification of human crania. According to Morton, "Having had the occasion, in the summer of 1830, to deliver an introductory lecture to a course on Anatomy, I chose for my subject 'The different forms of skull as exhibited in the five races of men.' Strange

---

[7] Patterson, pp. xxvi–xxviii; Meigs, pp. 20–21; for the influence of Paris on Philadelphia medicine, see Richard H. Shryock, "The Advent of Modern Medicine in Philadelphia, 1800–1850," *Yale Journal of Biology and Medicine* 13, no. 6 (July, 1941): 728–35; Richard H. Shryock, "Trends in American Medical Research During the Nineteenth Century," *Proceedings of the American Philosophical Society* 91 (February, 1947): 59.

[8] Morton published some of his findings in these areas in the journal of the society. See "Analysis of Tabular Spar, from Bucks county, Penna.," pp. 46–49; "Description of a new fossil species of Ostrea," pp. 50–51; "Description of the Fossil Shells which characterize the Atlantic Secondary Formation of New Jersey and Delaware," pp. 72–100; "Description of two new species of Shells of the genera Scaphites and Crepidula; with some observations on the Ferruginous Sand, Plastic Clay, and Upper Marine formations of the United States," pp. 107–119; "Note: containing a notice of some Fossils recently discovered in New Jersey," pp. 120–28; all in *Journal of the Academy of Natural Sciences of Philadelphia* 6 (1829). See also notices of S. G. Morton in the *Proceedings of Natural Sciences* vols. 1–5 (1841–51). Other articles of Morton's on geology and fossils were published in *American Journal of Science and Arts*. In several of these articles Morton reveals his fascination for identifying new species. It is useful to note in the context of Morton's interest in geology and biology the excellent article by Maurice Mandelbaum that discusses geology's influence on biology: "Scientific Background of Evolutionary Theory in Biology," in *Roots of Scientific Thought A Cultural Perspective*, ed. Philip P. Weiner and Aaron Noland, pp. 517–36.

to say, I could neither buy nor borrow a cranium of each of these races. . . . Forcibly impressed with this great deficiency in a most important branch of science, I at once resolved to make a collection for myself."[9]

Morton's reference to the differences in the crania of the five races of man raises questions in the context of phrenological thought of the day. Phrenologists claimed that the brain was the organ of the mind; that the brain was composed of individual faculties that controlled personality, thought, and moral action; that the strength of these faculties could be determined by protuberances on the skull; and that each race manifested its cultural traits through the shape of the cranium. Thus, phrenologists believed, each race possessed a typical, or national, cranium.

As Morton's statements reveal, his interest in acquiring crania began after the 1830 lecture; however, he may have begun collecting before that. It is unlikely that as a student Morton would have remained untouched by the excitement that phrenology generated in Edinburgh, London, and Paris. When he was in Edinburgh, the followers of the new "science" were gathering adherents to the faith. Several notable scholars endorsed phrenology, and collections of crania and casts of heads became common. Medical journals published findings of the new science, giving it added scientific respectability.[10] In Edinburgh, Morton came into contact with the phrenologist Gregory and in Paris perhaps with Franz Joseph Gall, the founder of phrenology, who was quite influential in medical circles.[11] Thus Morton's

[9]Samuel G. Morton, "Account of a Craniological Collection; with Remarks on the classification of some families of the human race," *Transactions of the American Ethnological Society* 2 (1848): 217.

[10]T. M. Parssinen, "Popular Sciences and Society: The Phrenology Movement in Early Victorian Britain," *Journal of Social History* 8 (Fall, 1974): 1–20; Lucile E. Hoyme, "Physical Anthropology and Its Instruments: An Historical Study," *Southwestern Journal of Anthropology* 9 (1953): 408–30; Cassedy, pp. 147–53.

[11]Erwin H. Ackerknecht and Henri V. Vallois, *Franz Joseph Gall, Inventor of Phrenology and His Collection*, Wisconsin Studies in Medical History, no. 1 (1956): 7–12, 32–36. For an extensive discussion of phrenology and anthropology, see Paul Alfred Erickson, "The Origins of Physical Anthropology"

interest in phrenology, acquired in Scotland and perhaps furthered in France, may have led him to collect crania, an activity that eventually drew him to ethnology and endowed him with the sobriquet "father of American physical anthropology."[12]

Phrenology was certainly not the only or even the major factor that drove Morton into a career of craniology. It was, however, one of several new scientific interests that crossed the Atlantic and made an impact in the halls of the American Philosophical Society and the Academy of Natural Sciences, invigorating American research. One focus of these studies was the profound question of man's relationship to other forms of life, especially to other primates. The quandary this problem posed to eighteenth-century philosophes remained to perplex nineteenth-century scientists. Questions of troglodytes and tailed men proved less vexing to nineteenth-century thinkers than they did to Linnaeus and Lord Monboddo; more important was the issue of whether man constituted one species or many. The debate settled on races: were different races actually various species of man, or, if all were the same species, then how did separate races evolve? It was in this debate that Morton would play a major role. The debate, however, had its own history, and that history helped to shape Morton's contributions to ethnology.

(Ph.D. diss., University of Connecticut, 1974); and Paul Alfred Erickson, "Phrenology and Physical Anthropology: The George Combe Connection," *Current Anthropology* 18 (March, 1977): pp. 92–93. See also John D. Davies, *Phrenology: Fad and Science: A 19th-Century American Crusade*, pp. 145–48; Owsei Temkin, "Gall and the Phrenological Movement," *Bulletin of the History of Medicine* 21 (May-June, 1947): 275–321.

[12][Luther Burke] "Progress of Ethnology in the United States," *The Literary World* 3 (September 23, 1848): 663; Aleš Hrdlička, "Contributions to the History of Physical Anthropology in the United States of America: With Special Reference to Philadelphia," *Proceedings of the American Philosophical Society* 87 (July, 1943): 61–63; Hoyme, pp. 415–24; T. D. Stewart and Marshall T. Newman, "An Historical Résumé of the Concept of Differences in Indian Types," *American Anthropologist* 53 (1951): 22. For Morton's early interest in phrenology, see Samuel G. Morton to George Combe, October 4, 1838, George Combe Papers, NLS; and Samuel G. Morton, "Study of Ancient Crania," *The Boston Medical and Surgical Journal* 31 (1844): 422–23.

The great taxonomist Carolus Linnaeus and the anatomist Petrus Camper, noted for his measurement of the facial angle,[13] both helped to define the issue, but the greatest contribution toward clarifying the issue in the eighteenth century came through the work and theorizing of Frenchman Georges Louis Leclerc Buffon and German Johann Friedrich Blumenbach. Both men were monogenists, and both believed that environment was the main determinant of racial characteristics. Of the two men, Blumenbach was the most important for anthropology. His dissertation *On the Natural History of Mankind* (1775) went through several editions and remained a significant work in physical anthropology into the nineteenth century. In it Blumenbach examined a collection of eighty-two skulls of various races and noted that each race possessed a cranial shape peculiar to that race. At a time when others were basing their findings on travelers' reports and rumors and were propounding numerous races, Blumenbach identified five basic races from empirical observation: Mongolian, American, Caucasian, Malayan, and Ethiopian. Through his observations of skulls he identified the Caucasian as the original type from which other races had degenerated. According to Blumenbach, the Caucasian skull was the most symmetrical when viewed from both the top and the back, and, since the circle was the most beautiful shape in nature, it followed that this cranium was the original type created by God.[14]

[13] Dutch anatomist Petrus Camper, in his examination of both ape and human skulls, found a gradual increase in the facial angle from the former to the latter. Measuring the angle formed by the intersection of the line from the forehead to the upper lip with the line from the base of the nose to the auditory opening, he found that the angle increased as one moved from ape to African to European. For a discussion of Camper, see John C. Greene, *The Death of Adam: Evolution and Its Impact on Western Thought*, pp. 188–93; Winthrop D. Jordan, *White Over Black: American Attitudes Toward the Negro, 1550–1812*, pp. 225–26 and passim; Philip D. Curtin, *The Image of Africa: British Ideas and Actions, 1780–1850*, 1: 39–40; Thomas F. Gossett, *Race: The History of an Idea in America*, pp. 69–70; Léon Poliakov, *The Aryan Myth: A History of Racist and Nationalist Ideas in Europe*, pp. 161–62.

[14] Greene, pp. 222–30; Gossett, pp. 36–39; Earl W. Count, "The Evolution of the Race Idea in Modern Western Culture During the Period of the Pre-Darwinian Nineteenth Century," *Transactions New York Academy of Science* 8, ser. 2 (Jan., 1946): 145–47; John C. Greene, "Some Early Specu-

By the end of the eighteenth century others were also pondering racial differences and arriving at various conclusions. Lord Kames in Scotland in his *Sketches of the History of Man* (1774) suggested that races were so divergent that they could be accounted for only by recognizing their separate creations. He realized that such thinking countered Biblical history, so he carefully tried to mute criticism by reconciling his views with Genesis.[15] A bit later Charles White, an English physician, published *An Account of the Regular Gradations of Man* (1799) in which he utilized a series of drawings representing cranial development in animals and man and deduced that the cranial shape of the Negro was too different from that of the white for these races to be considered of the same species.[16] White believed that the Negro formed an intermediate type between the white man and the ape. To White, this type did not indicate evolution but constituted a fixed and permanent level of development. Although he opposed the institution of slavery, White nevertheless reasoned from anatomical data (that happened to coincide with growing social attitudes) that the Negro race and the white race were actually two different species. White pointed out that only in the Caucasian could one find:

---

lations on the Origin of Human Races," *American Anthropologist* 56 (1954): 34. For an account of George Forster, a contemporary of Blumenbach, who held remarkably advanced views concerning race classification, see Erwin H. Ackerknecht, "George Forster, Alexander von Humboldt, and Ethnology," *Isis* 46 (1955): pp. 85–86. See also the excellent article by Richard H. Popkin, "The Philosophical Basis of Eighteenth-Century Racism," in *Racism in the Eighteenth Century: Studies in Eighteenth-Century Culture*, ed. Harold E. Pagliaro, 3: 245–62; and the surveys in Jacques Barzun, *Race: A Study in Superstition*, chap. 3; Robert F. Berkhofer, Jr., *The White Man's Indian: Images of the American Indian from Columbus to the Present*, pp. 38–44; and Poliakov, pts. 1, 2.

[15]George W. Stocking, Jr., "Scotland as the Model of Mankind: Lord Kames' Philosophical View of Civilization," in *Toward a Science of Man: Essays in the History of Anthropology*, ed. Timothy H. H. Thoresen, pp. 84–85; Gossett, pp. 50–51.

[16]Charles White, *An Account of the Regular Gradation in Man, and in Different Animals and Vegetables; and from the Former to the Latter*, p. iv; Nancy Stepan, *The Idea of Race in Science: Great Britain 1800–1900*, p. 8; Gossett, pp. 47–48.

that nobly arched head, containing such a quantity of brain. . . . Where that variety of features, and fulness of expression; those long, flowing, graceful ring-lets; that majestic beard, those rosy cheeks and coral lips? Where that . . . noble gait? In what other quarter of the globe shall we find the blush that overspreads the soft features of the beautiful women of Europe, that emblem of modesty, of delicate feelings . . . where, except on the bosom of the European woman, two such plump and snowy white hemispheres, tipt with vermillion.[17]

Another English physician opposed to slavery was James Cowles Prichard. Like Blumenbach and Buffon, Prichard too was a monogenist. He saw that cranial variations were used to identify species when in fact the variations were merely between races. Increasingly Prichard also noted that cranial gradations were employed by some to determine differences in intellectual endowment. Prichard deplored such a move, as well as the tendency to see cranial variation not as the result of differences in the environment but as racially determined. A careful scholar who utilized physical, historical, and linguistic data, Prichard labored to prove that mankind was one species and that racial differences could be accounted for by environmentalism. He could not dispute that races appeared unequal, but he firmly believed that all races had the potential for equality.

The social, political, and economic events of the early nineteenth century, the expansion of the European frontier, and the debate over slavery increasingly brought environmentalism into dispute. Although not everyone agreed, many believed that racial differences were innate and, as exhibited by Indians and blacks, were marks of inferiority. The need was growing for more exact criteria by which to determine these racial differences and to ascertain what such variations really meant.[18]

It was the "determination of ethnic resemblances and discrepancies by a comparison of crania" that prompted

[17]Charles White, p. 135.

[18]Gossett, pp. 54–56. For the most extended discussion of Prichard's anthropology, see George W. Stocking, Jr., "Introduction," in James Cowles Prichard, *Researches into the Physical History of Man*, ed. George W. Stocking, Jr.

Morton to collect skulls and to endeavor to improve upon the criteria for classifying races.[19] It was his hypothesis that the interior of the cranium revealed brain size and that cranial capacity differed among races and could be objectively determined and ranked. According to Morton, brain size and intelligence were correlated; determining the rank of one determined the rank of the other. To the physical data he would add material drawn from philology and from an assessment of moral character determined by phrenological investigation. The phrenological theories of Franz Joseph Gall and Johann G. Spurzheim, which he had absorbed while in Scotland and perhaps also while in Paris, proved valuable. Phrenology not only provided clues to the intellectual quality of the brain but also offered a theory that correlated biology with national character. Thus not only could Morton correlate physical size and intelligence with racial characteristics, but also he could measure size against moral traits and cultural development.

Initially, Morton primarily sought American Indian crania, but later he added others from Egypt, India, and European countries. Although a quiet man, Morton had the ability to engender enthusiasm in others for his researches and to enlist their support. His connections with the Academy of Natural Sciences and the American Philosophical Society provided a useful network of individuals eager to aid him. He appealed on a professional basis to other physicians, both civilian and military, in the West and asked them to send him all the Indian crania they could locate. In time Morton amassed the largest crania collection in the United States.

The establishment of a network of field investigators actually proved easier than the procurement of crania. Extracting intact skulls from mound sites along the Ohio and Mississippi rivers proved extremely difficult; most were crushed, or disintegrated with exposure to air.[20] Many that

[19] Patterson, p. xxviii.
[20] G. Troost to Samuel G. Morton, March 4, 1837, Morton Papers, APS; Patterson, p. xxix.

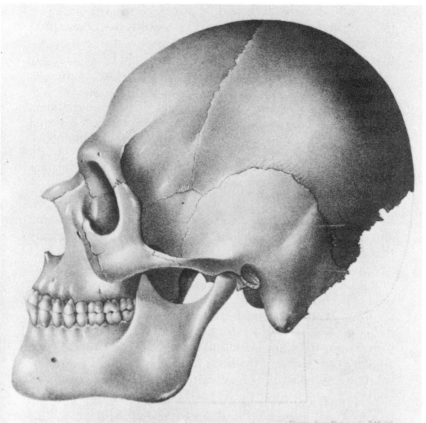

FROM THE GRAVE-CREEK MOUND
NEAR WHEELING, VIRGINIA

A skull from Grave Creek Mound in West Virginia. Lithograph by John Collins for Samuel G. Morton's *Crania Americana*.

did not disintegrate immediately often did so before they could be shipped to Philadelphia.

Other problems lessened the enthusiasm of field collectors. Although Indians seemingly expressed little concern over crania taken from the ancient mounds, they were acutely aware of Americans who robbed graves for the heads of recently deceased relatives. Such robberies at times brought retaliation against perpetrators. As one field collector wrote to Morton:

> It is rather a perilous business to procure Indians' skulls in this country—The natives are so jealous of you that they watch you very closely while you are wandering near their mausoleums & instant & sanguinary vengeance would fall upon the luckless ——— who would presume to interfere with the sacred relics . . . . There is an epidemic raging among them which carries them off so fast that the cemeteries will soon lack watchers—I don't rejoice in the prospects of death of the poor creatures certainly, but then you know it will be very convenient for my purposes.[21]

So great, however, were the collectors' passion for science and so little their regard for the Indians or their feelings that robbery of new graves continued.[22]

Apparently Morton was not the only physician gathering crania. Indian agent Henry Rowe Schoolcraft recorded a grisly tale from Sault Ste. Marie, Michigan. On September 26, 1826, a soldier reported seeing Robert McKain deliver an Indian head wrapped in a handkerchief to the hospital at Fort Brady. McKain later said that he had not robbed the Indian grave and that the head had been dug up by another soldier. According to Schoolcraft, however,

> Robert McKain has long had the reputation among his companions, of digging up dead bodies of Indians for pay. That sometime in the month of August last, between the 1st & 18th of that month, said McKain informed this deponent that he had been offered a good price by Doctor Lyman Foot for bringing him three Indian heads, and proposed to this deponent to assist in digging them up, which (this deponent) promptly declined. This deponent further says, that on the

---

[21] John Townsend to S. G. Morton, Sept. 20, 1835; William Wood to Daniel Drake, Sept. 28, 1833; Daniel Drake to Samuel G. Morton, Oct. 29, 1833, Morton Papers, APS.

[22] H. Galiotti to Samuel G. Morton, Dec. 27, 1841; Feb. 24, 1842, Samuel G. Morton Papers, LCP; Patterson, p. xxix. Other American physicians whose interests in phrenology led them to collect crania were John C. Warren, Charles Caldwell, and Elisha Bartlett. See Cassedy, pp. 148–49.

night of the 2nd of September instant, a light was seen in the Hospital during the night, as was reported among the soldiers at the guard house on the following morning. It was further added, that some of the guards went to the Hospital windows, suspecting that the heads of the Indians were in preparation, and saw kettles on the fire. And the guards who were stationed near the Hospital that night complained that a most abominable stench was experienced by them during the night arising from the Hospital, and suppose to be the effects of boiling the Indian skulls.[23]

The collecting of Indian crania appears to have been a cottage industry on the frontier.[24]

Crania of recently deceased Indians offered the opportunity to identify the tribe or band and to learn something about the individual. Occasionally, a field investigator could, in supplying a cranium, relate how a person had met his death and provide information on the identity, tribal position, level of intelligence, character, and defects of the deceased, all useful data for refining phrenological investigation.[25] This kind of information was especially valuable to Morton, who sought to correlate personality and intelligence with cranial size.

[23] Henry Rowe Schoolcraft to _____, Aug. 21, 1826, Letters Received, Sault Ste. Marie Indian Agency, Records of the Bureau of Indian Affairs, NA.

[24] This activity continued throughout the nineteenth century. On June 6, 1888, anthropologist Franz Boas recorded in his diary: "We discovered that someone had stolen all the skulls, but we found a complete skeleton without head. I hope to get another one either today or tomorrow. . . . It is most unpleasant work to steal bones from a grave, but what is the use, someone has to do it. I have carefully locked the skeleton into my trunk until I can pack it away. I hope to get a great deal of anthropological material here. Yesterday I wrote to the Museum in Washington asking whether they would consider buying skulls this winter for $600; if they will, I shall collect assiduously. Without having such a connection I would not do it." Quoted in *The Ethnography of Franz Boas: Letters and Diaries of Franz Boas Written on the Northwest Coast from 1886–1931*, ed. Ronald P. Rohner, p. 88. See also William H. Goetzmann, "The West and the American Age of Exploration," *Arizona and the West* 2 (Autumn, 1960): 265–78.

[25] John Bachman to Samuel G. Morton, March 17, 1837; Douglas Houghton to Samuel G. Morton, Nov. 21, 1837; J. Martin to Samuel G. Morton, Aug. 1, 1838, Morton Papers, APS.

In the same year that Lydia Child published *Anti-Slavery Catechism* and answered the question of the natural inferiority of blacks, based on the conformation of their skulls, Morton published *Crania Americana*, a record of his extensive findings on American Indian crania. The question Morton asked was taxonomic: did "the American aborigines, of all epochs, . . . [belong] to one Race, or to a plurality of Races"?[26] The significance of Morton's answer lay in his attempt to explain the northern tribes' lack of advancement when compared to the achievements of the Indians of Mexico and Peru. Morton attributed the confusion surrounding the question of Indian races, as well as the problem of race taxonomy in general, to the inadequate means of classifying races. Investigators, he wrote, resorted to either of two methods: the physical, in which man was grouped by "similarity of external conformation," or the ethnographic, "the arrangement based on analogies of language."[27] Although Morton saw merits in the ethnographic approach and claimed that he would draw upon such analogies in language and moral character, he plainly sided more with the physical approach. Unlike others who employed this method, Morton rejected the concept of environment as an agent capable of altering man's physical characteristics. The physical characteristics of the cranium, he believed, offered an excellent example for refuting environmentalism. According to Morton, the cranium proved remarkably resistant to environmental influences, and it had the added advantage of offering an accurate record of brain size and mental traits. Thus cranial measurements served both for race classification and as an index of mental capability. But if crania were to be useful as taxonomic devices, Morton had to prove that they were indeed immune to environmental forces.

To prove this immunity, Morton devoted part of *Crania Americana* to a comparison of the crania of prehistoric

---

[26] Samuel G. Morton, *Crania Americana; or, a Comparative View of the Skulls of Various Aboriginal Nations of North and South America: to which is prefixed an Essay on the Varieties of the Human Species*, p. 97.

[27] Ibid., pp. 3–4.

North and South American Indians with those of recently deceased Indians of both continents. His statistics revealed only slight differences between the crania of the "barbarous" Indians of North and South America and what he called the "demi-civilized" Indians (Incas, Mexicans, and mound builders).[28] Morton concluded that the Indians were one race but represented two great families of man. More important, his evidence suggested that no drastic change had occurred for centuries in either the size or the shape of Indian skulls. To Morton, statistical evidence proved conclusively that the environment had no effect on the physical characteristics of the skull.[29]

Once Morton proved this to his own satisfaction, he devoted his energy to determining brain size by race. He calculated brain size by sealing all the openings in a skull but one, filling the cavity with mustard seed (later lead shot), and weighing the seed to determine cranial volume.[30] He examined 256 crania, of which 147 were of Indians from both North and South America (and three of these were only partial crania). His examination led him to conclude that Indian crania were radically different from Caucasian, African, Mongolian, and Malayan crania.[31] By Morton's calculations, Indian crania were smaller in volume than those of the Malayan, Mongolian, and Caucasian groups. Since Morton believed that brain size (cranial volume) and intelli-

---

[28] As Stephen J. Gould has noted in "Morton's Ranking of Races by Cranial Capacity: Unconscious manipulation of data may be a scientific norm," *Science* 200 (May 5, 1978): 503–509, Morton actually averaged in the larger crania of North American Indians with the smaller crania of South American Indians, thus reducing the average cranial size of the Indians below that of the Caucasian crania. That he did not average the smaller crania of "Hindoos" in with other Caucasian crania because this procedure would lower the average of the Caucasian group belies Morton's bias. See also Stephen Jay Gould, *The Mismeasure of Man*, pp. 54–60. Another article critical of Morton's statistical methods is Daniel Wilson, "Physical Ethnology," *Annual Report of the Board of Regents of the Smithsonian Institution for 1862*, pp. 240–302. See also Bruce J. Trigger, "Sir Daniel Wilson: Canada's First Anthropologist," *Anthropologica* 8 (1966): 14–17.

[29] Morton, *Crania Americana*, p. 260.

[30] Ibid., pp. iii, 96–124, 141–62, 217–36.

[31] Ibid., p. 260.

gence were related, he concluded that Indian intelligence was inferior to that of groups with larger cranial volume.

Applying phrenological techniques, Morton next correlated cranial shape and size with mental traits as denoted by the customs and the habits of a people. In this endeavor the importance of an individual's history became evident, since, by matching known cultural characteristics with a particular Indian skull, Morton could extrapolate these phrenological findings to other Indian skulls. For example, as far as Morton could determine from the historical evidence, Indians had always possessed wild traits. Since his investigations revealed that no variation had appeared in cranial size and shape over vast periods of time, he assumed that the wild or savage ways of the Indian were derived not from lack of society but from mental attributes biologically determined. Furthermore Morton believed the Indian's "mental constitution" represented a very "low state of development" and that his meager intelligence had enslaved him to "savage" ways despite more than two hundred years of contact with the example of European civilization.

Since Morton seems to have begun his investigations with the assumption that all Indians were similar in mental attributes, it is not surprising that his data mirrored this opinion. In Morton's hands statistics not only delineated the Indian but also judged him: the hand of God, not the environment, shaped the Indian's cranium. For some reason God had seen fit to create such inferior varieties of man: "The Intellectual faculties of this great family appear to be of a decidedly inferior cast when compared with those of the Caucasian or Mongolian races. They are not only averse to the restraints of education, but for the most part incapable of a continued process of reasoning on abstract subjects."[32]

Writing after Morton's death, his colleague Henry Patter-

[32] Ibid., p. 81. An excellent article showing how Morton manipulated his data to arrive at certain conclusions is Gould, "Morton's Ranking of Races," and his chapter on Morton in *The Mismeasure of Man*, pp. 50–69.

son denied that Morton ever wholly subscribed to phrenological theories or took them seriously: "Morton's collection was ethnographic in its aim from the outset; nor can I find that he ever committed himself fully to the miscalled Phrenology."[33] Patterson, however, is not totally convincing in his denial, writing as he did after phrenology had "passed out of the hands of men of science" and had "become the property of itinerant charlatans, describing characters for twenty-five cents a head."[34] What Patterson could deny in the 1850s, after phrenology had ceased to be a science, would have been more difficult to deny in the 1830s when, by his own admission, phrenology made advocates of men of science. Thus it is important to examine Morton's involvement with phrenology in the context of its contemporary scientific value, for this helps clarify the attitudes and opinions toward Indians found in his famous work *Crania Americana.*

Morton used phrenological assumptions in his conclusions, but he never really affirmed his allegiance to the science. His reluctance to openly declare himself a phrenologist was consistent with his hesitant and cautious approach to any theory. Yet he did go so far as to call himself a student of the new science, and, when he was in Scotland, Morton attended the meetings of the Phrenological Society of Edinburgh. In the preface to *Crania Americana*, Morton proclaimed to his phrenologist friend J. S. Phillips:

> You and I have long admitted the fundamental principles of phrenology viz. that the brain is the organ of the mind, and that its different parts perform different functions. . . . We have not . . . neglected this branch of inquiry, but have endeavored to examine it in connection with numerous facts, which can only be fully appreciated when they come to be

[33] Patterson, p. xxxii.

[34] Ibid. Note also Lydia Marie Child, *Letters from New York*, pp. 247–57; Hunt in Gross, pp. 592–93. After working in the George Combe Papers and writing this chapter, I discovered Paul A. Erickson's *Phrenology and Physical Anthropology: The George Combe Connection*, Saint Mary's University Occasional Papers in Anthropology no. 6 (1979): 45–53, whose conclusions regarding Morton and phrenology are similar to mine.

compared with similar measurements derived from the other races of men.[35]

In a letter to his friend George Combe, the noted Scottish phrenologist, who lectured in the United States in 1839, Morton was quite enthusiastic about Combe's promoting phrenology in the United States:

> You may rest assured, my dear Sir, that your visit to this country has given immense impetus to inquiries of this sort [phrenology], which were before almost wholly neglected, & even regarded with suspicion & distrust. *Now*, the spirit of inquiry is abroad, which nothing can check, & the results, like seed sown in good ground, will produce abundant harvest of inconvertible facts.[36]

[35] Morton, *Crania Americana*, pp. iii–lv. See also S. G. Morton to George Combe, Oct. 4, 1838, Combe Papers, NLS.

[36] Samuel G. Morton to George Combe, May 24, 1840, Combe Papers, NLS. There are several letters in the Morton Papers of the American Philosophical Society that either urge Morton toward phrenology or reflect his interest in the subject: see J[?] E. Doornik to S. G. Morton, June 28, 1835; William Byrd Powell to Samuel G. Morton, Aug. 6, 1838; Powell to Morton, May 2, 1839; Gerard Troost to Samuel G. Morton, Feb. 6, 1837; Troost to Morton, March 4, 1837. See also the many letters from George Combe, the Scottish phrenologist, to Morton in the Morton Papers, APS. According to Combe, "I have had the pleasure of holding many consultations with Dr. Morton and Mr. Phillips about the best means of measuring the skulls to be described in this work [*Crania Americana*], . . . Dr. Morton has requested me to furnish an Appendix for his work. He is imperfectly acquainted with Phrenology himself, and has composed his text without reference to it. He perceives, however, that when he presents a correct drawing of an average specimen of a national skull, and describes historically the mental character of the nation, he places in juxtaposition the two elements on which Phrenology is founded; and he is anxious to obtain the means of enabling his readers to combine them, so that they may draw their own conclusions on the accordance or discordance of the forms of the skulls with the Indian characters. . . . My Appendix will consist of a brief outline of the phrenological faculties, of a drawing of a skull showing the regions of the animal, the moral, and the intellectual organs, with directions how to estimate their relative proportions; and some remarks on the influence of size in the brain on mental power. The reader of Dr. Morton's work, by applying the rules and examples thus furnished to the several skulls, delineated in it, will be able to draw his own conclusion." George Combe, *Notes on the United States of North America During a Phrenological Visit in 1838–9–40*, 1: 307–308. Morton was also one of a committee of seven elected to convey their appreciation to Combe for the lectures on phrenology he gave in Philadelphia, see Combe, *Notes*, 2: 357–58. In a letter acknowledging a letter from Morton,

These comments are significant because they signal Morton's sympathy with phrenology and, more important, his acceptance of a cardinal principle of the science: that the brain is the organ of the mind. As a corollary to this principle, phrenologists affirmed logically, but erroneously, that brain size directly indicated intelligence; thus, because a cranium's capacity reflected the size of the brain, the size of the head denoted the degree of intelligence. In phrenology, then, the sizes and configurations of "national skulls" served as indices of national mental traits, and the study of "national" crania could determine the intelligence of various races and the reasons races acted differently from one another.

Morton was cautious in relying upon phrenological theory that held that the skull could be mapped according to personality or character traits and that protuberances of the skull accurately reflected an individual's propensity for a particular trait. This approach did not suit his research methodology, which focused on the size of the brain rather than the functions of its individual parts. But Morton did believe that phrenology served as the best indicator of "national traits" and that it "explained" the reason Indians seemed childlike, often "mimicking" Euro-American customs when with whites, only to return to the woods to pursue their "wild and savage" ways at the first opportunity. Morton shared with other phrenologists the assumption that the Indians' rejection of civilization lay not in willfulness but in their mental inability, given the size of their brains, to absorb civilization.[37]

Henry R. Schoolcraft wrote, "I shall be pleased to receive the phrenological plates, connected with your forthcoming work, & although not myself skilled in this branch of mental philosophy, I take much interest in it, & hope to see the facts admitted to their proper standing in the science." Henry R. Schoolcraft to Samuel G. Morton, May 5, 1838, Morton Papers, APS. Note also Samuel G. Morton to George Combe, May 24, 1840, Combe Papers, NLS. For a different view of Morton's interest in phrenology, see Patterson, pp. xxxi–xxxiii, and William Stanton, *The Leopard's Spots: Scientific Attitudes Towards Race in America, 1815–59*, pp. 34–39.

[37]George Combe, *A System of Phrenology*, pp. 572–76. See also R. H. Collyer, *Manual of Phrenology, or the Physiology of the Human Brain.*

When Morton decided to include a chapter on phrenology in his *Crania Americana*, he probably acted more on his own inclination than on the advice of friends. Considering himself still a student, however, Morton sought out a phrenologist friend to write the chapter and construct a series of charts on phrenological measurements. When his friend could not oblige, Morton assumed the task himself. But before he could complete the tables, phrenologist George Combe arrived in the United States, and Morton prevailed upon him to write the chapter.[38] After initially hesitating, Combe wrote a noncommittal reply: "I shall have great pleasure in inspecting it [Morton's crania collection] on my arrival in Philadelphia. . . . If I shall then find that I can write anything on the skulls useful to Phrenology and to you, it will afford me the greatest pleasure to do so; but until I see them I cannot offer any more decided pledge."[39]

Apparently Combe found something useful to phrenology in Morton's collection, for he eventually wrote the chapter and also a lengthy review of *Crania Americana* for Benjamin Silliman's *Journal of Arts and Science*, again at Morton's request.[40] Although the chapter Combe wrote was not long, it was long enough to stress the principles of phrenology and their application to American Indian crania. It also provided a glimpse into Combe's own prejudices. Blacks received sympathetic treatment; Indians did not. Although Africans exhibited a nearly "unbroken scene of moral and intellectual desolation," there were some African tribes who "have advanced beyond the savage condition," having cities, "rude manufactures, agriculture, commerce, gov-

[38] Samuel G. Morton to George Combe, Oct. 4, 1838, Combe Papers, NLS.
[39] George Combe to Samuel G. Morton, Oct. 19, 1838, Morton Papers, APS.
[40] George Combe, "Appendix, Phrenological remarks on the relation between the natural talents and dispositions of nations, and the developments of their brains," in Morton, pp. 269–91; [George Combe], Review of *Crania Americana: or a Comparative View of the Skulls of Various Aboriginal Nations of North and South America*, in *The American Journal of Science and Arts* 38 (1840): 341–75; Samuel G. Morton to George Combe, March 19, 1839, Combe Papers, NLS.

ernment and laws." In comparison, the American Indians presented a deplorable condition:

> Surrounded for centuries by European knowledge, enterprise, and energy, and incited to improvements by the example of European institutions, many of the natives of that continent remain, at the present time, the same miserable, wandering, houseless and lawless savages as their ancestors were, when Columbus first set foot upon their soil. Partial exceptions to this description may be found in some of the southern districts of North America; but the members who have adopted the modes of civilized life are so small, and the progress made by them so limited, that speaking of the race, we do not exaggerate in saying, that they remain to the present hour enveloped in all their primitive savageness, and that they have profited extremely little by the introduction amongst them of arts, sciences and philosophy.[41]

Morton's concept of the Indian, as distilled in *Crania Americana*, can be understood by his statement that "there is a singular harmony between the mental character of the Indian, and his cranial developments as explained by phrenology."[42] Morton found much about the Indian to praise. Basing his opinion on missionary, travel, and government reports, Morton saw the Indian to be polite and quick to show gratitude. Furthermore the Indian was no more covetous, superstitious, idolatrous, or treacherous than other people in similar circumstances. But any positive traits that Morton acknowledged were blunted by what he considered the Indian's "repulsive" domestic habits. Morton's overall perception of the Indian was negative. When not on the hunt or at war, Indians, Morton claimed, were indolent, revengeful, dirty, cruel to their wives and children, and given to depraved and immoral acts of vice and sensuality. Their laziness and slowness to learn were manifest in their aversion to agriculture and their complete lack of maritime skills.[43]

This ambivalent picture mirrored Morton's craniological

[41] Combe in Morton, p. 272.
[42] Morton, *Crania Americana*, pp. iii–iv.
[43] Ibid., pp. 75–82.

and phrenological findings. In his examination of the crania of "barbarous tribes," Morton noted the small cranial size and concluded that not only were their intellectual faculties inferior to other races but also their "inventive and imitative faculties . . . [were] of a very humble grade." Furthermore their faculties pointing to a "predilection for the arts or sciences" were absent.[44] Apparently more child-like than adult, Indians as adults were sadly deficient in the niceties of social intercourse, their manners being nasty, brutal, and grotesque. According to Morton, deficiency of brain was the Indian's major handicap.

> However much the benevolent mind may regret the inap-
> titude of the Indian for civilization, the affirmative of this
> question seems to be established beyond a doubt. His moral
> and physical nature are alike adapted to his position among the
> races of men, and it is as reasonable to expect the one to be
> changed as the other. The structure of his mind appears to be
> different from that of the white man, nor can the two harmo-
> nise in their social relations except on the most limited scale.[45]

Given his acceptance of the relationship between brain size and intelligence, the "demi-civilized" tribes of South America, those he termed the Toltecans, were in complete variance with phrenological theory. Morton found himself utterly unable to explain this anomaly.

> It would be natural to suppose, that a people with heads so
> small and badly formed would occupy the lowest place in the
> scale of human intelligence. . . . The skull in these people
> [Toltecans] is remarkable for its small size. . . . The capacity of
> the cavity of the cranium, derived from the measurement of
> many specimens of the pure Inca race, shows, as we shall here-
> after see, a singularly small cerebral mass for an intelligent and
> civilized people.

The phrenologist Combe was also distressed by these find-ings while writing his review of *Crania Americana* for the *Journal of Arts and Science*, and he urged Morton to re-think his position on the Peruvian skull. Morton's response

[44]Ibid., p. 81.
[45]Ibid., p. 82.

was to admit that his findings might be erroneous. This upset Combe and he cautioned Morton against making such an admission, for he would lose the trust of his readers and the book's scientific reputation would suffer. Morton never fully resolved this contradictory evidence, which he felt threatened to nullify his thesis in *Crania Americana*.[46]

[46] Ibid., pp. 90–114. See also Combe, Review of *Crania Americana*, in which Combe notes this "discrepancy" according to phrenological theory. p. 363. In a series of letters Combe raised this issue with Morton and posed a solution. On February 28, 1840, Combe wrote to Morton, "The only part of your work which puzzles me is that which treats of the ancient Peruvian heads, & at once claims that they are compressed & yet ascribe to them high civilization. If I have read right, you consider the Toltecan to be the ancient race, that it extended over both Mexico & Peru, & was the creator of the ancient Tombs, Pyramids, etc. If the long narrow ancient Peruvian skulls were compressed, I could understand that the anterior lobe was not destroyed, or impeded in its growth, and only thrown back into another part of the skull, but still capable of performing its functions, if it were wanting, which the skulls, if uncompressed, would indicate to be the case to an extraordinary extent, how can we account for the civilization? In the thoroughly savage tribes, without arts & civilization, constructiveness, Ideality, Imitation & Reflection are all deficient. Nature is constant. How can these contradictory facts be reduced to consistency with Nature? There is no living people with heads rationally so deficient as these ancient Peruvians who are civilized or who construct. Finally—A superior race is never exterminated by an inferior one. How came the ancient Race to perish, if they were capable of such efforts as their remains indicate?"

On March 6, 1840, Combe wrote: "The account of No. 4 [ancient Peruvian] is printed, & I have said that it forms an exception to all the other facts, & also added that the conclusions you draw will need farther investigations. It occurs to me that it would be useful if you would address a Letter by return of post to Professor Silliman as Editor, saying that you had received his Remarks on the discrepancy between the developments No. 4 & the character given to the people, and on your assumption that this head was a fair average specimen of the ancient race, & on your conclusion that these heads were not altered by art, and in reply beg to mention so etc. . . .—This would prevent a world of discussion about that head & people. I could not print your present statement, because it is not made with due deliberation. Read your text, & then write, & write cautiously & considerate."

Finally on March 13, Combe wrote: "The fault of your letters to me of 2d & to him of 3d March, was too broad an admission of your own error, too strong a condemnation of what you had written about the ancient Peruvians, and too complete an abandonment of your own opinion and inferences. The effect would have been to reduce the reliance of your readers on your general care, caution, & accuracy, & to induce the public not to purchase this Edition, but wait for one more correctly prepared. I have avoided, as far as possible, this evil, & at the same time made your state[ment] the essential

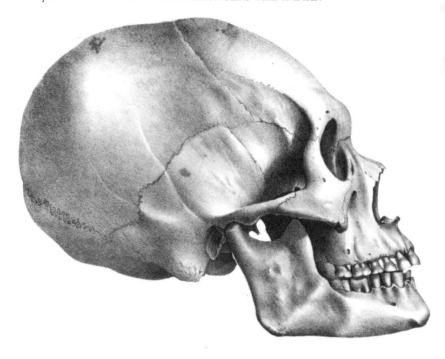

PERUVIAN
OF THE ANCIENT RACE.
From Arica
Drawn from Nature and on Stone by J. Collins

A Peruvian skull. Lithograph by John Collins for Samuel G. Morton's *Crania Americana*.

In his comparative study of national skulls, Morton attempted to delineate differences between racial types, dif-

---

fact that No. 4 is not the cranial type, & that you are engaged in procurring farther [sic] information." George Combe to Samuel G. Morton, Feb. 28, March 6, March 13, 1840, Morton Papers, APS. Morton followed Combe's advice, see Combe, Review of *Crania Americana*, p. 375, and Samuel G. Morton to George Combe, March 2, 1840, Combe Papers, NLS. Later Morton decided that the ancient Peruvian skull did indicate artificial elongation. See George Combe Manuscript Letterbook, 7390; George Combe to Samuel G. Morton, Jan. 29, 1845, Combe Papers, NLS.

ferences that could serve as indices of the Indian's capacity for progress. In a world in which varying degrees of progress existed between nations, differences in cranial size served to explain why some nations had not, or could not, advance. For Morton, as for many others, Indians never could be "civilized" because they lacked the necessary brains, and what brains they had were more animal than human. By linking racial differences to cranial measurements, phrenology seemingly provided scientific justification for popular conceptions of nonwhite racial inferiority.

The author who reviewed *Crania Americana* for the *American Phrenological Journal* found the book an important contribution to phrenology and was gratified to learn "that the Caucasian race, which is the most civilized, and is, in every respect superior to the others, possess, on an average heads *four cubic inches* larger in capacity than either of the other [Mongolian, American Indian, Malayan, and Ethiopian (black)] races, harmonising most strikingly with the fundamental principle in phrenology, that size, other things being equal, is a measure of power."[47]

Many nonphrenologists agreed with that point. Another reviewer noted the difference in cranial size between white and nonwhite races and pointedly informed readers that the measurements represented the mean of fifty-two Caucasian skulls "from the lowest and least educated class of society and [were] consequently likely to be rather below the true average."[48] The implications of Morton's work

[47]Review of *Crania Americana* in *American Phrenological Journal and Miscellany* 2 (1839): 143–44. Italics in original.

[48]Review of *Crania Americana* in *The North American Review* 51 (1840): 185. Historian George Bancroft was only one of many who viewed Indians in phrenological terms and used phrenology in describing Indians. According to Bancroft, "The unity of the human race is established by the exact correspondence between their respective powers; the Indian has not one more, had not one less, than the white man; the map of the faculties is for both identical. . . . When, from the general characteristics of humanity, we come to the comparison of powers, the existence of degrees immediately appears. The red man has aptitude at imitation rather than invention; he learns easily; his natural logic is correct and discriminating, and he seizes on the nicest distinctions in comparing objects. But he is deficient in the power of imagination to combine and bring unity into his floating fancies, and in the faculty

were obvious. The Caucasian race proved superior both in civilization and in intelligence. The reviewer pointed out that regardless of how people felt about the validity of phrenology, Caucasians were "not apt to attribute a high degree of mental capacity to heads of an *anti-Caucasian* formation."[49]

Accordingly, Morton's work on the "cranial peculiarities of races" did much "to clear up and elucidate an important point in the natural history of man" and also helped "prove" the racial inferiority of nonwhite races.[50] Thus phrenology lent a certain aura of scientific proof to observed deficiencies in Indian character, although such phrenological descriptions reflected more the cultural stereotyping by Americans than accurate observation based on phrenological method.

Although Morton rejected data drawn from the study of similarities in customs and philological comparisons as convincing proof regarding a people's origin or racial affinities, he did consider such data valuable in supporting the physical evidence. The philological discoveries of Gallatin and Du Ponceau that indicated Indian languages were similar in North and South America, although unlike any Old World languages, supported Morton's findings that Indians were one race physically. Morton also pointed to similarities in burial customs and patterns of warfare among Indians as further proof of his thesis. The main confirmation of this argument remained, however, physical evidence determined by racial inheritance.

It must be remembered that Morton wrote at a time when the question of what constituted a species was the

---

of abstraction to lift himself out of his dominion of his immediate experience. He is nearly destitute of abstract moral truths, of general principles; and, as a consequence, equalling the white man in the sagacity of the senses, and in judgements resting on them, he is inferior in reason and the moral qualities. Nor is this inferiority simply attached to the individual; it is connected with organization, and is the characteristic of the race." George Bancroft, *History of the United States, from the Discovery of the American Continent*, 3: 302.

[49] Review of *Crania Americana* in *North American Review* 51 (1840): 180.
[50] Ibid., p. 186.

subject of sharp debate. In both zoology and geology battle lines were drawn on this issue as well as on the issue of transmutation versus permanency of type.[51] Before Buffon, "species" referred only to larger classes of organisms easily distinguished by observable differences. With Buffon the concept of species became more narrowly defined.[52] Accordingly, each plant and animal represented a different species, created through a special act of God. Each constituted archetypes from which some variation would be permitted.

The generally accepted belief that man was a species and that the various races of man were mere variations of that same species showed signs of crumbling by the midnineteenth century. As Herbert Odom points out, although the concept of species was the usual expression of zoological classification, in nineteenth-century racial theories of man the species concept was replaced with the concept of type; that is, each race had a set of typical physical characteristics that identified its members and that were inherited from an original type.[53] In essence, this concept "asserts that every representative of a race conforms to the type and is separated from the representatives of any other race by a distinct gap."[54] Degrees of variation from the original type or norm of race could exist, but never to a magnitude to confuse one race with another. Each race

[51]A. Hunter Dupree, *Asa Gray 1810–1888*, pp. 216–32; Edward Lurie, *Louis Agassiz: A Life in Science*, pp. 252–302; Count, pp. 139–65. For an extended discussion of these problems at the time of Darwin, see William Coleman, *Biology in the Nineteenth Century*, pp. 57–91, and Herbert H. Odom, "Generalizations on Race in Nineteenth-Century Physical Anthropology," *Isis* 58 (Spring 1967): 5–18; Stocking, "Some Problems," pp. 407–25. A good summary of these issues as they evolved in England is Gay Weber, "Science and Society in Nineteenth Century Anthropology," *History of Science* 12 (1974): 260–83.

[52]Arthur O. Lovejoy, "The Argument for Organic Evolution before the Origin of Species, 1830–50," in *Forerunners of Darwin: 1745–1859*, eds. Bentley Glass, Owsei Temkin, and William L.. Strauss, pp. 394–95.

[53]Odom, pp. 6–7. See also Ernst Mayr, "Darwin and the Evolutionary Theory in Biology," in *Evolution and Anthropology: A Centennial Appraisal*, ed. Betty J. Meggers.

[54]Mayr, p. 3.

thus appeared as a natural, "knowable" type and, for the polygenists, as an individual unit of identity whose physical and mental traits identified it as a type especially created by God. This being so, for most polygenists it followed that the differences between types (or races) constituted a qualitative hierarchy from inferior to superior types. Thus slavery was justified for some people and extinction was justified for others, both in the name of progress.[55]

In his review of *Crania Americana*, Combe assured readers that Morton assumed "the unity of the human species." Morton, however, soon moved to a polygenist's position.[56] In a letter Morton wrote to his friend J. C. Nott in 1850, he claimed, "I avow my belief in a plurality of origins for the human species . . . when I took this ground four years ago, (and with some misgivings, not because I doubted the truth of my opinions, but because I feared they would lead to some controversy with the clergy)."[57]

Just how or when Morton arrived at this position is uncertain. He had access to a paper by B. H. Coates in which Coates demolished most arguments for Indian migration from the Old World and came close to laying the basis for a consideration of the Indians as autochthonous.[58] Although there were those in zoology who saw each organism as specially created for its own environment, Morton apparently arrived at this position independently through his own research.[59] A stable racial typology is implicit in the concep-

[55] See Richard Colfax, *Evidence Against the Views of the Abolitionists, Consisting of Physical and Moral Proofs, of the Natural Inferiority of the Negroes*, for one example of such thinking.

[56] Combe, Review of *Crania Americana*, p. 344.

[57] Quoted from Patterson, pp. xlix–l.

[58] B. H. Coates, "Annual Discourse, Delivered Before the Historical Society of Pennsylvania . . . On the Origin of the Indian Population of America," *Memoirs of the Pennsylvania Historical Society* 3 (1836): 3–63. Coates, after critically examining all the migration theories of the day, presented his own. He believed that the Indians of South America were Malayans and those of North America were Tartars. While Coates's theories were not new, his arguments were.

[59] Lurie, *Louis Agassiz*, pp. 255–71; Dupree, *Asa Gray*, pp. 226–28; Edward Lurie, "Louis Agassiz and the Races of Man," *Isis* 45 (September, 1954): 234.

tual framework of *Crania Americana*. Where others viewed man as one species divided into races or varieties, Morton saw races as original types. Furthermore, Morton, like many others, concluded that since physical characteristics repeated themselves in subsequent generations, logic held that mental characteristics, like intelligence, morality, and industry, would also breed true. With such typological thinking, Morton's *Crania Americana* provided a scientific foundation for a polygenetic racial history of man.

The issue of polygenism was a crucial one to a society that was splitting itself over the question of slavery, eager to expand its boundaries westward and south into Mexico, and proclaiming that none but whites should rule. The question of the capacity of the "inferior" dark races for progress had tremendous political and social implications. To many people it seemed obvious that Indians resisted civilization and were "blighted" by its contact and that blacks could be only partially civilized. What people wanted to know was why. For example, in the case of Indians, why did the gap between civilization and their "savagism" increase until it threatened Indians with extinction? What did questions on race mean for society and the future of progress? Even more noxious was the doubt polygenism cast on the Mosaic interpretation of Scripture, and clergymen rushed into the fray to defend the common humanity of man.[60]

The shrill public arguments on race penetrated Morton's study. Seemingly oblivious to the charged nature of these arguments, Morton chose to believe that in this area the insight and proofs of science were more correct, and hence more valuable, than those of religion. Where the theologian could only interpret Scripture, the scientist by empirical investigations of nature could clearly discern God's plan. It was science, not dogma, that would be the ar-

[60] For the clergy's reaction to polygenism, see Stanton, pp. 21–22; an extended view of the whole period is provided by Reginald Horsman, *Race and Manifest Destiny*; also dealing with these issues is Robert E. Bieder, "Scientific Attitudes Towards Mixed-Bloods in Early Nineteenth-Century America," *Journal of Ethnic Studies* 8 (Summer 1980): 21–22.

bitrator of this momentous issue. By the midnineteenth century the question of species or type, in the context of the debates on race, assumed greater importance.

By the early 1840s, Morton's interest had shifted to the investigation of the permanency of racial types. His early attraction to phrenology faded as phrenology became a popular fad. Although he continued to accept the major phrenologic premise that the brain was the organ of the mind, he exercised more caution in relying upon the facile correlations of character traits with designated cranial areas. Always the empiricist, Morton warned his students, "Let us be cautious how we attempt to localize organs which are beyond our sight and reach, and of which the exact position can only be ascertained by numberless comparisons, and these made without reference to preconceived opinions."[61] Although certain concepts of phrenology continued to underlie Morton's thinking, his concerns now centered on racial types and their immutability and the meaning of this for society.

In 1842, speaking before the Boston Society of Natural History, Morton reiterated and elaborated on his message regarding the racial inferiority of American Indians. Specifying that the object of his talk was to emphasize that Indians of both North and South America were of one race, he enumerated their physical, moral, and intellectual similarities. He admitted that the stunted Fuegians of Tierra del Fuego seemed a different race from other Indians, but he argued that their stature was the result of their environment, that beneath their external appearance remained the original Indian type. Morton repeated the old adage, "He who has seen one tribe of Indians has seen all," as a popular verification of his thesis.[62]

In their moral traits, Morton believed Indians to be similar to other people in the "savage" state; they lived generally in small groups and were cunning and constantly en-

[61] Samuel G. Morton, "Lecture No. 3," pp. 15–16, Morton Papers, LCP.
[62] Samuel G. Morton, *An Inquiry into the Distinctive Characteristics of the Aboriginal Race of America*, p. 6.

gaged in war with their neighbors. He found Indians to be unique, however, from other "savage people" in "their habitual indolence and improvidence, their indifference to private property, and the vague simplicity of their religious observances." According to Morton, these traits pointed to a "peculiar and eccentric moral constitution." In his consideration of the "demi-civilized" Indians, Morton found that the Aztecs shared the same cruel and bloody temperaments as did the more "barbaric" tribes. Their rule was based on fear and torture. The Incas were different to the extent that they tricked others into believing they had special power and so ruled over an "effeminate vassalage" by moral and physical influence. Once their empire disintegrated, however, the "gentle and unoffending Peruvian was transformed into the wily and merciless savage."[63]

In his Boston talk Morton again returned to his attack on Indian intellectual capacity. He told his audience that the "intellectual faculties" of the Indians were not high and that "as a race they are decidedly inferior to the Mongolian stock." He deplored as a "cheerless picture" the possibility of Indian intellectual progress: "Their minds seize with avidity on simple truths, while they reject whatever requires investigation or analysis. Their proximity for more than two centuries to European communities, has scarcely effected an appreciable change in the manner of life; and as to their social condition, they are probably in most respects the same as at the primitive epoch of their existence."[64]

Although Morton could not explain the variations that seemed to exist between the cultures of the "demi-civilized" tribes and those of the nomadic tribes, he did feel that the differences were more apparent than real. Drawing upon ethnology, Morton resorted to a chain model whereby one could "trace all the gradations, link by link, which connect" the diverse cultures. In Morton's mind, however, this scale did not reflect an evolutionary or developmental model, but rather depicted a degenerative slide where "a variety

[63] Ibid., pp. 10–12.
[64] Ibid., pp. 13–14.

of causes has long been urging them onward to deep degeneration and rapid extinction."[65]

When Morton addressed the Pennsylvania Medical College, also in 1842, he turned from analyzing the Indian as a type to considering why Indians differed from other races. He ridiculed as humiliating theories that linked "man to the monkey tribe" and attacked those who held that differences between races were the result of chance and environmental causes:[66]

> Some intelligent minds, influenced more, perhaps by feeling more than reflection, are unwilling to admit these differences among the several races of men, regarding them incompatible with the equal wisdom of and justice of Providence. Yet, on the other hand, it requires but little observation to convince oneself that these very differences form a universal, and no doubt essential feature in the so called social organization of our species.[67]

Nor, as he had reminded his students, did the differences in intellect between the races merely represent differences in degrees of education. Rather, said Morton, the races were unequal in their "congenital germ of mind." Intellectual differences between families were similar to those found between races. Although it was true that some improvement might result from educating Indians for several generations—"it would enlarge their minds and increase their capacity for knowledge . . ."—still it would never raise the Indian to the same intellectual level as the Caucasian. Not content with this qualification, however, Morton questioned whether raising Indians to such an intellectual level ought to be attempted, providing it were even possible. The differences in intellect between races might be an inequality decreed by God and might "be designed for the same purposes in *nations*, as it is among individuals. . . ."[68]

Still hesitant to declare openly his belief in polygenism,

[65] Ibid., p. 17.
[66] Samuel G. Morton, *Brief Remarks on the Diversity of the Human Species, and on Some Kindred Subjects*, pp. 13, 7.
[67] Ibid., p. 6.
[68] Ibid., his emphasis.

Morton stated ambiguously to his audience that the differences between races were primeval. The differentiating of races and their dispersal were coeval with the Deluge and had the "impress of obvious and original design." Rejecting the arguments of those who advocated the effect of environment on man, Morton turned their evidence to his advantage. He conceded that certain physical characteristics, such as skin color, helped one survive in certain climates, but he questioned whether this was not just proof that God had made each race in such a way as to best adapt to its environment. Morton considered blacks' immunity to certain diseases and their failure to become white on removal to America points in favor of his view.[69]

In Morton's opinion, mental attributes were even more important than physical characteristics. Standing before his audience of medical students, Morton declared that mental qualities, like physical qualities, were God-given and hence could not be changed. The "defects" in the Indian's mind were repeated generation after generation and could not be the result of chance. They were part of Indian character, distinctly stamped upon Indian minds thousands of years ago; they mirrored the "wise and obvious design" of God fitting Indians for the "original adaption" to their circumstances of "climate and locality." If God in His infinite wisdom had so "retarded" dark races, then His plans "for wise purposes, have given our race a decided and unquestionable superiority over all the nations of the earth." Divine intention seemed obvious to Morton: "Was it not for this same mental superiority, these happy climes which we now inhabit would yet be possessed by the wild and untutored Indian, and that soil which now rejoices the hearts of millions of freemen, would be yet overrun by lawless tribes of contending Barbarians. Thus it is that the white race has been able to plant and to sustain its colonies in every region of the habitable earth."[70] Here Divine intent, racial superiority, and nationalism combine in a scientific

[69] Ibid., pp. 9–11.
[70] Ibid., pp. 21–22.

rationale for removal of Indians to make way for a new race and a new day. Little concerned that others would dispute his facts, Morton, whether attacking disease or the question of Indian progress, was interested only in the "science of facts."[71]

Although many fervently believed that religion and education would change the Indians, thereby assuring their survival, Morton chose to place the concept of behavioral and physical change in a historical context. History, Morton believed, was the basic factor most often overlooked, especially by those who believed that by changing the environment of the Indian they could change the Indian. To Morton such thinking disregarded the evidence that there had been no change in the Indian for thousands of years.

What were the temporal parameters of Morton's history? Although no longer constrained by Bishop James Ussher's estimate of four thousand years for the age of the world, both monogenists and polygenists still worked within a rather restrictive time frame. In 1857 discoveries in European archaeology would help to overturn literal Biblical chronology for the age of man, but in the 1840s the telescoped time placed restrictions on ethnological theories and forced explanations of human change and development into a limited time span.[72] Through his work in geology, Morton undoubtedly possessed an awareness of the vastly increased age of the world; yet, strangely enough, he bound his theories to the Septuagint chronology, which dated man's time on earth at about six thousand years. That was ample, however, for Morton to establish his proof and demonstrate the error of those monogenists who clamored about the progress of nonwhites.

Because of the sketchy nature of Indian history, Mor-

[71] Morton, *An Inquiry*, p. 37. For an analysis of the importance of climate and locality in nineteenth-century thought, see Count, p. 152.

[72] J. A. Barnes, "Anthropology in Britain Before and After Darwin," *Mankind: Official Journal of the Anthropological Societies of Australia* 5 (July, 1960): 370–72; Coleman, p. 100; Jacob Gruber, "Brixham Cave and the Antiquity of Man," in *Context and Meaning in Cultural Anthropology*, ed. Medford E. Spiro, pp. 373–402.

ton turned to the history of blacks for evidence to refute the environmental assumptions upon which evolutionary schemes for nonwhites were erected. After the publication of *Crania Americana*, Morton became the leading physical anthropologist in America, and so his statements on race carried great import. In his next study, *Crania Aegyptica*, Morton endeavored to demonstrate that no change had ensued in the physiognomy or mentality of the blacks since the days of the Egyptian pharaohs. By Morton's calculations the pharaohs ruled some seven hundred years after the Deluge, or thirty-five centuries ago.[73] Examining crania, statues, and works of art of ancient Egypt (which usually showed blacks in servile positions), Morton proved to his own satisfaction that blacks had changed neither their physical appearance nor their servant status in three thousand years. The ruling class, then as now, was white.[74]

Armed with this fact, Morton and other polygenists proclaimed that monogenists deluded themselves by thinking that all races could change their particular colors and their physical and mental characteristics, either through environmental factors or degeneration, in the short span of seven hundred years between the Deluge and the rise of Egyptian civilization.[75] Clearly these data seemed uncontestable and refuted the optimistic, sometimes fantastic, hopes of humanitarians and philanthropists. To the poly-

---

[73] Samuel G. Morton, *Crania Aegyptica; or, Observations on Egyptian Ethnography, Derived From Anatomy, History, and the Monuments*, p. 2. Although published in 1844, much of this material was presented before the American Philosophical Society on December 16, 1842, and on January 6 and April 6, 1843.

[74] Ibid., pp. 60–61, 66.

[75] Ibid., p. 18. In a letter to Morton, J. C. Nott proclaimed: "You have gone far enough . . . to blow up all the chronologies although it may not be very *politic* to say so in these days of Christian intolerance. The Bible if of divine origin, was clearly not intended to include in its code of beautiful morals, the whole range of natural science, for it knows no knowledge beyond *human* knowledge of the day & its great ends did not require any other—even the Septeaguit [sic] account is far too short to take in the events of Egypt, to say nothing of geological formations which are now placed before the 'beginning' of Moses." J. C. Nott to Samuel G. Morton, Oct. 15, 1844, Morton Papers, LCP.

genists it was obvious that darker skin and inferior mentality differentiated mankind's races one from another since
the Deluge and probably since creation. History seemed to
collaborate with zoology to support polygenism. Those who
sought to suppress nonwhites and deny their basic humanity eagerly embraced these scientific conclusions.[76]

There was a good deal if not of truth then of prescience
in the observations of a writer in 1850 in the *American
Whig Review*:

> The scientific study of humanities, from being for a century
> back the theme of a few speculative philosophers, is become at
> last a topic of general and even popular interest. It has been
> remarked as a peculiarity of the late European revolutions,
> that they were propagated by divisions of race. Such a feature
> is in fact an evidence that this great idea of the age is at work
> not merely in the scientific, but even in the practical and po-
> litical world. The very destination of the movement implies
> the concurrence of both operations; the principle which is to
> be the organizers of future societies must be preparatively the
> disturber or destroyer of the present.[77]

The writer's prophecy bore fruit a decade later and indeed
has remained a specter ever since. At midcentury forces in
society converged in a way to promote, as William Coleman pointed out, "the notion of aboriginal differences
among men. . . ." The solution "was to isolate the superior
races and determine the varying degrees of inferiority of
other peoples."[78]

Throughout the 1840s and 1850s the debate between

---

[76] For an extended discussion of this issue, see Stanton, p. 50. Several re-
cent writers have taken issue with Stanton's interpretation, see George M.
Fredrickson, *The Black Image in the White Mind: The Debate on Afro-
American Character and Destiny, 1817–1914*, pp. 76–82; Reginald Horsman, "Scientific Racism and the American Indian in the Mid-Nineteenth Century," *American Quarterly* 27 (May, 1975): pp. 152–68; Horsman, *Race and
Manifest Destiny*, chap. 7. Also informative on this topic is John S. Haller,
Jr., *Outcasts from Evolution: Scientific Attitudes of Racial Inferiority,
1859–1900*; and Bieder, "Scientific Attitudes," pp. 21–27.

[77] "Unity of the Human Race," *American Whig Review* 12 (1850): 567.

[78] Coleman, p. 97.

monogenists and polygenists raged, fanned by Morton's investigations. Intellectuals both inside and outside science assumed positions on the questions involved. The debate, as expected, colored the attitudes of many toward the Indian. Monogenists, who continued to see Indian salvation in terms of education and Christianity, were morally outraged.

The polygenists, in contrast, struck a more confident stance. When Morton turned his attention to questions of hybridity—an issue which, although only tangentially related to American Indians, was still much associated with the ethnological issues of the day—a growing number of Morton's disciples continued their leader's racial studies and expanded upon his assumptions. Their works filled out Morton's theories and popularized them. This small, avid group of polygenists, designated as the American School of Anthropology, recognized Morton as their leader and dedicated themselves to the further dissemination of his ideas. Their belligerence belied their small numbers, and their aggressive attack on the "delusions" of "fuzzyheaded" monogenists moved with a certainty that bordered on contempt.[79]

The battle even enlisted Louis Agassiz, the famous Swiss naturalist then teaching at Harvard, who sided with the polygenists. Although long a believer in special creation for the lower animals, Agassiz became convinced after seeing blacks for the first time in Philadelphia that they had different origins than Caucasians. He assumed this position in his enormously successful lectures in Charleston, where he confirmed the truth of polygenism and asserted that "the brain of the Negro is that of the imperfect brain of a 7 month's infant in the womb of the white."[80] But Agassiz was a zoologist and little interested in taking a stand on the South's "peculiar institution." His cause was building and

[79] Horsman, "Scientific Racism," p. 167.
[80] Quoted from George Gliddon to Samuel G. Morton, Jan. 9, 1848, Morton Papers, LCP. For a more extended account of Agassiz's racial feelings, see Lurie, "Louis Agassiz," pp. 227–42.

stocking a natural history museum at Cambridge, and it led him in January 1865 to make a request of Secretary of War Edwin M. Stanton:

> Now that the temperature is low enough . . . permit me to re-call to your memory your promise to let me have the bodies of some Indians; if any should die at this time. . . . All that would be necessary . . . would be to forward the body express in a box. . . . In case the weather was not very cold . . . direct the surgeon in charge to inject through the carotids a solution of Arsenate of soda. I should like one or two handsome fellows entire and the heads of two or three more.[81]

Evidently this was not Agassiz's first request for such "speci-mens." Several years earlier he had received for his mu-seum "one head of a North American Indian, in alcohol." With Agassiz the enthusiasm for collecting crania had taken another grisly turn.[82]

The most prolific expounder of Morton's ideas was his for-mer student Josiah C. Nott, a southern physician. Nott was an outspoken advocate of slavery who liked to mix his sci-entific investigations, which he termed "niggerology," with a dash of politics. Although he did not engage in politics, he liked to press his "scientific" conclusions upon poli-ticians who could make the best use of them. Nott was also not above tweaking the noses of fundamentalist clergy. He seemed to like nothing better than to indulge in scraps with clergymen who professed literal interpretations of the Bible. Nott also conveyed his militant stand in his let-ters. Writing to Morton in 1850, Nott expressed delight in Agassiz's support. Agassiz, lionized at Harvard, had become a hero to southern proponents of slavery. Nott gleefully pointed out to Morton that "with Agassiz in the war the battle is ours. This was an immense accession for we shall not only have his name, but the timid will come out from their hiding places."[83] Unlike Agassiz, Nott did use "sci-

---

[81] Quoted from Lurie, *A Life in Science*, p. 338.
[82] Ibid., p. 304, and Lurie, "Louis Agassiz," pp. 227–42.
[83] J. C. Nott to Samuel G. Morton, May 4, 1850, Morton Papers, LCP; Lurie, *A Life in Science*, pp. 256–61.

ence" in defense of slavery, and in his eagerness to do so, he became a hero in the South. As he expressed it in a moment of modest reflection, this stand "has given me more popularity and respect than I deserve."[84] To be sure, Nott, often buttressed with Morton's facts, proved a most agile opponent of monogenism.

In 1847, when the proslavery arguments were warming up, Nott presented "Two Lectures on the Connection between the Biblical and Physical History of Man" before the Louisiana legislature.[85] The offer to Nott to lecture was extended by J. D. B. De Bow, a professor of political economy, commerce, and statistics at the University of Louisiana and editor of the influential *De Bow's Review*. Apparently De Bow shared Nott's opinion "that the white, black, and other races, *now* present peculiar moral and physical characters, which should not be overlooked by the statesman, whose legitimate aim can only be the prosperity and happiness of all nations and all races."[86] Although Nott's "Two Lectures" are concerned primarily with differences between whites and blacks, there is much in them germane to Indians. Nott assumed the inferiority of the Indian, an assumption he based on Morton's "scientific" investigations of Indian physiology and physiognomy. According to Nott, Indians, like blacks, degenerated in a free state. Whereas blacks could reach their optimal potential only in slavery, Indians, being difficult to keep in slavery, were doomed to extinction. At one time Nott considered that there may have been an Indian race superior to the one then existing. This race, he believed, had built the civilizations of Mexico and Peru, but "they were [still] immeasurably below the Caucasian race in civilization at the time of conquest, and were . . . evidently retrograding at that epoch. The cranial developments, too, of this race, prove conclusively that

---

[84] J. C. Nott to Samuel G. Morton, June [?], 1847, Morton Papers, LCP.

[85] J. C. Nott, *Two Lectures on the Connection Between the Biblical and Physical History of Man.*

[86] J. D. B. De Bow, "Prefatory Letter," in Nott, *Two Lectures*, his emphasis, p. 6.

they were incapable of very high attainments."[87] While Nott admitted that the heads of Mexicans and Peruvians were exceedingly small, their "intellectual lobes" were "relatively large (compared with the rest of the brain) . . . thus affording a real confirmation . . . of phrenology." Still, they constituted

> a degenerate, mixed, and, therefore retrograding race. . . . Though superior, even at the present day, in some respects to the savage tribes around them, they show no disposition to adopt the higher civilization. Some of the mixed bloods have held civil and military posts under the present government, but not one thorough-bred Mexican has ever yet attained even to mediocrity. Where has the white race ever been similarly situated; nay where has it ever existed, even in slavery, that individuals did not burst through all trammels and assert their intellectual superiority?[88]

Admittedly, Nott claimed that whites had robbed and cheated Indians of their lands, but it was because of the Indians' mental habits and general inferiority that power and wealth gravitated to the whites and some "mixed breeds." The cause, if there was one, lay in the Indians' inability to progress rather than in American cupidity and duplicity. Drawing on Morton's work, Nott announced, "The full-blooded Indians are now, what they always have been, lazy, intemperate, improvident savages."[89] To substantiate this opinion Nott cited congressional reports and remarks from Indian agents and army officers. He even pointed out that a Dr. B. Randall, who lived among the Cherokees and Choctaws, "the most *civilized of our savages*," had claimed that "I have never met with full-blooded Indians who have adopted the industrial habits of the whites, or given evidence of a disposition for steady advancement in civilization or mental cultivation."[90] Similar sentiments were echoed by Joseph Campbell, another polygenist, who de-

[87] Ibid., p. 32.
[88] Ibid., p. 33.
[89] Ibid., p. 34.
[90] Ibid., his emphasis.

creed, "No dark race of men has ever been equal to a white race . . . the dark race must submit to the fair, the two cannot exist together in the same community on terms of equality."[91]

Nott's, Randall's, and Campbell's statements underscore a continuing pattern of thought about the Indians during the 1840s. Furthermore, articles such as "Our Indian Policy," published in 1844, by the monogenist Henry Rowe Schoolcraft attempted to justify government removal policy by expressing similar sentiments: "It is proved by history, that two essentially different states of society, with regard to arts and civilization, cannot both prosperously exist together, at the same time."[92]

Other polygenists, however, were not as dogmatic as Nott and Campbell. In *An Investigation of the Theories of the Natural History of Man*, William Van Amringe, another disciple of Morton, insisted that polygenism was a fact that could not be denied. His sifting of the findings of physiology, philology, and history proved mankind was differentiated by intellectual power, mental anatomy, and physiology. According to Van Amringe, the Indian, for example, was marked by his dark skin and callous temperament. Nervous insensibility, not heroic natures, enabled Indians to suffer excruciating tortures with less feeling or emotion than whites.[93] This "inferior" sensibility caused their low position among the species of mankind. Van Amringe defined the Indians' "psychical" attributes as "moderately mental; not originative, or inventive, but speculative; roving, predatory, revengeful, and sensual. . . . War like [sic] and destructive." Van Amringe believed that because of such attributes Indians were not suited for "high moral and intellectual attainments." In addition, their general progress

[91] John Campbell, *Negro-Mania: Being an Examination of the Falsely Assumed Equality of the Various Races of Men*, p. 6.

[92] [Henry R. Schoolcraft] "Our Indian Policy," *Democratic Review* 14 (1844): 169.

[93] William Frederick Van Amringe, *An Investigation of the Theories of the Natural History of Man, By Lawrence, Prichard, and Others. Founded Upon Animal Analogies and an Outline of a New Natural History of Man, Founded Upon History, Anatomy, Physiology, and Human Analogies*, pp. 380–81.

was precluded, and educating them would be very nearly useless. In a passage reminiscent of Morton, Van Amringe asked, "How does it happen now, that with the benefit of the example, guided by the benevolence, and, still more, the wonderful display of power acquired by knowledge, exhibited by the Shemitic species, no impression of any great extant, or importance, has yet been made. . . ." on the Indians.[94]

Van Amringe cited attempts to educate Indian children who "have been, when young, brought to our schools and colleges, in the hope that, by educating them, they would be efficient instruments for the improvement of their people." These hopes remained unfulfilled, however, for upon graduating "they bounded away to their forest," never to be heard from again.[95] "The mental capability of these species is incapable of receiving such improvement. . . . [Their] faculties cannot comprehend what is beyond their reach."[96] In time this defect in temperament might be overcome, Van Amringe thought, but it would take generations of instruction. The hope, if any, for their "improvement" rested upon the benevolent and patient nature of the white species. "This is the only species endowed with any power to drag cumbrous dark races out of the slough, in which they have been wallowing for ages."[97] Van Amringe thus expressed hesitant optimism for the Indian, but optimism tinged with dark shadows of doubt.

Nott, however, was far more pessimistic about the Indians' worldly future. In 1846 he wrote of them:

> Their wants would seem to be few, their capacity limited, and incapable of development, if we are to judge by the success of missionaries and others; and their earthly destiny is now so rapidly fulfilling, that, after a few generations, the red men will all be gathered to the tombs of their forefathers, in darkness. Their destiny, in another world, rests in the hands of an Omnipotent God, whose laws we have no right to call in

[94] Ibid., p. 489.
[95] Ibid., pp. 209–10.
[96] Ibid., pp. 210–11.
[97] Ibid., pp. 713–14.

question. A powerful argument against their Adamic origin, is the impossibility of civilizing or Christianizing them. In spite of all the attempts of missionaries, and all the flattering accounts they give, no advance has yet been made. The Indians cannot live where civilization and christianity [sic] exist, and are rapidly vanishing as these approach. They will die without appreciating, and, most of them, without hearing the sound of the gospel. . . .[98]

Nott's comments, tinged with a regret that suggests a final and imminent farewell, characterize many Americans' views of Indians during the 1840s. Although Indians no longer represented a physical threat in the eastern U.S., they did constitute a problem for whites, a problem many believed was slowly working itself out to a terrible and final solution.

Many, of course, had prophesied a tragic end for the Indian even before Morton began his investigations, but Morton seemed to provide the scientific proof for Indians' inevitable extinction. In a biographical sketch of Morton published in 1861, Sanford B. Hunt summed up Morton's scientific findings, stressing their political and social implications with respect to the Indian. Drawing upon Morton's findings, Hunt asserted that government cannot decree equality. "In history, we find that, so far as the welfare of nations is concerned, there is no such thing as equality; that the strong hand, guided by the intelligent brain, has ever conquered." According to Hunt, the small-brained Toltecs were conquered and driven out by the stronger, larger-brained Indians of the north, who in turn were forced from their lands and driven to their "forest graves" by even larger-brained Teutons. "It was not conquest or subjugation, but annihilation. Rank by rank, and tribe by tribe, the red man faded from his possessions."[99]

The primary element of contention, Hunt claimed, was not the demand to replace the forest with civilization, but rather the usurpation of Indian hunting grounds. The battle was a primal one between white fur trapper and Indian; it

[98] J. C. Nott, "Unity of the Human Race," *Southern Quarterly Review* 9 (January, 1846): 7.
[99] Hunt in Gross, pp. 597–603.

was a battle pitting race against race, with the Indian biologically doomed to give way. Eighty-four cubic inches of Indian brain had to compete against, and would eventually succumb before, ninety-six cubic inches of Teuton brain. "Had the Indian been capable of subjugation to slavery he would still be found among us." Through slavery whites could have exercised for the Indian that same guardianship they offered to blacks, that "paternal care and superior wisdom in guiding, protecting, and elevating [the race], in such a manner . . . as is best fitted to its capacities." Unfortunately the Indian had "faded, and passes away from the broad lands they once claimed as their own. Without a claim to the soil, without a vestige of national organization, and in competition with a vastly superior race . . . annihilation . . . has . . . dogged the retreating footsteps of the Indian. . . ."[100] Morton's theory of the Indian's biological inferiority must have comforted many Americans, for now they could find God's hand and not their own directing the extinction of the Indian.

But these passages suggest more than mere scientific rationale; they point to the broader concepts that found expression between 1830 and 1860. Morton began his work at a time when environmentalism was under attack. The great social and educational programs for the Indian initiated at the beginning of the century had failed. These much-touted experiments, based on environmentalism, did not measure up to the glowing expectations with which they were launched.[101] Their failure and the consequent dis-

---

[100] Ibid.

[101] For an excellent discussion of the decline of philanthropic and humanitarian hopes for Native Americans, see Bernard W. Sheehan, *Seeds of Extinction: Jeffersonian Philanthropy and the American Indian.* Of course not all efforts ceased on behalf of improving the condition of the Indians. Many abolitionists sought to also help Indians along with blacks, but freeing the slave was their prime goal. See Linda K. Kerber, "The Abolitionist Perception of the Indian," *Journal of American History* 62 (September, 1975): 271–95. More concerned with humanitarian reform in Indian affairs after the Civil War is Robert Winston Mardock, *The Reformers and the American Indian,* and Francis Paul Prucha, *American Indian Policy in Crisis: Christian Reformers and the Indian, 1865–1900.* Prucha points out, however, that abo-

crediting of environmentalism caused the image of the Indian held by his would-be benefactors to suffer. Critics such as Morton and other polygenists could applaud the goals of the humanitarians but believe their actions to be misguided. To these critics it was not so much human nature that thwarted philanthropic goals as it was racial or biological differences, divinely ordained and immutable. In the polygenists' view, one could educate the Indian all he liked, but in the end the Indian would remain an Indian with all the negative connotation that implied. In other words, the Indian could never achieve equality with a white man. In a society that would not share power, respect, or land with nonwhites, the Indian was an anomaly. Slavery was the only effective institution Americans had developed for controlling nonwhites and since Indians made poor slaves, necessity seemed to decree that they be removed from the white man's sphere of activity until nature took its course. Removal of Indians across the Mississippi River was an expedient but temporary measure. For the humanitarian, who fervently believed the Indian could be made to accept civilization, removal was a final opportunity. For the polygenist critic, Indian removal was the next logical step toward Indian extinction.

At the same time Swiss scientist Louis Agassiz lectured before thousands in Boston and New York on God's "Plan of Creation in the Animal Kingdom," in Philadelphia, Morton was trying to comprehend God's plan of creation as it related to man. Undoubtedly, Morton shared with Agassiz the premise that through scientific study of nature man would not only better understand his own place in the universe but also better comprehend the beauty and wisdom of God's grand design.

Through piecing together broken skulls, Morton constructed the scientific proofs of polygenism. He began his

---

litionists as a group had little effect on Indian policy especially after the Civil War. See also Brian Dippie, *The Non-Vanishing American: White Attitudes and U.S. Indian Policy*, pp. 95–106.

studies believing in the unity of mankind and the various races as the product of environment or chance, but his research led him to abandon this position and advocate a plural origin for man, an assertion made with "great difficulty and delicacy."[102] He was correct in anticipating the outcry that would follow his announcement of such a theory. A religious man, Morton did not wish to tamper with another man's faith, but only wished that science could pursue the truth regardless of where it led. His opponents accused him of abetting the collapse of Christianity and the demise of social and political rights. This they believed would follow if the doctrine of polygenism were accepted. To Morton this was a spurious deduction. All men, regardless of species, had certain rights, if only because they also were created by God. But to Morton, it made "little difference whether the mental inferiority of the Negro, the Samoiyede, or the Indian, is natural or acquired; or if they ever possessed equal intelligence with the Caucasian they have lost it; and if they never had it, they had nothing to lose. One part would arraign Providence for creating them originally different, another for placing them in circumstances by which they inevitably became so. Let us search out the truth, and reconcile it afterwards."[103]

The philanthropists' hope for the Indian hinged on the Indians' intelligence; it was this trait in particular that assured the promise of advancement. Thus, with the Indians' intelligence cast in doubt, so also was the philanthropists' hope for the Indians' eventual "civilization." It is little wonder that many philanthropists and others who sought the Indians' advancement could not accept such dour findings.

Through painstaking research, often late into the night after his duties as a teacher and physician were completed, Morton pursued his search for nature's truth. But after numerous measurements on hundreds of crania, he arrived

[102] Samuel G. Morton, *A Letter to Rev. John Bachman, D.D., on the Question of Hybridity in Animals, Considered in Reference to the Unity of the Human Species*, p. 14.
[103] Samuel G. Morton to George Gliddon, quoted in Patterson, p. lii.

not at nature's truth but at his own.[104] Both the history and archaeology of Egypt and the archaeology of the Ohio and Mississippi valleys came to his aid in his classification of man and the confirmation of the permanency of type. Like many other naturalists of his day, Morton believed that collecting, classifying, and arranging served as explanation. The record that he read in history, combined with his minute examination of individual crania and classification of them by type, revealed for Morton that each race continued physiologically and intellectually as it had always been—a separate creation. Morton believed in an orderly universe and felt that rational investigation of the facts of nature would reveal its timeless permanency. To admit to physical agents of change, to see races as varieties of a single species or type produced by environment or chance, opened up chaos and confusion in God's universe. Unlimited varieties of man could be produced under these conditions. It was much grander to see God's hand in the creation of species over time than to attribute the plenitude of nature to rampaging material causes.

Morton could be sympathetic toward the Indian and feel remorse that Indians had suffered so much injustice at the hands of the white man, but it was the same sympathy he could feel for a whipped horse. The Indian was a tragic figure who had reached his highest level in "savagery" and who could progress no further. But if he was a tragic figure, he was also a specimen for science. Indians represented primordial types possessing peculiar physical, mental, and moral traits. Morton, of course, was not the only one who saw Native Americans as such, but he was a teacher who taught Americans that by viewing the Indian's skull—the seat of the Indian's intelligence—one could both discern the Indian's past and predict his future. Morton's work helped to sanction the activities of those who, in the name of science, traveled to the West to collect Indian crania for phrenological purposes and for museums. And if for Morton and

[104] For a discussion of how Morton arrived at "his truth," see Gould, *The Mismeasure of Man*, pp. 50–69.

Agassiz the Indian became a zoological specimen, so also might others begin to perceive him as such. Within this broader context one can see the serious aspect of the remark made in fun by a member of a government exploring expedition who suggested that the group catch one of the Indians they met along the trip and "preserve him in alcohol as a zoological specimen. . . . " [105] In the case of Agassiz, this was a grotesque reality.

By the 1860s, Morton's proofs of polygenism and polygenism itself began to collapse under the devastating weight of new research. [106] In the decades before the Civil War, however, Morton's ethnological theories seemed to many in accord with the facts and possessed the power to explain Indian behavior. Even historian Francis Parkman attributed the Indian's demise to biological inferiority and leaned toward separate creation as an explanation. [107]

Morton's theories on Indians were accepted by many not only because they agreed with the observations of others who saw what they wanted to see, but because they were viewed as scientific and seemed to fit the facts. Morton worked to make ethnology an empirical science, just as medicine had become, and he hoped to draw up the fundamental principles for a scientific ethnology. Death, however, prevented this. Morton stressed that ethnology must be considered broadly and must be studied in connection with "general zoology, geology, and chronology; and even astronomy." [108] History, he claimed, also was useful, but not as valuable as archaeology in trying to decipher the Indian's mysterious past. As the geologist explored the layers of earth to discern God's plan from the fossils, so too was it

[105] Joseph C. Ives, *Report Upon the Colorado River of the West*, 36th Cong., 1st Sess., 1861, Sen. Exec. Doc. 90, pp. 97–98.

[106] Wilson, pp. 240–302; Trigger, pp. 14–17; Stewart and Newman, p. 22.

[107] Parkman was a close friend of the polygenist E. G. Squier and was sympathetic to many of Squier's "scientific" ideas. See Don C. Seitz, ed. *Letters From Francis Parkman to E. G. Squier*, pp. 28–29, and Robert F. Berkhofer, Jr., *The White Man's Indian: Images of the American Indian from Columbus to the Present*, pp. 95–96.

[108] Morton, *A Letter to Rev. John Bachman*, p. 19.

incumbent upon the archaeologist to dig into the past to answer the riddles in the Indian's historical record.

One who rose to the challenge and fully accepted the task, as well as Morton's leadership, was Ephraim George Squier, a sometime teacher and journalist. Through his archaeological investigations of the Ohio River mounds, Squier became Morton's American historian.

4

Ephraim George Squier
and the Archaeology of Mental Progress

RECENTLY several histories of anthropology have cited the work of Ephraim George Squier (1821–1888). Mention of Squier is generally confined to the field of archaeology, as a result of his book on the New York mounds and another book he coauthored with E. H. Davis on the mounds of the Ohio and Mississippi valleys. Squier's contributions to ethnology, however, were more than just archaeological. He also analyzed American Indian legends and symbols and assessed their importance for ethnological investigations. Although Squier's work and theories are now outdated, they remain valuable in the history of ethnology because they mirror issues and problems concerning the direction of ethnology and the morality of Indian-white relations in the middle of the nineteenth century.[1]

In his 1843 lecture "Condition and True Interests of the Laboring Class of America" before the New York State Me-

[1] For brief notices of Squier's archaeological and ethnological career, see Gordon Willey and Jeremy Sabloff, *A History of American Archaeology,* pp. 42–87; Leo Deuel, *Conquistadores Without Swords: Archaeologists in the Americas,* pp. 18–20; Robert Silverberg, *Mound Builders of Ancient America: The Archaeology of a Myth,* pp. 109–34; Gordon Willey, "One Hundred Years of American Archaeology," in *One Hundred Years of Anthropology,* ed. J. O. Brew, p. 33; William Stanton, *The Leopard's Spots: Scientific Attitudes Towards Race in America, 1815–59;* Don Seitz, ed., *Letters from Francis Parkman to E. G. Squier,* pp. 9–15; Robert E. Bieder and Thomas G. Tax, "From Ethnologists to Anthropologists: A Brief History of the American Ethnological Society," in *American Anthropology: The Early Years, 1974 Proceedings of the American Ethnological Society,* ed. John V. Murra, pp. 11–12; Curtis M. Hinsley, Jr., *Savages and Scientists: The Smithsonian Institution and the Development of American Anthropology, 1846–1910,* pp. 35–40; Thomas G. Tax, "The Development of North American Archaeology, 1800–1879" (Ph.D. Diss., University of Chicago, 1973).

chanic Association, E. G. Squier stated that "manual labor is conducive to the development of mind; and that he who, while he labors, still thinks and studies, will attain a mental strength and stature, to which the pampered and effeminate son of wealth can never arrive."[2]

Squier spoke from experience. Born in 1821 in Bethlehem, New York, the son of a Methodist minister, Squier had limited educational opportunities. As a youth working on a farm he was able to acquire sufficient education to become the local school teacher. In his free time he studied civil engineering, but the depression of 1837 made that trade unfeasible and prompted him to turn to journalism. He soon moved to Albany where he had little success; his *Poet's Magazine* failed after two issues, and his employment on the *New-York State Mechanic* ceased when the paper failed in 1843. Squier next left Albany for Connecticut and became the editor of the Hartford *Evening Journal*. A rather flamboyant journalist, Squier had a tart, castigating wit that was a source of enjoyment for the Whigs and a distress to the Democrats. But problems in Connecticut led him to move again in 1845, this time to Chillicothe, Ohio, where he published the *Scioto Gazette* and in 1847 served as clerk of the Ohio House of Representatives.[3]

Surrounded in his new location by Indian mounds believed to be the remains of ancient civilizations, Squier and a friend, Dr. E. H. Davis, explored them systematically. Just what motivated Squier in this endeavor is not known, although there are some clues worth following. First was the wonderful romantic image of the mounds—situated in gloomy forests and cloaked with mystery—which the press evoked. Romances were written based on the mythical ancient civilizations purported to have been situated in the Ohio and Mississippi valleys, civilizations that supposedly

[2]Ephraim George Squier, "Two Lectures on the Origin and Progress of Modern Civilization," Misc. Mss., Squier Papers, NYHS. See also, Ephraim George Squier, *Lecture on the Condition and True Interests of the Laboring Class of America, The Working Man's Miscellany*.

[3]Herman J. Deutsch, "Squier, Ephraim George," *Dictionary of American Biography*, ed. Dumas Malone, pp. 488–89; Seitz, pp. 9–15; E. Squier to E. George Squier, Dec. 18, 1845, Squier Papers, WCL.

had ruled North America in fabled splendor. Examples of this genre were "The Prairies," a poem by William Cullen Bryant published in his collection of *Poems* (1832), and the romance *Behemoth: A Legend of the Mound Builders* (1839), by Cornelius Mathews.

To explore these mounds and to discover facts about these ancient civilizations probably seemed a grand adventure to an imaginative young man. Squier was also influenced by William Henry Prescott's *History of the Conquest of Peru*, which he read while laboring in the fields around Chillicothe. The gloomy mystery, the romance, and the importance of salvage archaeology, so replete in Prescott's writing, appealed to Squier.[4] He was not, however, entirely motivated by Romantic literature about the mounds. His concepts of progress, civilization, and history undoubtedly strongly influenced his interest in archaeology.

In 1841–42, while still in Albany, Squier wrote two lectures on civilization and progress that reveal the influence of François Guizot's *History of Civilization*, published in 1837.[5] A popular book, Guizot's *History* by 1841 had gone through three editions in America, as well as three in England. One reason for the numerous American editions was the widespread use of these Sorbonne lectures as a college text.

Guizot's concept of civilization embodied two themes:

[4]Many years later the influence of Prescott was acknowledged by Squier not only on his mound explorations but also on his work in Central and South America; see E. George Squier, *Peru: Incidents of Travel and Exploration in the Land of the Incas*, pp. 1–2; Deuel, p. 19. For a perceptive study of Prescott's romantic view of Indians, see David Levin, *History as Romantic Art*, pp. 126–59. The ties between archaeology and the romantic movement in England are explored briefly in Stuart Piggott, "Prehistory and the Romantic Movement," *Antiquity* 11 (1937): 31–38. That this connection was also true for America, see Silverberg, *Mound Builders*.

[5]The first English edition of this work was published in 1837. The work first appeared in three volumes in France in 1828 as *Histoire de la civilisation en Europe*. In England this work was published as *General History of Civilization in Europe* and also as *Lectures on European Civilization*. Evidently Squier had access to one of these two English editions. For a brief account of François Guizot's life and influence, see Stanley Mellon, "Editor's Introduction," in François Guizot, *François Guizot: Historical Essays and Lectures*, ed. Stanley Mellon, pp. xvii–xlv.

the progress of society and the progress of the individual, which in combination led to "the melioration of the social system and the expansion of the mind and faculties of man." Christianity was vital to both themes. Taking these two themes and adding a third, the influence of Christianity in European history from the downfall of Rome to the French Revolution, Squier prepared his "Two Lectures on the Origins and Progress of Modern Civilization."[6] A projected third lecture developing these themes for the much shorter period of American history apparently was never written; at least, no trace of it remains.

Squier's lectures' basic theme, lifted from Guizot, was the gradual development of civilization from savagism. Using European history as example, Squier sought to demonstrate that in spite of the chaos of barbarian invasions, multiple wars, and social breakdown, civilization and progress always moved forward. Although admitting to periods of decline, Squier believed that history on the whole demonstrated inevitable progress; chaos and social breakdown did not necessarily signal a setback. True, reverses did occur, but to Squier they proved necessary, since out of confusion and disorder man sought order and improvement. Man was impelled to improve his material world; even the barbarian aspired to civilization before he could possibly achieve it.

Other premises, also derived from Guizot, emerged in Squier's lectures. Savage life was democratic, although savages were incapable of self-government. Environmental forces were important. "The general climate, the character or appearances of the county [sic] all have a wonderful and at the same time unaccountable influence on the character of man."[7] Squier repeatedly emphasized that he was not concerned with history per se, but rather with revealing the path of progress and its effect on human and social development, the path of man's struggle against an environment that shaped his destiny and in turn was shaped by him. By expounding upon this path of progress before

[6] E. George Squier, "Two Lectures on the Origin and Progress of Modern Civilization."

[7] Ibid., p. 47 and passim.

working-class men in the Mechanics Institute, Squier sincerely believed he could give them a philosophy to improve their lives. Perhaps years later, while exploring the secrets of the Ohio Valley mounds, Squier hoped to discern better this struggle between man and his environment and to detect the beginnings of progress in America.

Contemporaries judged the work of Squier and Davis a turning point in the study of the mounds.[8] There had been speculation on the contents of the mounds and their builders since the eighteenth century. By the 1790s reports filtered back from travelers and military men in the Ohio and Mississippi valleys that aroused the attention of eastern scholars.[9] The founding of the American Antiquarian Society was premised partly on the need to pursue further investigations into this area of history.[10] The major debate centered on whether the builders were Indians or a more civilized people. Scientists and explorers such as Benjamin Smith Barton, Jonathan Heart, William Bartram, Jonathan Carver, and Caleb Atwater held the opinion that a popu-

[8]Albert Gallatin to Joseph Henry, June 16, 1847, Gallatin Papers, NYHS; Samuel F. Haven, *Archaeology of the United States*, Smithsonian Contributions to Knowledge 8 (1856): 32. See also S. F. Haven to John Russell Bartlett, June 4, 1846, Bartlett Papers, JCBL.

[9]Amos Stoddard, *Sketches, Historical and Descriptive of Louisiana*; Daniel Drake, *Natural and Statistical View, or Picture of Cincinnati and the Miami Country*; DeWitt Clinton, *An Introductory Discourse Delivered Before the Literary and Philosophical Society of New York on the Fourth of May, 1814; Memoir on the Antiquities of the Western Parts of the State of New York*; A.B., "To the Editor," *The North American Review* 1 (May, 1815): 21–22; Timothy Flint, *Recollections of the Last Ten Years in the Valley of the Mississippi*, ed. George R. Brooks; J. W. Monette, "Indian Mounds; Or, American Monuments, In the South-West," *South-Western Journal: A Magazine of Science, Literature and Miscellany* 1 (July, 1838): pp. 228–31; George Bancroft, *History of the United States, from the Discovery of the American Continent*, dismisses reports of mounds as "feeble fortifications," 3: 307–309.

[10]James Bowdin, "A Philosophical Discourse Publicly Addressed to the American Academy of Arts and Sciences," *Memoirs of the American Academy of Arts and Sciences* 1 (1785): 1–20. See also William L. Joyce, "Antiquarians and Archaeologists: The American Antiquarian Society, 1812–1912," *Proceedings of the American Antiquarian Society* 91 (1982): 307.

lous nation had built the mounds, a nation that must have had an advanced civilization based on agriculture and laws.

By the early nineteenth century the two conflicting views on the identity of the mound builders were elaborated in the works of Bishop James Madison and the Reverend Thaddeus Harris. Madison held that the mounds were the work of a people no further advanced toward civilization than present-day Indians. Harris, however, disagreed and assigned their construction to ancient Toltecs who later migrated south. Both men formed their opinions based upon personal inspection of the mounds; they had firsthand knowledge of their size and extensive nature. Harris's views prevailed for most of the century, however, perhaps because he was connected with the American Antiquarian Society.[11]

Those who agreed with Harris that the mound builders were more civilized than contemporary Indians disagreed on the builders' identity and origin. Debated with great intensity and concern were questions of whether the builders had been Indian or white, whether they had come from the south (Mexico) or had migrated to Mexico, whether the mounds were of great antiquity or were built just prior to the arrival of whites in the New World, and whether the builders still survived or had been destroyed by the present-day Indians.[12]

[11] James Madison, "A Letter on the Supposed Fortifications of the Western Country from Bishop Madison of Virginia to Doctor Barton," *Transactions of the American Philosophical Society* 6, pt. 1 (1804): 132–42; Thaddeus Mason Harris, *The Journal of a Tour into the Territory Northwest of the Alleghany Mountains, Made in the Spring of the Year 1803*; Benjamin Smith Barton, *New Views of the Origin of the Tribes and Nations of America*; Jonathan Heart to Benjamin Smith Barton, n.d., Barton Papers, APS; Caleb Atwater, "Description of the Antiquities Discovered in the State of Ohio and Other Western States," *Transactions and Collections of the American Antiquarian Society* 1 (1820): 105–299; Jonathan Carver, *Three Years' Travel Throughout the Interior Parts of North America*; Haven, *Archaeology*, p. 31; Silverberg, *Mound Builders*.

[12] Henry Marie Breckinridge, *Views of Louisiana . . .* ; Drake, *Natural and Statistical View*; Clinton, *An Introductory Discourse*; Atwater, "Description of Antiquities"; Hugh Williamson, *Observations on the Climate in Different Parts of America . . .* ; John Haywood, *The Natural and Aborig-*

In the swirl of controversy little firm support existed for any particular theory. The answer to the mystery, however, would not be found in eastern libraries. What was needed were field investigators who could dig and theorize. The rather irascible Caleb Atwater of Circleville, Ohio, filled this position. With the assistance of the American Antiquarian Society, Atwater undertook a survey of the principle mounds in his neighborhood. His results were published in 1820 in the first volume of *Archaeologia Americana*.[13] Atwater concluded that the mound builders lived in a society more complex than that of contemporary Indians; that they had a regular form of government and a society complete with laws, arts, and institutions; and that they had fixed settlements inhabited over long periods of time. According to Atwater, although the mound builders were from Asia, they were not the ancestors of the local Indians. The mound builders, he believed, had originated in southern Asia, whereas the Indians were descended from the Tartars.[14]

inal History of Tennessee, Up to the First Settlements Therein By the White People in the Year 1768; Constantine S. Rafinesque, "Ancient Annals of Kentucky; or Introduction to the History and Antiquities of the State of Kentucky," in H. Marshall, *The History of Kentucky*; N. Harris, *Journal of a Tour in the Indian Territory in the Spring of 1844*; William Henry Harrison, "A Discourse on the Aborigines of the Valley of the Ohio," *Transactions of the Historical and Philosophical Society of Ohio* 1 (1839): 219–67; John Delafield, *An Inquiry into the Origin of the Antiquities of America*; Alexander W. Bradford, *American Antiquities and Researches into the Origin and History of the Red Race*; Josiah Priest, *American Antiquities and Discoveries in the West . . .* ; William Bartram, *Travels of William Bartram*, ed. Mark Van Doren; James Harris McCulloh, Jr., *Researches on America: Being an Attempt to Settle Some Points Relative to the Aborigines of America, etc.*

[13]Atwater, "Description of the Antiquities." One study of Atwater found him an aggressive eccentric. A contemporary saw Atwater as a "queer talking, . . . a disappointed, unhappy man." See Francis P. Weisenburger, "Caleb Atwater: Pioneer Politician and Historian," *Ohio Historical Quarterly* 68 (1959): 18–37. Joyce, p. 307.

[14]Atwater, pp. 209–15; Caleb Atwater, *Remarks Made on a Tour to Prairie Du Chien; thence to Washington City in 1829*. See also Samuel L. Mitchell, "Communications from Dr. Samuel L. Mitchell," *Archaeologia Americana, Transactions and Collections of the American Antiquarian Society* 1 (1820): 321–32, 344–55.

Atwater based his final conclusion on the existence of mounds in Asia and on the discovery of a Hindoo-like vase found near Nashville, Tennessee. He believed these facts supported Mosaic chronology and monogenism:

> Let those who are constantly seeking for some argument, with which to overthrow the history of man by Moses, consider this fact [the existence of ancient works, as found in the Ohio Valley, Asia, and Europe]. Such persons have more than once asserted, that there were different stocks or races of man; but this similarity of works almost all over the world, indicated that all men sprung from one origin . . . [that similarities among works] lead us to the conclusion, that the more carefully we examine the Antiquities of this . . . country the more evidence will be found, tending to establish the truth of the Mosaick history.[15]

Others, however, saw little in the mounds that gave evidence of a more complex civilization than that of the "primitive Indian." One historian, James H. McCulloch, at first accepted the arguments of Harris, but after a later survey of the evidence reversed himself and sided with Bishop Madison. McCulloh charged that those who advocated that the mound builders were an advanced race of people did not argue from the evidence. Nothing yet found indicated any other than a primitive people. Territorial governor of Michigan and Indian scholar Lewis Cass agreed in an article for the *North American Review*.[16] The debate revolved around several important issues. Were contemporary Indians descended from the mound builders, and did they suffer a decline from a higher civilization? Or were the mound builders a separate race of man? Acceptance of the former cast doubt on the progressive development of man. If the latter proved true, what had happened to this mysterious race?

[15] Atwater, "Description of the Antiquities," p. 205.
[16] James Haines McCulloh, Jr., *Researches, Philosophical and Antiquarian, Concerning the Aboriginal History of America*; [Lewis Cass], Review of *Manners and Customs of several Indian Tribes . . .* [and] *Historical Notes Respecting the Indians of North America*," in *The North American Review* 22 (January, 1826): 70.

The identity of the mound builders held implications beyond scholarly dispute, affecting even government Indian
policy. When the debate over the government's stand for
Indian removal stirred the nation, President Andrew Jackson based his rationale in part on the theory that Indians
had at an earlier time driven the mound builders from their
homes and perhaps had even destroyed them.[17] In a sense,
by interpreting the mound builders as an advanced civilization and attributing their downfall to "savage hordes," civilization was justified in warring against Indian tribes. The
white race in the name of civilization would do to the Indians
what the Indians had once done to the mound builders. The
final victor would be civilization.

Although both McCulloh and Cass were persuasive, the
weight of opinion seemed to rest on the other side. Books
and articles on the mounds and their builders continued to
flow from the presses, but none advanced the debate or
mustered sufficient additional proof to sway one side or the
other.[18] The work of Josiah Priest in 1834 was probably the
most popular. According to his publishers, twenty-two thou-

[17] After justifying government actions on removing Indians across the Mississippi River, President Jackson reported that they were doing well. He
noted that Indians were rapidly dying off and would eventually be extinct.
This, according to Jackson, must be accepted and reconciled by those who
sought to help and preserve the Indian. That such a fate was not unusual in
the course of history he noted by pointing out that the very Indians who now
suffered removal had driven off or killed the Indians who had built the
mounds long before white contact. "In the monuments and fortresses of an
unknown people, spread over the extensive regions of the west, we behold
the memorials of a once powerful race, which was exterminated, or has disappeared, to make room for the existing savage tribes. Nor is there anything
in this, which, upon a comprehensive view of the general interests of the
human race, is to be regretted." Andrew Jackson, "Message from the President of the United States to the Two Houses of Congress . . . December 7,
1830," U.S. 21st Cong. 2nd House Doc. No. 2 (1830): 19–22. See also Silverberg, pp. 159–60; Willey and Sabloff, pp. 47–48.

[18] For example see Haywood, *The Natural and Aboriginal History of Tennessee*; Rafinesque in Marshall, *The History of Kentucky*; Joseph W. Moulton
and J. V. N. Yates, *History of the State of New York including its Aboriginal
and Colonial Annals*; Flint, *Recollection of the Last Ten Years*; Clinton,
Memoir on the Antiquities; Breckenridge, *Views of Louisiana*; "On the Aborigines of the Western Country," *The Port Folio* 1 (June, 1816): 457–63.

sand copies of Priest's *American Antiquities and Discoveries in the West* were sold to subscribers in the first thirty months. There were five editions by midcentury. Despite its immense popularity, however, Priest's book met with some criticism. One reader saw the work as a mere "collection of odds and ends of theories and statements . . . a sort of curiosity-shop of archaeological fragments, whose materials are gathered without the exercise of much discrimination, and disposed without much system or classification, and apparently without inquiry into their authenticity." [19]

One writer who aspired to greater scholarly precision was Henry Rowe Schoolcraft, author of "Observations Respecting the Grave Creek Mound in Western Virginia." [20] When a stone tablet containing what appeared to be writing or an alphabet was discovered at the Grave Creek Mound, eastern scholars responded with excitement. Was it genuine or a fake? The issue seemed to place the mound builders in an entirely new light, and the stone added evidence to the arguments of those who believed the mounds were built by Europeans long before Columbus. Scholars were not alone in their fascination regarding the find; the public also seemed consumed with the marvelous discovery, a fact not missed by the owner of the mound. As Squier wrote to John R. Bartlett, a member of the American Ethnological Society,

> I visited also, the celebrated Grave Creek Mounds. The earth around the shaft has tumbled in, and it is really "a sight to see!" The Engraved Stone, I understand, has gone to Richmond Va., where it ought, if possible, to be secured by your Society. Not that I attach much value to it, but with a view of determining its genuineness. From what I could learn, both at Grave Creek and Wheeling, of the character of the younger Mr. Tomlinson who opened the mound, I am satisfied that very little reliance can be placed upon his word in matters when his *interest* is involved. He opened the mound, not through an enlightened,

[19] Haven, p. 41.
[20] Henry Rowe Schoolcraft, "Observations Respecting the Grave Creek Mound in Western Virginia," *Transactions of the American Ethnological Society* 1 (1845): 366–420.

nor for that matter, an unenlightened, curiosity, but as a specu-
lator, boarded it round, put on pad-locks, hung up his skele-
tons in horrible ghostliness and sat down at the gate expecting
that the universal Yankee native would come trecking to see it,
at "a quarter a head, children half price."[21]

Schoolcraft, commissioned by the American Ethnological
Society to look into the case of the Grave Creek Mound,
arrived at no firm conclusion.

A more extensive survey of American mounds was needed.
This Squier and Davis provided.

Compared to Atwater's survey, the proposed investigations
of Squier and Davis were to be far more extensive and
promised greater results. When the two men approached
the American Antiquarian Society and the American Ethnological Society in 1846 for funds to carry out the explorations, they received enthusiastic encouragement but no
funds. Although the American Antiquarian Society, along
with Benjamin Silliman's *Journal of Arts and Science*, offered to publish articles on the team's findings, and the
American Ethnological Society committed itself to publishing the completed results of the investigations, no
funds for the actual archaeological explorations were made
available.[22]

Undaunted by lack of financial support, Squier and Davis,
who had begun mapping, drawing, and digging in the Ohio
Valley in 1845, by 1847 had amassed a monumental amount
of material. It soon became apparent to the American Ethnological Society that it could not raise the funds necessary
to publish the voluminous findings in a way appropriate to
the scope of the work, which included extensive maps and
engravings. Fortunately for both the American Ethnological Society and the archaeologists, the newly created
Smithsonian Institution, casting about for a scientific manu-

[21] E. George Squier to John R. Bartlett, Aug. 24, 1846, Bartlett Papers, JCBL.
[22] E. George Squier to John R. Bartlett, Sept. 21, 1846, Bartlett Papers, JCBL.

An engraving of Grave Creek Mound from *Ancient Monuments of the Mississippi Valley*, by E. G. Squier and E. H. Davis.

script that would draw attention to its initial volume of *Contributions to Knowledge*, settled on the work of Squier and Davis.[23] Physicist Joseph Henry of Princeton, who served as the first secretary of the Smithsonian Institution, was devoted to the advancement of science and used his position to further this goal. Henry possessed very decided views on what constituted science, and he was determined

---

[23] The Smithsonian Institution was founded in 1848 through the bequest of James Smithson, an Englishman, who desired that the money go to found "an establishment for the increase and diffusion of knowledge among men." See Wilcomb E. Washburn, "Joseph Henry's Conception of the Purpose of the Smithsonian Institution," in *A Cabinet of Curiosities*, p. 105. See also Joseph Henry to John R. Bartlett, Nov. 4, 1847, Bartlett Papers, JCBL.

to publish only that which contributed to its advancement.[24] Once he agreed to publish the manuscript on the mounds, he demanded that Squier and Davis eschew all speculative theorizing and confine themselves to facts and to describing only what they had found. In Henry's view, too much nonsense on the mounds had already been perpetuated in the name of science.

Squier and Davis were in sympathy with Henry's demands, for they were severely critical of much of what at that time passed for archaeological investigation. In a letter from Davis to Squier, Davis castigated the methodology of a contemporary, the southern archaeologist Dr. Montroville W. Dickeson:

> The great difficulty with the Doctor is that he is extending his observations over too large a field and expending his energies on too many subjects—He has in his list of subjects for special attention—Geology—Mineralogy—Paleontology—Conchology—Asteology with a dozen more beside *Moundology*— The Natural history of Man—Habits of Negroes—Animals and birds—as well as botany in all its various branches. He is [an] *artifact* in fossil geology, but has something yet to learn in moundology—His manner of collecting facts is too loose, and not always to be relied on—for instance—he sets down too many hearsay facts—and secondly, his mode of opening the mounds is not calculated to furnish the most accurate scientific knowledge.[25]

Davis described Dickeson's methods as more similar to a picnic outing than to real scientific investigation. Dickeson used slaves to dig while he sketched the mound and its contents. Wrote Davis, "This is all very cozy and not very expensive pastime—which may furnish considerable information for a journalist. But there is none of that close measurement and accurate investigation which characterizes *our labours.*"[26]

[24] Arthur P. Molella and Nathan Reingold, "Theorists and Ingenious Mechanics: Joseph Henry Defines Science," *Science Studies* 3 (1973): 323–51; Hinsley, pp. 34–52. See also "Introduction," in Joseph Henry, *The Papers of Joseph Henry*, eds. Nathan Reingold, et al., pp. xvi–xxi.
[25] E. Davis to E. George Squier, Dec. 29, 1846, Squier Papers, LC.
[26] Ibid.

Davis and Squier's *Ancient Monuments of the Mississippi Valley* contains little speculative theory, offering instead a thorough presentation of the facts as the authors saw them. On the whole, the book provided a rather dry description of the various kinds of mounds—enclosure mounds or "forts," sepulture mounds, and anomalous mounds—as well as an elaborate description of their contents. Although Squier and Davis refrained from speculation, they did believe that the data gave evidence of a large and rather advanced population with contacts to Central and South America. As Squier pointed out with respect to the mound builders,

> It may safely be claimed . . . that a large local population can only exist under an agricultural system. Dense commercial and manufacturing communities, the apparent exception to the remark, are themselves the offspring of a large agricultural population, with which nearly or remotely they are connected, and upon which they are dependent. [Furthermore] if the mound-builders were a numerous, stationary, and an agricultural people, it follows of necessity that their customs, laws, and religion, had assumed a fixed and well defined form,—a result inseparable from that condition.[27]

The authors claimed that proofs for these assumptions and for the mound builders' connections with Central and South American civilizations came from the mounds themselves. Squier and Davis theorized that the skull of the true mound builder was of a kind described by Morton as Toltec, which indicated to them that the mound builders and the Indians of Central and South America were the same people. In their opinion the architectural style of the mounds was strongly similar to that of the monumental structures found in Mexico, and the unearthed art and religious objects showed signs of southern religious practices. On this point Squier noted there was indeed need of further study.

---

[27] Ephraim G. Squier and Edwin H. Davis, *Ancient Monuments of the Mississippi Valley: Comprising the Results of Extensive Original Surveys and Explorations.* Smithsonian Contributions to Knowledge 1 (1848): 301–303.

If, again, as from reason and analogy we are warranted in sup-
posing many of these sacred structures are symbolical in their
forms and combinations, they indicate the prevalence among
their builders of religious beliefs and conceptions, corresponding with those which prevailed among the early nations of the
other continent, and which in their elements seem to have
been common to all nations, far back in the traditional period
before the dawn of written history.[28]

The mounds and their artifacts suggested to Squier a progressive force in religion. He would return to this argument in subsequent writings.

Further statements based on meager data were also
made. Squier and Davis conducted their investigations before adequate dating techniques were developed, and so
accurate dates for the construction of the mounds could not
be made. This, however, did not prevent the authors from
concluding that the mounds were very ancient. Given the
extensive geographic range of the mounds in the Middle
West—some were even reported in Oregon—Squier and
Davis argued that the builders of these mounds were "a
people advanced from the nomadic or radically savage
state," that they were a numerous slowly migrating people
with an agricultural economy and with "established habits,
customs, and modes of life."[29] Thus, although not highly
civilized, the mound builders were more civilized than the
Indians found by Europeans. According to Davis and Squier,
the mound builders possessed a more complex religion and
social organization than contemporary Indians. Although
their populous agricultural settlements at one time were
found extensively in North America, in time they moved
slowly down the Mississippi River. Eventually their civilization reached its culmination in Mexico. These conclusions were not at all startling. The American Ethnological
Society committee that the Smithsonian Institution asked to
review the work found it wholly acceptable for publication.
"Its chief features are a Scientific arrangement, simplicity

[28]Ibid., p. 304; see also pp. 288–92.
[29]Ibid., p. 186.

& directness of statement, and legitimate deduction from the facts, with no attempt at mere speculation or theory." Even the conservative theorizer Albert Gallatin could accept the work. Writing to Joseph Henry to recommend the publication of *Ancient Monuments*, Gallatin stated that the work was animated by the "love of truth" and was "worthy of entire confidence." In a later letter Gallatin described *Ancient Monuments* as an "impartial" account that would go far to lay to rest the conjectures of earlier writers.[30]

Squier won his ethnological credentials in the fields along the Ohio River, but his real education in ethnology took place in New York City. There from 1848 to 1849 as a member of the New-York Historical Society and the American Ethnological Society, he discussed ethnology over tea and oysters. He became friends with philologist W. W. Turner and with John R. Bartlett, who, along with Charles Welford, ran a bookstore specializing in works on ethnology. It was also at this time that Squier met John L. Stephens and William Catherwood, two men widely acclaimed for their works on the ruins in Mexico. With other members of the American Ethnological Society, Squier enjoyed dinners at Gallatin's house and conversed with ethnologist Henry Rowe Schoolcraft about Indian legends.[31]

[30] Ibid., p. 44. Squier and Davis also offered an alternative theory of northward migration, but they were more convinced that the mound builders moved southward and eventually to Central America. For the American Ethnological Society report, see Edward Robinson, John R. Bartlett, W. W. Turner, "Report," June 12, 1847, Squier Papers, LC. See also Albert Gallatin to Joseph Henry, June 12, 1847, quoted in Squier and Davis, pp. vii–ix. In a later letter Gallatin described the manuscript of "Ancient Monuments" as an impartial account that would go far to lay to rest the fantastic conjectures of earlier writers. Albert Gallatin to Joseph Henry, June 16, 1847, copy, Gallatin Papers, NYHS. See also Joseph Henry to John R. Bartlett, June 23, 1847, Squier Papers, LC; Joseph Henry to Elias Loomis, June 5, 1847, BLY; Joseph Henry to E. G. Squier, June 23, 1847; E. G. Squier to Joseph Henry, June 26, 1847, draft, Squier Papers, LC. Other testimonials include Samuel G. Morton to Joseph Henry, June 8, 1847, copy; George P. Marsh to Joseph Henry, June 19, 1847, copy, Squier Papers, LC.

[31] For a brief discussion of the activities and members of the American Ethnological Society, see Bieder and Tax, "From Ethnologists to Anthropologists," in Murra, *American Anthropology*.

Unfortunately, at this time Squier's study of ethnology was often interrupted by his desperate financial situation. From his room in Judson's Hotel, Squier constantly fretted about delays in publication of *Ancient Monuments*, whose sale he hoped would ease his financial problems. Joseph Henry's lethargic pace did not suit Squier, who tried valiantly to live by writing. In a letter to a friend Squier confided, "Meanwhile, I shall have the felicity of working hard and—*starving*." Dependent upon subscriptions to publish other works, Squier found himself in a predicament. "Getting subscribers on empty pockets is a prospect not the most delightful to contemplate, and I fear my note of hand would not command a heavy premium in Wall St."[32]

In 1848, Squier gratefully accepted two hundred dollars from the Smithsonian Institution and the New-York Historical Society to survey the mounds of New York state. Unfortunately, he could not entirely dodge misfortune. He started work in the fall of 1848, and the first autumn rains innundated him in "oceans of mud," hampering his digging. Later in western New York he tried valiantly to survey

---

[32] E. George Squier to John R. Bartlett, Feb. 1, 1848, Bartlett Papers, JCBL. That Squier apparently blamed Henry for the delays in publication, perhaps with some justification, is indicated in a letter by George P. Marsh: "Professor Henry left for N.Y. last evening or this morning. I rec'd yesterday a letter from Mr. Squier which he desired me to deliver to Mr. Henry, but as I knew that Mr. H. had been for some days on the point of departure for your city, with a view of attending to the publication of Mr. S's book, I thought it better not to deliver it, but to leave the matter to be settled in a personal interview between them. I have no doubt that Squier has been ill used. He is a little hasty perhaps, but from my observation of Mr. Henry's manner of transacting business, I presume S. is in the right of the controversy. In all matters of business, Prof. H. is as imbecile a person as I ever met, & a man more utterly unfit for his place could hardly be found. Still the aid of the Institution is important to S. & I hope your influence with him may prevent an outbreak between him & Prof. H." G. P. Marsh to John R. Bartlett, March 31, 1848, Bartlett Papers, JCBL. On Squier's constant financial embarrassment, see Joel Squier to E. George Squier, July 13, 1846, Squier Papers, WCL; E. George Squier to Peter Force, Oct. 11, 1851; E. George Squier to Peter Force, Oct. 25, 1854, Force Papers, WCL. About this time Squier attempted to start an ethnological journal, but friends were not encouraging, and they finally convinced him that there were already enough journals to handle ethnological publications. See Samuel G. Morton to E. George Squier, Sept. 25, 1848, Squier Papers, LC.

and dig in the mounds in the midst of snowstorms. Once in the field he also discovered that the amount of labor required to do an adequate job was triple what he had expected.[33]

In 1848 and 1849, Squier published several articles in ethnology.[34] His work on the mounds of Ohio and New York and his reading of McCulloh and Schoolcraft had led him to believe that, in investigating man's past, the study of ancient religious systems and legends might possibly be as important as archaeology. To Squier both mound architecture and the objects found within the mounds indicated a well-defined religious system "which in their elements seem to have been common to all nations, far back in the traditional period, before the dawn of written history." According to Squier, in order to really investigate the history of the American Indians, their religious systems had to be compared with those of the "primitive nations in the old world."[35] Such a comparison would yield information that would firmly place the Indians' position on the path of progress.

Squier's views on Indian religion prompted him to look at the manuscript notes of C. S. Rafinesque, which a friend had placed in his hands.[36] Using these notes Squier in 1848 wrote a series of articles on Indian legends. Following

[33] *Eighth Annual Report of the Smithsonian Institution*, p. 164. E. George Squier to John R. Bartlett, Oct. 26, 1848; Squier to Bartlett, Nov. 7, 1848; Squier to Bartlett, Nov. 12, 1848; Squier to Bartlett, Nov. 27, 1848, Bartlett Papers, JCBL.

[34] Squier's articles for the period include: "Observations on the Aboriginal Monuments of the Mississippi Valley, with Maps and Illustrations," *Transactions of the American Ethnological Society* 2 (1848): 131–207; "Ne-She-Kay-Be-Nais, or the 'Lone Bird,'" *The American Review: A Whig Journal* 8 (September, 1848): 255–59; "Manabozho and the Great Serpent," *The American Review: A Whig Journal* 8 (October, 1848): 392–98; "New Mexico and California," *American Review* 2 n.s. (November, 1848): 503–28; "Historical and Mythological Traditions of the Algonquins," *American Review* 3 n.s. (February, 1849): 273–93.

[35] Squier and Davis, p. 304.

[36] Ibid., p. xxxvi. See also E. George Squier to Henry R. Schoolcraft, Feb. 15, 1849, Schoolcraft Papers, LC; Henry R. Schoolcraft to E. George Squier, Feb. 16, 1849, typescript, Squier Papers, NYHS; Squier, "Ne-She-Kay-Be-Nais," pp. 255–59; Squier, "Manabozho," pp. 392–98.

Schoolcraft, who had recently published his *Algic Researches*, a monumental study of Indian legends, Squier pointed out, in his article "Ne-She-Kay-Be-Nais, or the 'Lone Bird,'" that the legends of the "semi-civilized nations" and the "savage" tribes "would open to the world a new view of the aboriginal mind."[37] He believed much more information on Indian history and mentality could be gleaned by an analysis of the elements and symbols found in such legends and their comparison with the tales of other peoples. He noted, for example, that certain elements, such as the serpent symbol, appeared in the legends and religious systems of the more "refined civilizations" of both Asia and Europe. To Squier this was more than just a matter of incidental interest; it was, he believed, a discovery of a progressive developmental structure in Indian symbolism. In the religious systems in America, Squier wrote, the serpent as "intermediate demi-god was not less clearly recognized than in those of the old world; indeed, as those systems were less complicated, because less modified from their primitive forms, the Great Teacher appears with more distinctness. Among the savage tribes his origin and character were, for obvious reasons, much confused, but among the more advanced semi-civilized nations he occupied a well defined position."[38]

In another article, Squier again underscored the importance of comparative study of legends, when he quoted William Prescott on the subject: "'The existence of similar religious ideas in remote regions inhabited by different races, is an interesting subject; furnishing as it does, one of the most important links in the great chain of communication which binds together the distant families of nations.'" To Squier, where history stood silent on the military, civil, and political life of a people, "the religious conceptions and observations, . . . authentic traditions of the aboriginal nations," were of vital significance for determining a people's rank "in the scale of human development."[39]

[37] Squier, "Ne-She-Kay-Be-Nais," p. 256.
[38] Squier, "Manabozho," p. 392.
[39] Prescott as quoted in Squier, "Historical and Mythological Traditions," p. 275.

With this view of the significance of Indian symbols and "mythology," Squier regarded the Walum-Olum legend, which he discovered in the Constantine Rafinesque papers, as a document of great importance. Squier accepted Rafinesque's account that the Walum-Olum was found in Indiana in 1822 and translated with the aid of David Zeisberger's Delaware dictionary. The legend consisted of five parts. The first two parts recounted traditions of the creation and a flood. The other three parts referred to various migrations of the Lenni-Lenape, or Delaware, Indians and a listing of their ninety-seven chiefs. That the legend was illustrated with "mnemonic symbols" increased its value, Squier believed, for ethnologists. Henry Rowe Schoolcraft, however, distrusted its historical value in depicting the creation, flood, and subsequent wanderings of the Lenni-Lenape Indians. Squier nonetheless believed the use of mnemonic symbols revealed mental development in man and the progress of ideas. He praised the symbols as "the first advances beyond a simple oral transmission of ideas . . . from which we may trace upwards the progress of human invention to its highest and noblest achievements, the present perfected form of written language."[40]

In all his works published in 1848 and 1849, Squier sought to convince other ethnologists and the American public that Indian societies were not as primitive as believed and that these societies were progressive or "evolutionary." Squier's arguments ran counter to the growing doubts of many that Indians were capable of achieving civilization and their beliefs that the high civilizations of Central and South America had developed from foreign influence. Many Americans believed that these advanced civilizations were the result of diffusion from the Old World, but they stoutly rejected the notion that such contacts had penetrated North America above Mexico. Many Americans were prone to see Central and South American Indian societies with a romanticism they did not extend to northern Indian societies. Some Americans accounted for the differ-

[40] Squier, "Historical and Mythological Traditions," p. 293. Henry R. Schoolcraft to E. George Squier," Feb. 16, 1849, typescript, Squier Papers, NYHS.

ence in level of civilization among Indian groups by theorizing that the advanced people of the south really were not Indians at all or, if they were, that their origin was entirely different from that of their more "wild" northern neighbors.[41]

Squier's 1848 article "New Mexico and California," about the Indians of the American Southwest, and his 1849 article "American Ethnology" must be seen in that context. To Squier the New Mexico Indians seemed at a stage between the advanced people of Central America and the more nomadic and primitive people farther north. Squier was a bit more certain in this opinion than Gallatin had been. He based his theory upon United States Army reports, concluding that the Pueblo Indians and Southwest ruins represented a higher level in the scale of progress than the ruder structures found along the Mississippi and Ohio river valleys, albeit not so advanced as the elegant structures in Mexico. The New Mexico structures all stood as testimonials illustrating "the Grand Law of Development, the stages of which nature has graven in the imperishable rocks, and the truth of which history as a whole is an example and a witness."[42] In Squier's mind there seemed to exist a gradation from north to south, from "primitive" to civilized, and the New Mexico Pueblos provided the connecting link.

[41] See especially E. George Squier, "American Ethnology: Being a Summary of some of the Results Which Have Followed the Investigation of this Subject," *American Review* 3 n.s. (April, 1849): 395. Bradford's study saw the development of Indian cultures in completely opposite terms. He believed that the idea of the progress of man from rude beginnings was completely counter to the historical facts and "contrary to the course of events in all antiquity." He believed that progress could only come from outside a culture: "We then find knowledge transmitted from nation to nation—its first beams always coming from without, rather than originating from an internal impulse," pp. 177–78; see also review of *American Antiquities, and Researches into the Origin and History of the Red Race* in *New-York Review* 10 (January, 1842): 88, 91–92; Haywood, pp. 89–90.

[42] E. George Squier, "New Mexico and California," pp. 525–26. That Squier had formed some of these ideas from his work on the Ohio mounds, see E. G. Squier, "Observations on the Uses of the Mounds of the West, with an Attempt at Their Classification," *American Journal of Science and Arts* 3, n.s. (1847): 247, and "Aboriginal Monuments of the Mississippi Valley," pp. 178–95.

In his "American Ethnology," Squier was even more explicit in his arguments that Indians in both North and
South America were one people and that they possessed a
capability for progress. Marshaling a host of authorities—
Morton, Gallatin, Du Ponceau, Humboldt, and others—to
support his stand, Squier argued that, the Eskimos ex-
cepted, all peoples of North and South America were members of one great family.[43] True, this family could be broken
down into two groups as Morton had done, but in general
they were all one people unrelated to any people of the Old
World. Squier's acceptance of polygenism seemed to grow
out of his disagreement with the attitude of many monogenists who smugly assumed that Indian advances toward civilization resulted from their contacts with more advanced people before migrating to the New World or from
the subsequent diffusion of art and science from the Old
World. Monogenists who argued this view grounded their
theory on the similarity of Indian customs with those of the
Old World. Squier criticized such thinking as injurious to
the Indian and as not recognizing the Indian's ability to
progress and create his own civilization. Squier, however,
differed from other polygenists by refusing to recognize
any innate differences in the mental structures or capabilities among different groups.[44]

To Squier's way of thinking, despite their separate origins, all men were "alike in the elements of their mental
and moral constitutions," and they all possessed common
hopes and aspirations. With this as a basis, Squier went on
to postulate that all of humankind began with certain inherent predispositions or "sentiments." These sentiments,
part of man's "psychical" inheritance, over time developed
in a determined direction. Although there might be some
possible leeway in this development as a result of certain
environmental factors, in general "all psychical development must of necessity be in a single direction, and must
pass through precisely the same stages, whenever an advance is made." Thus "the nearer we approach the first

[43] Squier, "American Ethnology," pp. 390–91.
[44] Ibid., p. 395.

stages of human development, the more numerous and the more striking will be the coincidences and resemblances" of the various traits. This being so, it followed, according to Squier, that in the area of religious symbols and rites any particular state in a people's linear progress possessed "a like uniformity" with those symbols and rites of another people at the same state of development.[45]

Using sun worship as an example, Squier noted that it formed the basic element in all primitive mythologies extending back beyond "the historical and even beyond the traditionary period" of man. It could be traced among all American tribes from the most primitive "through every intermediate stage of development, to the imposing systems of Mexico and Peru, where it took a form nearly corresponding with that which it at one time sustained on the banks of the Ganges, and on the plains of Assyria." The differences that existed at any particular stage Squier believed could be accounted for through environmental circumstances.[46]

These two works contain some of the clearest expressions of Squier's belief in the progressive, "evolutionary" development of "culture" through stages. Noteworthy, too, in the light of Squier's polygenism, is that he saw all mankind (all the different "species of man") as endowed with the same "mental and moral" constitutions or "psychical sentiments," which progressed unilinearly, modified only by environmental factors. All "human species" were equal and capable of progress. For Squier then, not only did all mankind share the same mental constitution, but these mental propensities also evolved in a determined direction. Although Squier applauded Morton's researches in craniology and the work of the German C. T. Ph. von Martius, who also believed Indians were autochthonous, he was sharply critical of the derogatory and pessimistic views that polygenists held of Indians. Disavowing the polygenists' pejorative views of Indian mentality, Squier wrote,

[45]Ibid., p. 395.
[46]Ibid., p. 393.

It has not yet been satisfactorily shown that the American race is deficient in intellect, or that there is that wide difference in their "moral nature, their affections and consciences," which some have asserted. . . . A race of men which . . . [produced] the Iroquois confederation, . . . cannot be said to exhibit the "incapacity of infancy." A people who, like the Peruvians, had civil and social institutions nearly perfect as machineries of government and national organization . . . cannot be said to exhibit the "unpliancy of old age," or to be incapable of the highest attainments to which humanity may aspire. Nor can it be said that a people peaceable but brave, virtuous, honest, and approaching nearer than any other example which history affords, to the poetical idea of Arcadian simplicity and happiness, like those who inhabited the country above the Gila and the valley of New Mexico—that such a people "have never felt the blessings of divine descent," but have been left to their own dark natures and "preternatural" vicious instincts![47]

Squier denied the charge that Indians could not benefit from cultural contact. He pointed to the Florida Indians, who stood in evidence as a people who were not "one whit inferior to that of their white neighbors on the frontier." To Squier the hope for Indian advancement rested upon their better treatment. They should not be damned out of hand for lack of progress when, in justice, they had experienced only ill-treatment at the hands of whites.

When the Indians shall be treated as human beings, and not as wild animals; when they shall be relieved from the contamination of unprincipled hunters and traders, and the moral charlatanism of ignorant and narrow-minded missionaries; when we shall pursue towards them a just, enlightened, and truly Christian policy; then, if they exhibit no advancement, and ultimately reach a respectable rank in the scale of civilization, it will be quite time enough to pronounce upon them the severe sentence of a deficient intellect and an unhallowed heart—dead to sympathy, and incapable of higher developments. Till then, with the black catalogue of European wrongs and oppressions before him, and the grasping hand of powerful avarice at his throat, blame not the American Indian if he

[47] Ibid., p. 398.

sternly and gloomily prefers utter extinction to an association with races which have exhibited to him no benign aspect, and whose touch has been death.[48]

Reading this, one senses that Squier owed much to Gallatin: the preoccupation with the fate of Indians, the cogent arguments for man's progressive nature, the strong emphasis on the environment as an agency of change, and, despite Squier's polygenism, the belief in the psychic unity of humankind. Furthermore, there is an attitude toward race that Squier seems to share with Gallatin. Because all men are capable of progress, race is not the factor upon which to decide an individual's aptitude for civilization, but rather it is man's intellect and the environment in which this intellect is shaped that really make the difference. The similarity in the two men's works might also be attributed to the fact that when Gallatin was closely reading the army reports from New Mexico and coming to conclusions on the Pueblo Indians, Squier was in close contact. But although there are definite theoretical parallels between Squier and Gallatin, there are other sources for Squier's "eighteenth-century view" of man that should not be discounted.

Returning again to Squier's Albany lectures and his reading of Guizot, one cannot help but see how little Squier moved from his interpretation of man and history. In these lectures environment stood as a potent force for change. Long before he read Gallatin, Squier pointed out that besides a "new event" or "altered circumstances," the "general climate, the character or appearance of the country all have a wonderful and at the same time unaccountable influence on the character of men." In Squier's opinion such conditions could determine national personality. "Who doubts that the vivacious Frenchman and the free Switzer, have had their character much modified by condition or course of life which the peculiarities of their several countries compelled them to adopt." Culture and climate "have weight in determining man's character and have a powerful effect on the course of civilization." And what was civilization? Civilization was the combined progress of society

[48] Ibid.

and the progress of humanity, "the melioration of the social system [and] the expansion of the mind and faculties of man."[49] Reading Gallatin probably only strengthened and confirmed Squier's belief in the validity of his earlier assumptions.

Still, by the late 1840s, Squier's views remained only hypotheses. His swift rise in ethnology rested precariously upon his archaeological work in the Ohio Valley and a spate of articles on archaeology and mythology, and one on the Indians of New Mexico. His praise of Indian civilization and his admonitions against their ill-treatment by whites probably sounded a bit hollow since he had had little, if any, contact with Indians. Unlike his friend and, later, bitter rival Henry Rowe Schoolcraft, Squier had neither the publications nor the "fieldwork" experience to lend weight to his theories. Squier did have a settled opinion of what ethnology was and where it ought to be headed, but he needed field experience to back up his arguments. He also needed a secure financial position. It is in this context that Squier's application in 1849 for a position in the diplomatic corps in Guatemala should be seen. Here was a chance to serve both science and country. As he wrote to Joseph Henry:

> In studying the archaeology of our country, I have had my attention constantly and with increasing force directed to the Central parts of the Continent, concerning the Ancient remains of which Del Rio, Dupaix, Waldeck, Stephens and others have given us so many but so unsatisfactory glimpses. They furnish probably the most interesting subjects for archaeological investigation which the world affords. How far they may serve to reflect light upon the early history of man in America remains yet to be determined.

They had to be studied, however, in a scientific manner, and Squier was eager to accomplish the task. According to Squier "the magnificent connections" between the mounds

---

[49] Squier, "Two Lectures," pp. 47–48. See Guizot for similar arguments. Like Guizot, Squier emphasized the role of religion in shaping civilization and lifting man to new heights. For another example of similar sentiments by Squier, see his *Lecture on the Condition . . . of the Laboring Class*, pp. 10, 14–15.

of North America and those of Central America "are eminently suggestive." It would be important, he wrote, "to know how far they may serve to explain and illustrate each other."[50]

With friends from the New-York Historical Society and the American Ethnological Society, as well as such illustrious supporters as William Prescott, Washington Irving, and Edward Everett lobbying on his behalf, Squier obtained the appointment and found himself not in Guatemala but in Nicaragua confronting "skunks . . . alligators, and scorpians" and bedeviled by naked children who "trot about with their protruding bellies, with an air of the greatest nonchalance."[51]

Experiences in Central America changed neither Squier's attitude toward Indians nor his interpretation of the purpose of ethnology. Squier may not have seen the Indian as a "noble savage," but he certainly viewed him in romantic terms. To Squier the "pure" Indian seemed endowed with a natural nobility and a generosity that some "Indian experts" derided as purely romantic. Some evidence perhaps of Squier's feelings towards the Indian can be found in *Waikna; Adventures on the Mosquito Shore*, a novel set in Central America which Squier wrote under the pseudonym of Sam Bard. The novel depicts scenes from Squier's first field experience.[52] It relates Bard's dealings with the British and with the Indians in Central America. At the end of the novel, as Bard sits sadly contemplating his departure from the tropics and his return to "the dull, unsympathizing heart of the crowded city," his Indian guide, Antonio, approaches him. On this sad, moon-filled, tropical night, Antonio reveals to Bard that the Indians are not the defeated race they seem to be. A new era is dawning, an uprising is to soon happen, and he, Antonio, has been designated by his people to lead it.

[50] E. George Squier to Joseph Henry, March 10, 1849, Henry Papers, SIA.
[51] E. George Squier to John R. Bartlett, April 5, 1849; E. G. Squier to John R. Bartlett, June 10, 1849, Bartlett Papers, JCBL; William Prescott to Hon. B. C. Northrup, n.d., Henry Papers, SIA.
[52] Samuel Bard [E. George Squier], *Waikna; or, Adventures on the Mosquito Shore*.

I was silent and thoughtful when he had finished; but when, after a long pause, he asked, "Will my brother go with me to the lake of the Itzaes?" I grasped his hand and swore, by a name holier than that of Votan, to justify a friendship so un- wavering by a faith as boundless as his own. And when I left the outposts of civilization, and plunged into the untracked wilderness, with no other friend or guide, never did a suspi- cion or a doubt darken for an instant my confidence, or impair my faith in the loyal heart of Antonio Chul—once the mild- eyed Indian boy, but now the dreaded chieftain and victorious leader of the unrelenting Itzaes of Yucatan![53]

The work, of course, is romantic, and Squier did not "go native," as far as is known. As a metaphor, however, the novel reflects a certain empathy that he felt for the Indian and his plight, an empathy that found expression in both Squier's earlier and later ethnographic works. Squier did not take part in an Indian revolution, but he did attempt to instill in ethnology a more positive regard for the Indian as a creator of an original civilization. In Squier's opinion the Indian was certainly more than he seemed to be.

During his years in New York and Central America, Squier read extensively in ethnology and mythology. In the latter field, he read not only the available mythologies of Europe, Asia, Africa, and the Middle East but also the works of Wilhelm and Alexander von Humboldt, George Glidden, Sir William Jones, and Jacob Bryant, in order to develop a comparative view of religious and mythological systems. Whether Squier's early religious training led him to pursue such lines of investigation or whether his rejec- tion of strict Protestantism moved him to examine the rela- tive nature of all religions is uncertain. It is clear, however, that he combed travel and ethnological literature for infor- mation on the Indians of both continents in order to dis- cover the nature of their religious practices and the various symbols and ceremonies they employed.[54] Squier believed

[53]Ibid., pp. 327–32.
[54]The theme of religion runs through nearly all of Squier's works, not just his lectures before the New York State Mechanic Association, and it raises some question as to its influence on Squier's theoretical posture. Apparently by 1846, Squier no longer fully accepted his father's religious path. His fa-

the true essence of the Indians' being and nature lay in their religions.

The symbolic use of serpents in religion had early intrigued Squier, and he continued to be fascinated with what he saw as their extensive role in American Indian religion.[55] Research for his study *The Serpent Symbol* provided him with the opportunity to explore further this role and, he thought, to strike a blow against monogenism.[56] In this study Squier returned to the themes he had enunciated in "American Ethnology" two years before. He repeated that a close fit existed between environment and levels of civilization; yet, he continued, ethnologists had to exercise care in their investigations in order to separate what was fundamental to man from what was incidental or the result of environmental circumstance. Emphasis upon the latter generally obscured both the basic psychological unity of man and the similarities between the different Indian tribes. Fortunately, religious beliefs and sentiments found deep in the psyche proved less amenable to environmental influences than were art and economic institutions. By focusing on the former and revealing the permutation of such ideas, Squier believed it was possible to chart the course of progress in a people.[57]

---

ther, a Methodist minister, wrote in 1846, "I hope you have not forgotten this subject [salvation], yet I fear you are too much disposed, to neglect and defer the great preparation for death. Surely this subject has been early inculcated on your mind both by instruction and the spirit of the Lord. . . . The question is often asked me, 'Is your son pious?' I can assure you, it gives me much pain to have to give a negative answer." Joel Squier to E. G. Squier, Jan. 4, 1846, Squier Papers, WCL. Although he perhaps was less religious than in his youth, there is no evidence to brand Squier an atheist, as does Hinsley, p. 28.

[55] See E. H. Davis to John R. Bartlett, Oct. 28, 1846, Bartlett Papers, JCBL, where Davis claims in reference to a rattlesnake artifact: "My friend, Mr. Squier, is so enthusiastic upon this subject, that he goes off half-cocked sometimes (as the Western phrase is)."

[56] E. George Squier, *The Serpent Symbol, and the Worship of Reciprocal Principles of Nature in America.* American Archaeological Researches, No. 1 (1851).

[57] Ibid., pp. 11–17. Squier, of course, was not the first to see religious and psyche development in an evolutionary perspective. The English ethnologist J. C. Prichard also viewed religion in such terms. See George W. Stock-

At the very beginning of *The Serpent Symbol*, Squier established the book's relationship to the pressing ethnological issue of the day. In his opinion it was unfortunate that ethnology had so long labored under the negative influence of the Bible. Scientists had been forced to assume that the American Indians were "the descendants of some one or more of the diversified nations to which earliest history refers" and therefore directed their "inquiries to *which* of these their progenitors may be with most exactness referred." Consequently, such assumptions had led scientists to suggest a fantastic array of progenitors for the Indians, including almost all peoples of the Old World. Most often, however, theorists, basing their opinions on the manners and customs of the Indians, linked them with the Jews, forgetting "that all people, at some stage of their advancement, must sustain many resemblances towards each other, resulting . . . from a coincidence in circumstances, they have founded their conclusions upon what is conditional and changing, instead of what is fixed and radical."[58]

Squier asserted in his book that he would proceed from a different set of assumptions, ones that would enable him to explain "identities" between cultures "without claiming a common origin for man."[59] Assuming mankind's separate creation, Squier went on to examine religious beliefs and traditions in order to verify both parallel development and polygenism. Whereas all men were "alike in the elements of their mental and moral constitutions" and responded to similar impulses and motives, "it is not surprising that there should exist among nations of men . . . widely separated[,] a wonderful unity of elementary beliefs and conceptions."[60] Squier felt that, if he could convincingly demonstrate this similarity of beliefs among primitive peoples of the world, he would strengthen the polygenetic theory

ing, Jr., "From Chronology to Ethnology James Cowles Prichard and British Anthropology 1800–1850," in James Cowles Prichard, *Researches into the Physical History of Man* (1813, reprint 1973), p. 97.

[58] Squier, *Serpent Symbol*, p. 17.
[59] Ibid., p. 18.
[60] Ibid.

of a "community of origins." At the same time he would continue in his efforts to bring together all the facts relating to American monuments and other information that would illuminate the history of the Indians and their relations with other people.[61]

In order to demonstrate how man's "similar conditions, and like constitutions, mental, moral, and physical, may serve to approximate institutions, religions, and monuments to a common type," Squier had to show how similarities between the Old World and the New did not result from migration and diffusion but from a progression of man's inherent stages of mental or psychical development. Beginning with the premise that the Indians were all one people or race and that humankind, although separately created, was endowed with an invariable human nature, Squier asserted:

> It yet remains to be seen how far an investigation of the religious conceptions and notions of the American race shall serve to confirm the results of physiological and philological researches. But this will prove an inquiry of great difficulty; for if we assume that the religious sentiment is inherent, and its expression in accordance with natural suggestions, then the nearer we approach the first stage of human development, the more numerous and the more striking will be the coincidences and resemblances in the religious systems of the globe, however widely they may appear to differ at the present time.[62]

Squier's investigations revealed to him that the fundamental American Indian religion was nature worship, especially sun worship. Repeating some of the same assertions he made in "American Ethnology," Squier claimed to have traced this trait from the Eskimos of the north through every intermediate level until he reached "the imposing system of Mexico and Peru." Subsequent research disclosed this same system in use on the banks of the Ganges and the plains of Assyria. Even the symbols used for religious expression were the same because, Squier noted,

[61] Ibid., pp. 17–18.
[62] Ibid., p. 17.

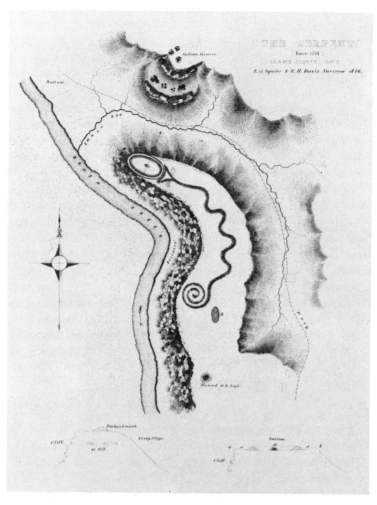

Great Serpent Mound in Ohio. From *Ancient Monuments of the Mississippi Valley*, by E. G. Squier and E. H. Davis. Squier also included an illustration of Serpent Mound in his work *The Serpent Symbol*.

mankind, even in different places, in similar circumstances thought in the same way.[63]

In subsequent chapters Squier focused on the universality of nature worship among primitive peoples; their use of phallic, serpent, and egg symbols; and the inclination to worship from high places. Following Sir William Jones, Squier interpreted phallic worship as sun worship, the worship of the procreative power of nature. He interpreted the serpent and egg as symbolizing creative powers; the serpent representing "productive energy," the egg, the "passive elements of nature."[64]

Squier also believed he had discovered a link between the developmental sequences of symbolic worship and the construction of places of worship. Accordingly, when sun worship prevailed among all primitive people, the serpent and egg symbols—"far too refined and abstract to be adopted by wandering, savage tribes"—could only be found among more advanced nations.[65] Likewise, the construction of dirt mounds rather than stone structures for elevated places of worship indicated a lower technological level and hence represented an earlier state of social development.[66] Thus, both in religious symbols and mound construction, a progression could be seen that implicitly denoted an advance in mental development.

In spite of lengthy notes and extensive citation, Squier, however, could not prove what he had set out to prove. He had hoped to demonstrate the sequential cross-cultural development of both religious ideals and architecture and to define what motivated a particular culture to shape its religious ideals in a way that corresponded to those of other cultures at the same level of advancement. This he did not and could not do. He succeeded only in demonstrating the possibility of his hypothesis. That Squier's objections to diffusion theory proved stronger than his arguments in favor of parallel invention and development soon became acutely

[63] Ibid., pp. 18–21. Squier, "American Ethnology," pp. 392–93.
[64] Squier, *Serpent Symbol*, pp. 146–58.
[65] Ibid., p. 224.
[66] Ibid., p. 76.

apparent to him. Recognizing halfway through his work that he could not prove that similarity of symbols had not resulted from diffusion, he asked, if diffusion were accepted, "how are we to determine whether the impression has been from Asia on America—or, as certain facts would imply, from America on Asia?"[67] Admitting at the end of his book that the data presented could support either theory, Squier acknowledged that his inclination toward the converse view stemmed from his desire to question whether "resemblances and coincidences" between Old World cultures and Indian cultures derived from the diffusion of customs and inventions from the former to the latter or resulted from independent developments in the Western Hemisphere.[68]

Although the book's argument is weak, the volume's importance is that it focuses more sharply on the central issues of Squier's ethnology than did anything else he wrote. He considered the Indians, excepting the Eskimos, a unique race, one entirely different from all peoples of the Old World, with a mentality potentially equal to that of the white race. In Squier's opinion, Indians developed their own civilizations without Old World influence. In his view the counter assumption, advanced by many monogenists, that cultural similarities between Indians and Old World cultures were proof of migration from and dependence upon the Old World, carried with it the inescapable conclusion that Indians did not have the ability to erect civilizations of their own. Squier found this denial of Indian ability and potential to progress particularly obnoxious. These concerns and the issues the book treats—the stages of progressive development and the uniformity of human nature and polygenism—must be seen in the context of Squier's groping to bring science into accord with his eternally optimistic view of man's potential.

In addition to making clear Squier's ethnology, *The Serpent Symbol* is important because it integrated various

[67] Ibid., p. 89.
[68] Ibid., p. 253.

themes dominant in American ethnology and attacked the growing number of pejorative interpretations of Indian civilization. In *The Serpent Symbol*, Squier dismissed the negative implications of polygenism that also found the Indian incapable of advancing in civilization, and relied instead on the older progressive view of Indian mental development and culture. Squier conceded that although degeneration was always possible, it was unlikely, since the history of man seemed to affirm that progress would always be the rule.

In the end, *The Serpent Symbol* proved a failure. Even Squier conceded that it was not worth much. It had been printed at his own expense, and Squier confided to a friend that "I must buy my own copies if I am foolish enough to want such a book."[69] Schoolcraft found it utterly impossible to consider the work a "contribution to American archaeology," and he sharply attacked it.[70]

The book, however, did provide Squier with an opportunity to assert his decided opinions on the direction ethnology should take. These views were further elaborated in letters to his friends. He was disturbed that too often philology, archaeology, physiology, and ethnology were heading in different directions. What was needed for sound development in "archaeological and ethnological science" was a comprehensive approach, a "concurrence of facts of different kinds."

> It is not therefore by pursuing a single branch of investigation that the grand results of this science are to be obtained. The

[69] E. George Squier to Peter Force, March 16, 1851, Force Papers, WCL. The rather tentative nature of the work is underscored by Squier in the introduction of the work: "I reserve to myself . . . the privilege of revising, altering, and if need be, of wholly rejecting, whatever may be advanced in this or succeeding volumes." p. x. Squier's friend Francis Parkman did write a favorable review. Review of *The Serpent Symbol and the Reciprocal Principles of Nature in America* in *The Christian Examiner* 51 (July, 1851): 140–41.

[70] Henry Rowe Schoolcraft, *Historical and Statistical Information Respecting the History, Conditions, and Prospects of the Indian Tribes of the United States*, vol. 4, p. 116.

philologist, the physiologist, the historian, the antiquary, all pursue independent paths of inquiry, and each may approximate truth; but their results cannot stand independently; they must concur in all essential respects before we can flatter ourselves that we have reached absolute and ultimate truth.

Squier explained that only in physiology and philology did research approach scientific accuracy. This now had to be achieved in ethnology, in the study of Indian religious, civil, and social institutions and in their arts and their sciences.[71]

What this synthesis meant for ethnology was one thing; what it meant for Squier personally was another. With the deaths of Morton and, especially, of Gallatin, Squier sought to assume the unofficial deanship of ethnology and to rouse the American Ethnological Society from the doldrums into which it had settled. Bringing together the monogenists and polygenists would constitute a long step in that direction, but it would be no easy task. On the eve of the Civil War many members of the society had assumed rigid attitudes toward questions of race, and any discussion of this subject during meetings was sure to provoke a shower of sparks.

Squier, having constantly misread Gallatin, was firmly convinced that Gallatin was a polygenist. Gallatin's statements to the contrary were dismissed by Squier as unavoidable declarations made to assure the acceptance of his works and to allay the fears of partisans of "the popular dogma of the Unity of the Human race."[72] Squier sought to

---

[71] E. George Squier to George Gliddon, n.d. but probably in the year 1853 or 1854, copy, Squier Papers, LC. Letter is labeled Honduras, and Squier was there during these years. Gliddon undoubtedly was at work with J. C. Nott on *Types of Mankind* (1854) and wrote to Squier asking what results had been made in American archaeology and what was firmly known. See also E. George Squier, *Nicaragua: Its People, Scenery, Monuments, and the Proposed Interoceanic Canal*, vol. 2, pp. 328–32; and E. George Squier, "Observations on the Archaeology and Ethnology of Nicaragua," *Transactions of the American Ethnological Society* 3 (1853): 93–94, 117.

[72] E. G. Squier to George Gliddon, n.d., pp. 3–4, Squier Papers, LC.

convince Gallatin's monogenistic followers to accept this view and to cross over and accept polygenism. Gallatin's followers, however, read their venerable leader's works correctly and refused to cross the line.

Any possible rapprochement between monogenists and polygenists suffered another blow when a feud between Squier and Schoolcraft, smoldering since the early 1850s, suddenly broke out in marked virulence. It is not known precisely what triggered the falling out between the former friends, but throughout the mid-1850s and until Schoolcraft's death, they traded swipes in private letters and in print. Schoolcraft was old and well known, his stature enhanced by his government position and the task of writing a "national work" on the Indians. It was natural for him to feel that he should assume the mantle that Gallatin had dropped at death. From Schoolcraft's perspective, Squier was an irksome upstart who had merely coauthored one good piece of ethnology, *Ancient Monuments*, and had failed miserably in all subsequent attempts. Squier was also a polygenist whose "pseudo-ethnology" Schoolcraft believed appealed to the degenerate while being offensive to the sensibilities of the genteel.[73]

Squier, by contrast, was young and aggressive. His archaeological publications and travels had given him an international reputation. Squier saw Schoolcraft as a monogenist fossil who, while plodding along in his lumbering "national work," held a stranglehold on the public treasury. Whereas Schoolcraft saw the "pagan" Indian as a miserable creature most likely doomed to suffer extinction, Squier perceived the Indian in more noble terms, seeing a people whose past achievements guaranteed great promise for future accomplishments. The scramble for recognition as dean of American ethnology exacerbated the feud between

[73] Schoolcraft, *Historical and Statistical Information*, p. 116. See also Henry R. Schoolcraft to E. H. Davis, April 8, 1858, copy; E. H. Davis to Henry R. Schoolcraft, April 5, 1858; E. George Squier to Henry R. Schoolcraft, Jan. 2, 1858, Schoolcraft Papers, LC; and Henry R. Schoolcraft to George Bancroft, July 27, 1853, Bancroft Papers, MHS; Henry R. Schoolcraft to R. W. Griswold, July 27, 1853, Griswold Papers, BPL.

the two men and split the American Ethnological Society even more.[74]

In New York the lethargic American Ethnological Society never fully recovered from the crippling blow of Gallatin's death. It was not a likely place for Squier to initiate a theoretical and methodological revolution. The society never really had been a scientific society in the strict sense of the word. It had no fixed meeting place. The members were not "professional scientists," even given the standards of the day. Membership consisted of "amateur ethnologists": lawyers, teachers, librarians, clergymen, and others from the professional class, few of whom had any ethnological field experience. Most were content to be armchair travelers to exotic cultures. Generally, unless a missionary returning from the field could be found and induced to speak about the languages or customs of Africans, Asians, or Indians, the papers presented to the society were the products of library research. Once in a while members in the field or people interested in ethnology sent in reports of an ethnological nature or artifacts for discussion. Moreover by the 1850s most of the active membership, those who had made vital contributions to the society or had engaged in fieldwork, such as Stephens, Schoolcraft, and Bartlett, had died or moved away from New York. Remaining members seemed more interested in the antiquities of the Near East than in the study of the American Indian, and, much to the polygenists' dismay, they maintained a literal interpretation of the Bible as a baseline for ethnological research. Ethnology was at times even scuttled for discussions on the critical analysis of medieval literature. Physical anthropology was carefully avoided, for as Squier pointed out, "the question of human unity could not be discussed without offense to some of the members and its casual introduction was made a ground of impassioned protest."[75]

[74]E. G. Squier to George Gliddon, n.d., Squier Papers, LC, pp. 2–3; Schoolcraft, *Historical and Statistical Information*, 4:116; Bieder and Tax, "Ethnologists to Anthropologists," in Murra, *American Anthropology*.

[75]E. George Squier, "Proceedings Preliminary to the Organization of the Anthropological Institution of New-York," *Journal of the Anthropological In-*

The unstable condition in which the American Ethnological Society found itself in the 1850s continued into the
1860s.[76] Although the controversy between polygenist and
monogenist eased after the Civil War and the publication in
1859 of Charles Darwin's *Origin of Species*, Squier still encountered resistance in his crusade to make ethnology truly
the "science of man" and in particular the science of the
American Indian.[77] Attending the International Congress of
Anthropology and Prehistoric Archaeology in Paris in 1867
as a delegate of the American Ethnological Society, Squier
was impressed by the French anthropologist Paul Broca,
also a polygenist, and the Société d'Anthropologie de Paris.
Upon his return to the United States, Squier attempted to
reorganize the American Ethnological Society along lines
similar to those of the French organization, even to the extent of trying to substitute anthropology, with its European
emphasis on physical rather than cultural research, for ethnology. Squier encountered heavy resistence among many
of the members.[78] By 1872 the long simmering clash of goals

---

stitute of New-York 1 (1871–72): 14–20; W. De Haas to H. R. Schoolcraft,
Feb. 26, 1858, Schoolcraft Papers, LC, gives a good account of some of the
controversy that raged in the American Ethnological Society at the time. See
also Bieder and Tax, "Ethnologists to Anthropologists," in Murra, *American
Anthropology.*

[76] W. E. Turner to E. George Squier, Nov. 26, 1852, Squier Papers, LC.

[77] It should be noted that Darwin's effect on the demise of polygenism is
overrated, for many polygenists merely reformulated their arguments to coincide with Darwin's theory. That Morton could have accommodated such a
theory is indicated in some of his manuscripts published after his death. See
Nott and Gliddon, *Types of Mankind*, pp. 324–26. See also George W. Stocking, Jr., *Race, Culture, and Evolution: Essays in the History of Anthropology*, pp. 42–68; and Francis Schiller, *Paul Broca: Founder of French Anthropology, Explorer of the Brain*, pp. 224–35.

[78] Bieder and Tax, "Ethnologists to Anthropologists," in Murra, *American
Anthropology*, pp. 14–16. Squier was very much interested in anthropological affairs in Paris. In 1867 he attended the International Congress of Anthro-
pology and Prehistoric Archaeology in Paris as a delegate of the American
Ethnological Society and served as the vice-president of the Paris meetings.
In 1868 he was elected a member of the Société d' Anthropologie de Paris.
Paul Broca to E. George Squier, Jan. 9, 1868, Squier Papers, LC; W. W. Tur-
ner to E. George Squier, Dec. 3, 1852, Squier Papers, LC. Paul Broca, the
most noted French anthropologist of his day, considered Squier the foremost
American archaeologist. See Schiller, *Paul Broca*, pp. 157–58.

and personalities erupted. The older members continued as the American Ethnological Society; those younger, who constituted a majority, voted to change the name and form the Anthropological Institute of New-York. This new society, more congenial to archaeology and physical anthropology, published one volume of *Proceedings* and then, with the curtailment of Squier's activities resulting from his personal problems and illness, ceased to exist.[79]

Squier died in 1888. In 1894 his theory of an advanced civilization of mound builders was destroyed by Cyrus Thomas, an Illinois entomologist who was commissioned by the Bureau of American Ethnology to survey the mounds and to decide definitively whether they represented the work of a higher civilization or whether they were the product of "primitive" Indians.[80] By the 1890s, of course, the mounds were less important, less in the imagination of Americans. Many of the mounds, their grandeur now diminished after repeated plowings, lay as mere swells of earth. Many others were gone completely. New generations of Americans had moved farther west beyond the mound country and were more concerned with living Indians than with the remains of a people long gone. The "moundologic" tradition of local antiquarian interest that had supported the work of Squier and Davis still lived on among a few who prowled the river bottoms of the Midwest in search of artifacts from past civilizations. But never again would the mounds capture the imaginations of eastern scholars as they had when Squier and Davis conducted their research, and when a man who would eventually be president, William Henry Harrison,

[79]C. H. Berendt to John R. Bartlett, Oct. 4, 1874, Bartlett Papers, JCBL. As Squier pointed out to a friend, "Now we have reorganized the old Ethnological Society as the Anthropological Institute of New-York." E. George Squier to Marshall Anderson (copy), Feb. 17, 1872, Squier Papers, HEH. On the continued interest in the old American Ethnological Society, see Henry T. Drowne to John R. Bartlett, March 3, 1871; Drowne to Bartlett, April 9, 1873; Drowne to Bartlett, Feb. 14, 1874, Bartlett Papers, JCBL.

[80]Cyrus Thomas, "Report on the Mound Explorations of the Bureau of Ethnology," *Bureau of American Ethnology Annual Report for 1891* (1894); Willey and Sabloff, p. 49; Silverberg, *Mound Builders*, pp. 182–221.

addressed a Cincinnati gathering and told of a vast ancient civilization that lay beneath the cornfields of southern Ohio.[81]

Squier moved beyond the antiquarian state and eventually published numerous books on archaeology, but his works lacked focus and depth and eventually assumed a superficial, almost travelogue quality. In many ways he always remained a "lay ethnologist," an ethnologist by avocation. But then, in his time one could only be an ethnologist by avocation. His call for a holistic anthropology went unheeded in the absence of structured institutional support. Although he acquired his reputation in ethnology, he was compelled to support himself through government jobs, journalism, lecturing, business, and writing travel books. If he had had a secure career post, Squier might have had greater opportunity to think through his ideas, instead of following his friend Francis Parkman's advice: "Publish and keep publishing."[82]

Yet Ephraim G. Squier, for all his shortcomings as a scholar, still is important, for he illuminates the ethnological concerns of antebellum America. More than any other thinker of his day, Squier tried to bring competing theories together. His love of progress and his optimistic view of man rooted in his early learning, reading, and youthful activities would not permit him fully to accept the racial implications of polygenism that saw nonwhite races forever locked in the inferior position of "almost civilized." To Squier the future was open-ended for all men, and civilization remained within everyone's grasp. Squier, like Gallatin, strongly supported the theory that all men rose by stages to civilization and that their rate of progress was controlled primarily by their environment. Because man's mind was everywhere the same and was subject to environmental influences, changes in environment produced changes in man. Squier tried to demonstrate this by depicting the unfolding of Indian religious beliefs and practices, but he was unsuccessful. It proved a difficult and unrewarding task to

[81] Harrison, "A Discourse."
[82] Seitz, *Letters from Parkman*, p. 46.

use similarities between two cultures, rather than unique attributes, to build a case against diffusion.

Squier's ethnological work in Central and South America and his stand on polygenism seemed to orient him toward English and later French anthropology. In the 1860s and 1870s, Squier attempted to transplant the "French anthropological tradition" to America, but America proved unreceptive. Squier conceived ethnology in older terms; he was interested in defining stages of development and, as a polygenist, was little interested in tracing historical migrations and origins of people. Unfortunately, although Squier admired progress, his limited perspectives shut him off from recognizing the implications of evolutionary theory and its importance for further anthropological research.

5

Henry Rowe Schoolcraft and the Ethnologist as Historian and Moralist

WHEN COMPARED with the ethnologists considered thus far, Henry Rowe Schoolcraft (1793–1864) stands out because his ethnological work drew largely from field experience rather than from reading and questionnaires. As a government Indian agent Schoolcraft worked for thirty years in close contact with Indians. During this time he was involved daily in their problems. This experience made him a valuable resource to ethnology and accorded him certain prestige among those who wrote in the field.

A prolific writer, Schoolcraft is best known today for his six-volume *Historical and Statistical Information Respecting the History, Condition, and Prospects of the Indian Tribes of the United States* and his two-volume *Algic Researches*. His ethnology was heavily influenced by his personality, his changing attitudes toward Indians, and his concern for their welfare. It was also shaped first by Schoolcraft's romanticism and later by his religious experience, which led to his moralistic and eventually pessimistic outlook. An examination of Schoolcraft's writings in the context of these influences reveals how much his ethnology was a product of the time and of the social concerns of his day.

In July of 1822, Henry Rowe Schoolcraft arrived at Sault Ste. Marie, a settlement hardly meriting the designation of village. A frontier post on the American and Canadian border, Sault Ste. Marie possessed a wild and colorful population of Indian, French-Canadian, and English residents all engaged in some aspect of the fur trade. For Schoolcraft, his arrival was a return to the frontier as well as a return to Sault Ste. Marie.

Born in 1793, Schoolcraft spent his youth in upstate New York. He learned glassmaking from his father and with him operated glassmaking shops in both New York and Vermont. Failures in business, however, prompted Schoolcraft to seek his fortune in the West, and in 1819 he traveled down the Ohio River to Missouri with the intention of exploring the mineral resources of the West.[1] As a result of this trip he wrote *A View of the Lead Mines of Missouri*,[2] which attracted the attention of Secretary of War John C. Calhoun. So impressed was Calhoun with the work that he offered Schoolcraft the position of geologist on the government's exploring expedition to the Northwest Territory under the leadership of Lewis Cass, territorial governor of Michigan. Schoolcraft accepted this offer, and in 1820 he stopped with the expedition at Sault Ste. Marie on the way to Lake Superior and the country beyond. Schoolcraft evidently impressed Cass on this trip, for Cass asked him to take part in an Indian treaty negotiation the following year in Chicago. In 1822, at Cass's urging, Calhoun appointed Schoolcraft as Indian agent at Sault Ste. Marie.[3]

Schoolcraft, still more interested in geology than in Indians or ethnology, looked on this assignment as a temporary one. He noted in his journal, "I had now attained a fixed position; not such as I desired in the outset, and had striven for, but one that offered an interesting class of duties, in the performances of which there was a wide field of honorable exertion, if it was embraced, also of historical inquiry and research."[4] For several years Schoolcraft had en-

---

[1] On Schoolcraft's failure in the glassmaking business, see Henry Rowe Schoolcraft to William Doornik, May 15, 1853, Schoolcraft Papers, LC. See also Richard G. Bremer, "Henry Rowe Schoolcraft: Explorer in the Mississippi Valley, 1818–1832," *Wisconsin Magazine of History* 66 (Autumn, 1982): 40–59; and a less useful work by Michael T. Marsden, "Henry Rowe Schoolcraft: A Reappraisal," *The Old Northwest: A Journal of Regional Life and Letters* 2 (June, 1976): 153–82.

[2] Henry Rowe Schoolcraft, *A View of the Lead Mines of Missouri*.

[3] Henry Rowe Schoolcraft, *Personal Memoirs of a Residence of Thirty Years with the Indian Tribes on the American Frontiers*, p. 88; Lewis Cass to Henry R. Schoolcraft, July 1, 1822, Sault Ste. Marie Indian Agency, Letters Received, Records of the Bureau of Indian Affairs, NA.

[4] Schoolcraft, *Personal Memoirs*, p. 87.

joyed no fixed occupation or steady income, and so he welcomed this position while he waited for an opportunity to find employment as a "mineralogist." In the meantime he willingly took advantage of his location on the frontier to pursue his interest in history and science.

Schoolcraft, critical of publications in science that were "founded on an imperfect acquaintance with the country" and rife with "assumed premises," believed that scientific investigations had to be based upon empirical observation and that the scientist must perform the tedious tasks of collecting and cataloging data before attempting to spin theories.[5] Imbued with these precepts, Schoolcraft welcomed the opportunity that the frontier post provided for data collecting, for exploring the unknown mineral wealth of the area, and for making ethnological studies of the Indians not only for his own amusement but also to aid others.

Sault Ste. Marie proved an excellent place for ethnological studies. Upon his arrival Schoolcraft noted in his journal that it was "carnival" time for the Indians. Hundreds had poured into the little village, decked out in their finest outfits, to barter their furs, to dance, to sing, and to drink. Schoolcraft delighted in the vivid scenes presented daily in the numerous encampments. After impressing upon the Indians his position and importance as agent, Schoolcraft resolved to cultivate a rapport with "this powerful and hitherto hostile tribe, namely the Chippewas."[6]

In pursuing this goal Schoolcraft was fortunate to be able to draw upon the help of the Johnston family. John Johnston had come to America from Ireland in 1793, entered the Canadian fur trade, and married Susan, the daughter of Wabojeeg, a respected band chief of the Lake Superior Chippewas. Johnston became a noted merchant and outfitter and a man of considerable influence among the Indians, the French, and the English at Sault Ste. Marie. He raised a family of eight children, who grew up fluent in Chippewa, English, and French, and it was as a boarder in this

[5] Schoolcraft, *View of the Lead Mines*, pp. 4–7.
[6] Schoolcraft, *Personal Memoirs*, pp. 95–103.

household that Schoolcraft learned Chippewa customs, stories, and language. Here, too, he could compare information gleaned from Indians visiting his agency. According to Schoolcraft, Mrs. Johnston proved invaluable "on abstruse points of the Indian ceremonies and usages." He claimed that the Johnston family was the only one "in North America who could, in Indian lore, have acted as my 'guide, philosopher, and friend.'"[7]

Schoolcraft needed no urging to apply himself to literary and scientific studies. Growing up in an America that to him promised unlimited opportunities to those who were morally upright and diligent, Schoolcraft believed that by cultivating such traits he could surmount any difficulty and achieve his goal. He emphasized duty, diligence, and virtue in his everyday dealings and exerted himself to the fullest to impress Cass, who had so generously acted as his patron.

Underlying Schoolcraft's investigations was his firm belief that science ought to be pursued for useful ends. American science was still largely justified on a purely pragmatic rationale, and Schoolcraft in his studies of Indian cultures echoed this outlook when he proclaimed, "Our Indian policy cannot be understood without looking at the Indian's history."[8] Although Schoolcraft still possessed romantic notions concerning the Indians, increasingly his view of them was shaped by his duties as agent and his investigations of them, which were performed out of his sincere desire to accord them better government treatment.

To Schoolcraft, two centuries of contact with rapacious white frontiersmen had left the Indians in such a state of degeneration that they had forgotten their old manners, ceremonies, and customs; had become dependent upon liquor; and were "prone to despond and easily sink into

[7] Henry Rowe Schoolcraft, "Memoir of John Johnston," ed. J. Sharpless Fox, *Collections of the Michigan Pioneer and Historical Society* 36 (1908): 53–94; Schoolcraft, *Personal Memoirs*, pp. 107–108, 662–63; Henry R. Schoolcraft to George Johnston, Aug. 28, 1826, Schoolcraft Papers, LC; Schoolcraft to Johnston, Aug. 7, 1828, Johnston Papers, BHC.

[8] Schoolcraft, *Personal Memoirs*, p. 131.

frames of despair."[9] According to Schoolcraft, the Indian was altered by recent circumstances. Lost was "much of that native energy and resource which belong to the hunter state." Now no longer able to hunt, the Indian could not or would not farm. Schoolcraft saw Indians as children. Officially he held that "as a people so incapable of self government, whose customs, laws, & manners are so relaxed, and whose spirit is sunk so low, . . . [the Indians] ought not to be . . . considered [as independent nations], except for the mere purpose of treating for the sale of their lands and the settlement of annuities." Considering their childlike state, Schoolcraft firmly believed that both justice and humanity required the government, and particularly him, as an extension of the government, to "superintend and protect them." Knowledge of their customs, language, and history, he believed, would allow a benevolent government to orient them on more productive paths and to direct them towards civilization.[10]

In April 1823, Schoolcraft learned that the superintendency of western mines, a position he had actively sought, was not to be his. A dejected Schoolcraft recorded in his journal, "It is a year since I received from the President (Mr. Monroe) a commission as agent for these tribes; and it is now more probable than it then was that my residence here may assume a character of permanency. I do not, however, cease to hope that Providence has a more eligible situation in reserve for me."[11] The news forced Schoolcraft to accept the fact that he was no longer a sojourner, that his position as Indian agent was a permanent one, and that Sault Ste. Marie was to be his permanent residence. Schoolcraft turned from his disappointment to a deeper involvement in ethnology and, equally important

[9]Ibid., p. 111; Henry R. Schoolcraft to Lewis Cass, Dec. 2, 1822, Sault Ste. Marie Agency, Letters Sent, Records of the Bureau of Indian Affairs, NA.

[10]Schoolcraft, *Personal Memoirs*, p. 111; Henry R. Schoolcraft to Lewis Cass, Dec. 2, 1822; Sept. 11, 1822, Sault Ste. Marie Agency, Letters Sent, Records of the Bureau of Indian Affairs, NA.

[11]Schoolcraft, *Personal Memoirs*, p. 176.

for ethnology, to marriage with Jane, the Johnston's oldest daughter.[12]

When Schoolcraft left for Sault Ste. Marie in 1822, Lewis Cass slipped into his hand a questionnaire on Indian customs. Cass admonished Schoolcraft to attend to it and to forward to him whatever he could learn on such matters. As territorial governor and superintendent of Indian affairs, Cass was intimately involved with Indian matters.[13] Thus when Schoolcraft moved into the Johnston household as a boarder, Cass was delighted and instructed Schoolcraft to make full use of the good fortune at having such a family as a resource.

> I am anxious that Mr. Johnston and his family furnish full and detailed answers to my queries, more particularly upon all subjects connected with the language, and, if I may so speak, the polite literature of the Chippewa. . . . There is no quarter from which I can expect such full information, upon these topics as from this. I must beg you to aid me in the pursuit. Urge them during the long winter evenings to the task. The time cannot be more profitably or pleasantly spent, and, as I am told you are somewhat of an aboriginophile, you can assist. A perfect analysis of the language is a great desideratum. I pray you, in the spring, to let me have the fruits of your exertions.[14]

[12]John F. Freeman, "Henry Rowe Schoolcraft" (Ph.D. diss. Harvard University, 1960), pp. 88–90.

[13]In 1828, Secretary of War Peter B. Porter requested Lewis Cass and William Clark, superintendent of Indian affairs for the Missouri Territory, to devise measures to reform the Indian office. The Indian policy of the eighteenth century was no longer adequate in the early nineteenth century. American expansion westward required more land, and sounder policies had to be worked out for dealing with the many new tribes encountered. It was within this context of rethinking Indian policy that Cass particularly desired to obtain data on Indians and that he found Schoolcraft's material extremely valuable. For an extensive discussion of the Cass and Clark plan, see Francis Paul Prucha, *American Indian Policy in the Formative Years: The Indian Trade and Intercourse Acts, 1790–1834*; and *Lewis Cass and American Indian Policy*. For an example of Cass's questionnaire, see William N. Fenton, "Answers to Governor Cass's Questions by Jacob Jameson, A Seneca [ca. 1821–1825]" *Ethnohistory* 16 (Spring, 1969): 113–39.

[14]Schoolcraft, *Personal Memoirs*, pp. 89, 181, 184.

Cass was incensed by what he considered the irresponsible and incorrect views of eastern critics of government Indian policy and frontier treatment of the Indian. He was angered also by the tendency of many eastern scholars to see the Indian as more noble and more civilized than he really was. In a series of articles for the *North American Review*, Cass sought to create a "frontier ethnology" that would both defend government policy and disprove the false allegations of eastern ethnologists, such as Du Ponceau, who had no direct contact with Indians. Although Cass relied heavily on Schoolcraft to supply him with "facts," the close relationship between the two men was really symbiotic. Since throughout his early career Schoolcraft was very solicitous of Cass's favor, when Cass urged him to carry on the fight against the "eastern establishment," Schoolcraft took up the cudgel and used Cass's articles as models. Because Schoolcraft's early works imitate Cass's articles in their structure, handling of data, conclusions, and even attacks on eastern writers, it is useful to take a closer look at Cass's works.

In an 1827 article, Cass agreed that Indian languages offered new insights into Indian history, but to him they also revealed a low level of Indian ratiocination. To Cass, Indians appeared as a "moral phenomenon," seeming to lack all those mental traits whites had found so useful in constructing their civilization.

> A principle of progressive improvement seems almost inherent in human nature. Communities of men, as well as individuals, are stimulated by a desire to meliorate their condition. . . . We are all striving in the career of life to acquire riches, or honor, or power, or some other object, whose possession is to realize the day dreams of our imaginations; and the aggregate of these efforts constitutes the advance of society. . . . But there is little of all this in the constitution of our savages.[15]

[15] [Lewis Cass] Review of *Indian Treaties, and Laws and Regulations relating to Indian Affairs; to which is added an Appendix, containing the Proceedings of the Old Congress, and Other important State Papers in relation to Indian Affairs. Compiled and published under Orders of the Department of War* in *The North American Review* 24 (April, 1827): 365–442.

A year later Cass renewed his critique of ethnology as written by easterners, but this time he attacked the work of Rev. John Heckewelder, the Moravian missionary whose years among the Delaware Indians had made him an authority on their language and culture. Whereas Heckewelder's work dripped with sentimentality, according to Cass, Schoolcraft's "abounds in accurate and animated descriptions, and in just and philosophical reflection." Schoolcraft's position as Indian agent, Cass proclaimed, provided him with "favorable opportunities for investigating the character and condition of these people, and he has surveyed them with the eyes of a cautious and judicious observer."[16]

Two years later, Cass returned to the subject of the Indian's "moral condition" in "Removal of the Indians." With the debate over Indian removal raging, Cass viewed his article as an ethnological contribution. He claimed that legends shaped the Indian's moral condition. Filled with magic and sorcery, bravery and chicanery, they fixed the Indian's mind and made it immune to civilization. So effective were superstitions in claiming the Indian's mind, and so controlling an influence did they exert against change, that Cass reasoned there must be something inherently unprogressive in the Indian mentality. He concluded that Indians might always remain like children. "Their moral and their intellectual condition have been equally stationary. . . . There must then be an inherent difficulty, arising from the institution, character, and condition of the Indians themselves."[17] For the Indians to be rescued from their past and

[16][Lewis Cass] Review of *Travels in the Central Portions of the Mississippi Valley . . .* [and] *A Vindication of the Rev. Heckewelder's History of the Indian Nations,* in *The North American Review* 26 (April, 1828): 365–66.

[17][Lewis Cass] Review of *Documents and Proceedings relating to the Formation and Progress of a Board in the City of New York, for the Emigration, Preservation, and Improvement of the Aborigines of America* in *The North American Review* 30 (January, 1830): 72–73. This theme was echoed in another review by Cass. See [Lewis Cass] Review of *A Narrative of the Captivity and Adventures of John Tanner, (United States' Interpreter at the Sault de Ste. Marie,) during thirty years residence among the Indians, in the interior of North America* in *American Quarterly Review* 8 (September, 1830): 108–110, which states, "The laws of nature seems to us well marked; man

prepared for the future, reasoned Cass, their mental character must be studied further. The Indian mind must be altered. Herein lay the secret for their change and eventual acceptance of civilization. Until that happened, however, Cass called for Indian removal from white contact to across the Mississippi River, in accordance with government plans.[18]

The ethnological theories that Cass developed in his articles were based primarily on data supplied him by Schoolcraft rather than on firsthand observation. The questionnaires Cass had sent to Indian agents and others were evidently of little use, for he discovered, as had Gallatin, that the quality of information depended on the intelligence of both the consultant and the persons who collected the information. As Cass confided to Schoolcraft, there was very little quality to the data collected, especially concerning linguistics. "There is a lamentable obtuseness of intellect manifested in both collector and contributor, and there is no systematic arrangement, no analytical process, and in fact no correctness of detail." As to Schoolcraft's data, however, Cass stated, "What I receive from you is more valuable than all my other stock. . . . I must beg you to continue your labours, as the greatest favor you can render me."[19]

In 1831, when Cass became secretary of war and ex officio in charge of Indian policy, he became less interested in ethnology and more absorbed in national affairs. Although Schoolcraft continued to supply Cass with information, the agent increasingly assumed the task of educating both the public and government officials on Indian matters. Cass's retreat from active support of ethnology did not end his particular influence on the science. To a large measure

---

may retard but cannot arrest its operation. For wise purposes doubtless, however, inscrutable they may be, it has been decreed by Providence, that the civilized and the savage man never shall live for any length of time upon the same soil." For more extensive surveys of Cass's career and views towards Indians, see Frank B. Woodford, *Lewis Cass: The Last Jeffersonian* and Willis E. Dunbar, *Lewis Cass*.

[18][Cass] Review of *Documents and Proceedings*, pp. 72–122.

[19]Lewis Cass to Henry R. Schoolcraft, Oct. 19, 1823, Schoolcraft Papers, LC.

Schoolcraft inherited Cass's views and benefited from his reputation. Not only did he receive his introduction to the publishing world through Cass, but, following Cass, he continued to collect ethnological data for the purpose of shaping government Indian policy.

As noted, Schoolcraft's early view of Indians was tinged with romanticism. Despite what he saw as the Indians' "deterioration of character," he recognized that hidden beneath the mien of poverty they "disclose traits of character which they are not thought to possess, and give us proofs of firmness, foresight and independence which have rarely been observed."[20]

This contradiction between "deterioration of character" —a childlike dependence—and resourcefulness extended to the Chippewa language. Given his conception of the simplicity of Chippewa culture, Schoolcraft was surprised and later annoyed to discover the language's complex structure. Learning Chippewa did not prove easy. What Schoolcraft had expected to be a simple task, "a novel and pleasing species of amusement" during the long winter months of 1822–23, turned into sheer drudgery and the mere "acquisition and treasuring up of facts." Several times Schoolcraft wavered on the verge of giving up the study of Chippewa entirely. He believed it easier to learn Greek or Hebrew and complained that Chippewa was as different from English as any language could possibly be. It was inefficient, encumbered with a great deal of verbiage, and tended towards "repetition and reduncy [sic] of forms." As a means of communication, he felt Chippewa would always prove inferior because the "paucity of terms leads not only to the use of figures and metaphors, but is the cause of circumlocution."[21]

By the end of the winter Schoolcraft had made some headway, but the vocabulary and grammar he had hoped to complete remained unfinished by summer. Through his contact with Indians other than Chippewas and his collec-

[20] Schoolcraft, *Personal Memoirs*, pp. 138–39.
[21] Ibid., p. 171.

tion of the latter's vocabulary, Schoolcraft discovered that the language was part of a larger group of languages denoted as Algonquin. The Algonquin-speaking tribes—most of whom lived east of the Chippewas—had a tradition that they had come from the East. Schoolcraft believed that, based on similarities in vocabularies, he could now confirm the validity of this tradition.[22]

Even more significant to Schoolcraft, however, was what language—linguistic categories—revealed of the Indian mind. Did linguistic categories disclose how Indians perceived their world, that is, how they thought? Did they carry messages that would yield insights into Indian culture? Schoolcraft believed that they did. He noted that the Chippewa language lacked generic and numerical terms and that "the Indian mind appears to lack the mathematical element." Their language was replete with words of magic, sorcery, and necromancy, reflecting an emphasis on the occult which Schoolcraft had observed daily in Chippewa behavior. He went on to theorize that, since language changes slowly, conceptions of the world expressed in grammatical patterns also must change slowly. Schoolcraft did not know how long it had taken the Indians to devise their grammatical patterns and ways of expressing thoughts and ideas, but he believed he had opened a door into the Indian past. Philology, rather than being merely one of the keys to knowledge about the Indian, became the most important key. "I am inclined to think," Schoolcraft later recorded, "that more true light is destined to be thrown on the history of the Indians by a study of their languages than on their traditions, or any other feature" of their culture.[23]

Schoolcraft ranked the study of Chippewa language high on his list of priorities. Philology, he calculated, was the subject most likely to attract the attention of European and American "savants" and to provide him with a secure base on which to build his growing scientific reputation. Philology certainly seemed uppermost in his mind in an article

[22]Ibid., pp. 267, 281.
[23]Ibid., pp. 129–36, 141, 149, 165, 171, 176–77, 181, 184.

published in the *North American Review* in 1828. Although the piece provided glimpses into Chippewa religious, political, and social customs, its greatest contribution was its analysis of Chippewa language. Schoolcraft wrote that grammatical rules revealed a certain mental propensity for order in the Indian mind, evidence which to him seemed significant, for it indicated a real potential for Indians' mental development. He asserted that history, too, could be served through language study: it is to language that "we must look for our chief aid in ascertaining the consanguinity of the various tribes, while we have scarce any other clue to guide us to the solution of the still more important problem of the original peopling of America."[24]

So profound did Schoolcraft's grasp and mastery of Chippewa appear to be that philologists such as Albert Gallatin, John Pickering, and Peter Du Ponceau expected much from him in linguistics. But he disappointed them. He turned from the analytic study of language to promoting its use in missionary work and to the study of Indian psychology. Although Schoolcraft criticized those who wished to translate the Bible into various Indian languages, he nevertheless believed that sermons should be preached in native languages. Because native missionaries had a knowledge of the grammar and an "instinctive" feel for what was correct, they had an advantage over nonnative missionaries. To facilitate mission work, Schoolcraft advocated teaching Indian languages in college. To promote this view he solicited the government to withhold some Chippewa treaty money in order that a dictionary of Chippewa could be completed for use in mission work and as an aid to civilizing the Indians.[25]

[24]Ibid., p. 114; [Henry R. Schoolcraft] Review of *La Découverte des Sources du Mississippi, et de la Rivière Sanglante . . .* in *The North American Review* 27 (July, 1828): 89–114.

[25]Schoolcraft, *Personal Memoirs*, p. 671; Henry R. Schoolcraft, *Travels in the Central Portions of the Mississippi Valley*; [Henry R. Schoolcraft] Review of *Proceedings and Fourteenth Annual Report of the Board of Managers of the Baptist General Convention, at the meetings held in New York, April 1828* [and] *A Discourse on the Occasion of Forming the African Mission*

A recent study suggests that Schoolcraft's switch from philology to other ethnological interests was motivated by his desire to return to directions Cass had delineated for ethnology, namely the collection of artifacts, legends, tales of migrations, and tribal connections.[26] There is some truth in this, although other factors also must be taken into account. When considered in the broad context of biography, the causes for Schoolcraft's retreat from philology throw light on his development as an ethnologist and his very decided opinion on the function of ethnology.

For instance, there is a question just how well Schoolcraft knew the Chippewa language. Du Ponceau was impressed with the analysis of Chippewa in Schoolcraft's two lectures at the end of his *Narrative of an Expedition through the Upper Mississippi to Itasca Lake*, and he praised him as a man of "genius and talent." He sensed that Schoolcraft had spoken the language for a long time.[27] There are indications, however, that Schoolcraft's knowledge of Chippewa was not very extensive. Throughout his official career he constantly employed interpreters despite his contempt for their command of the language beyond the narrow rudiments necessary in trade jargon. Furthermore, although he perhaps had an excellent command of the grammatical principles of Chippewa, he continued to depend heavily on his wife and her brother George Johnston for vocabulary.[28]

There are also certain indications that Schoolcraft did not

School Society, delivered in Christ Church in Hartford, Conn. on Sunday Evening, Aug. 10, 1828, in *The North American Review* 28 (April, 1829): 354–68; Review of *Archaeologia Americana: Transactions and Collections of the American Antiquarian Society Vol. 2d.* [and] *Inquiries respecting the History, Traditions, Languages, within the United States,* in *The North American Review* 45 (July, 1837): 34–59.

[26] John Finley Freeman, "Religion and Personality in the Anthropology of Henry Schoolcraft," *Journal of the History of the Behavioral Sciences* 1 (October, 1965): 309; see also Freeman, "Henry Rowe Schoolcraft."

[27] Schoolcraft, *Personal Memoirs,* p. 496; Peter S. Du Ponceau to Dr. E. James, Sept. 26, 1834, extract copies; Nov. 10, 1834, extract copies, Schoolcraft Papers, LC.

[28] Henry R. Schoolcraft to George Johnston, Aug. 28, 1826; Schoolcraft to Jane Schoolcraft, July 30, 1825, Schoolcraft Papers, LC; Henry Rowe Schoolcraft to George Johnston, March 30, 1849, George Johnston Papers, BHC.

feel entirely at ease in philology. In the 1830s the study of philology demanded a knowledge of more than one language; for comparative purposes it demanded a grasp of several. Schoolcraft did not have such a linguistic foundation. Both Gallatin and Du Ponceau, trained in Europe, were multilingual. Even Pickering, through his studies and travels in Europe, possessed an impressive superiority over Schoolcraft in this area. At one point, shortly after reviewing Gallatin's "Synopsis," which he did with some "reluctance," Schoolcraft noted in his journal the purchase of two Hebrew grammars. "I have a special motive in making myself acquainted with this ancient, and, I find, simple tongue. The course of my investigation of Algonquin language, has shown me the want of the means of enlarged comparison, which I could not institute without it."[29] That was perhaps as much as Schoolcraft could admit concerning his inadequacy as a linguist. He lacked an inclination for theory, however, and the Hebrew grammars—other than convincing him that Indian languages were Semitic tongues—were of little use to him as inspirations for comparative linguistics.

Schoolcraft was also aware that it would be difficult for him to compete as a philologist with those in the East. He deplored the insularity of his frontier situation. Lack of books, especially philological treatises, hampered his work in linguistics and put him at a disadvantage with philologists located in cities with bookstores. But more detrimental was his own attitude towards these philologists. He might disagree with their interpretations, but his basic distaste for initiating an argument with reputable scholars, who might someday be in a position to aid him, forced Schoolcraft to assume an inferior position. For example, although he disagreed with Du Ponceau and believed Algonquin to be basically a simple language, Schoolcraft confided that he "could not state this to a man of his learning and standing with the literary public, without incurring the imputation of rashness or assumption."[30]

[29]Schoolcraft, *Personal Memoirs*, pp. 557–60.
[30]Ibid., pp. 497–98.

To these factors that served to sway Schoolcraft from philological study was added the lack of American interest in the field. American journals were not inclined to publish esoteric philological essays that would entertain only a small portion of their readers.[31] Although they still published accounts of travels through the western Indian country and articles assessing church and government Indian policy, their pages also reflected the growing demand for romantic literature, Indian tales, and poetry that would stir sentimental emotions in eastern drawing rooms.[32]

Schoolcraft's shift from philology, however, is even better understood within the context of his religious experiences, his altered views on Indians, and his new perspective on the role or use of ethnology. On February 7, 1831, Schoolcraft noted in his journal, "This day is very memorable in my private history, for my having assumed, after long delay, the moral intrepidity to acknowledge, *publicly*, a truth . . . the divine atonement for human sin made by the long foretold, the rejected, the persecuted, the crucified Messiah."[33] Religious revivals periodically swept the frontier settlements of northern Michigan, and it was at one of these, in Mackinac, that Schoolcraft publicly made his confession of faith and joined the Presbyterian church. The religiosity expressed at that moment had been building slowly for several months.[34]

[31] Even at midcentury Gallatin cautioned Schoolcraft that only in Germany and France were philological treatises published. Great Britain and America preferred only "light literature." To only a select few was the esoteric subject of Indian languages of any interest. Schoolcraft, *Personal Memoirs*, pp. 622, 492, 508–509.

[32] Ibid., p. 631; Freeman, "Religion and Personality," p. 305; see also Louise K. Barnett, *Ignoble Savage: American Literary Racism, 1790–1890*; Hoxie N. Fairchild, *The Noble Savage: A Study in Romantic Naturalism*; Robert F. Berkhofer, Jr., *The White Man's Indian: Images of the American Indian from Columbus to the Present*, pp. 86–96, for discussion of this romantic perspective on the Indian in the first half of the nineteenth century.

[33] Schoolcraft, *Personal Memoirs*, p. 343.

[34] For this revival spirit at Sault Ste. Marie and at Mackinac, see the Jeremiah Porter Mss. Journals, 2–11, Porter Papers, CHS. Bremer believes that the death of Schoolcraft's son William in 1827 also contributed to Schoolcraft's turn to religion. See Bremer, "Schoolcraft," pp. 54–55.

In a November 1830 letter to his wife, Jane, Schoolcraft resolved that he and his household from that moment forth would serve the Lord. He thought this would be difficult for Jane, a mixed-blood, "brought up in a remote place, without any thing which deserves the name of a regular education; without the salutary influence of society to form your mind, without a mother, in many things to direct you, and with an overkind father." To Schoolcraft, she was filled with vanity and pride, and being a woman only made it worse because "it is the domestic conduct of a female that is most continually liable to error, both of judgement and feeling. Nothing is more clearly scriptural, than that a woman should forsake 'father & mother' & cleave to her husband, and that she should look up to him with a full confidence as, next to God, her 'guide, philosopher & friend.'"[35]

Although Schoolcraft may have sincerely wished to embrace the Lord, it is apparent in this letter that he also wanted to assert his own identity. During the first decades of the nineteenth century the Johnston family was still of some importance at Sault Ste. Marie despite economic losses suffered in the War of 1812. Since Schoolcraft lived under the shadow of the Johnston family, indebted to them for his living quarters, his acquisition of Chippewa ethnography, his social contacts, and probably his very reputation at the Sault, it seems likely that only through his spiritual regeneration could he assert his independence and, as he probably believed, his new moral superiority.

In subsequent letters Schoolcraft restated his dedication to lead a Christian life and expressed regret that he had spent so much time absorbed in science.[36] On the day he entered into church fellowship he noted that religion would probably give a *"coloring to all my future acts."*[37] He was right. Schoolcraft's new religiosity certainly altered his

[35] Henry R. Schoolcraft to Jane Schoolcraft, Dec. 8, 1830, Schoolcraft Papers, LC.

[36] Ibid.; Henry R. Schoolcraft to Jane Schoolcraft, Dec. 22, 1830, Schoolcraft Papers, LC.

[37] Henry R. Schoolcraft, Journal, entry for Feb. 6, 1837, Schoolcraft Papers, LC. His emphasis.

perspective towards the Indian. A graver and more unbending personality gradually emerged. To his role as agent and to his fancied role as "grand chief," which he half believed he had assumed as a result of his marriage to Jane Johnston, a granddaughter of Wabojeeg, Schoolcraft added another role—that of patriarch.

In his new role Schoolcraft increasingly viewed the Indians in moralistic terms and as children who needed to be led. According to Schoolcraft, their dark and gloomy future was compounded by their inability to cope with change. Unlike the white race, the Indians seemed unable to surmount calamities, and they constantly "required the proper course to be clearly pointed out" to them. Fortunately, however, once a proper course had been made clear, the Indians "can readily be induced to conform to it."[38] Schoolcraft thus saw himself as a kind and just father, but one constantly frustrated in his attempts to impress upon his unruly brood the need to labor, to think of the future, and to accept Christianity.

In seeking causes for the Indians' lack of progress, Schoolcraft determined that the roots lay in their moral depravity rather than in their economic insufficiency. To Schoolcraft, Indians as a race seemed unwilling and at times unable to accept the truths of Christianity. Schoolcraft wrestled with this dilemma and increasingly became less concerned with the Indians' economic advance and acculturation and more with their salvation. He no longer believed that civilization must precede conversion; "without a change of heart, whereby they are brought to see their true relation to God and to their fellow creatures, the attempt to induce a healthy state of society among them, must be as vain as hoisting a rope of sand."[39]

[38] Henry R. Schoolcraft to Lucius Lyon, Jan. 18, 1837, Lyon Papers, WCL. Also note Schoolcraft, *Personal Memoirs*, pp. 571, 573, 594–97. For other references to Schoolcraft's fatherly regard for Indians, see Henry R. Schoolcraft to Edwin James, Dec. 13, 1831, Schoolcraft Papers, LC; Freeman, "Religion and Personality," p. 310; and Bremer, "Schoolcraft," p. 55.

[39] Henry R. Schoolcraft to Rev. W. J. Boutwell, Feb. 14, 1832, copy; Schoolcraft to Hon. John Eaton, Secretary of War, Aug. 10, 1830, copy,

Henry Rowe Schoolcraft as he appeared in volume 6 of his *History of the Indian Tribes of the United States*, published in 1857.

Schoolcraft contrived with missionaries and mission boards to attack what he saw as Indian superstitution and paganism. The time to strike was at hand, he claimed: "Their simple arts of magic and manito-worship, are ready to totter with a touch. And there seems nothing but active, united, persevering efforts necessary, to win them over to the side of virtue, and lead them in the paths of eternal truth."[40] But the mission boards did not rise to the challenge, and Schoolcraft, his clarion call unheeded, retreated to delve deeper into ethnology. Years before, Schoolcraft had expressed disturbance in his journal, writing that "in making . . . Indian history and language a topic of investigation, the great practical objects of their reclamation may be overlooked."[41] Now, Schoolcraft believed, ethnology combined with missionization would eventually succeed in saving the Indian, but first ethnology must be made to yield an answer to the "great moral problem," the obtuseness of the Indian mind.[42]

Schoolcraft Papers, LC; Schoolcraft, *Personal Memoirs*, p. 325. For an extended discussion of this issue, see Robert F. Berkhofer, Jr., *Salvation and the Savage: An Analysis of Protestant Missions and American Indian Response 1787–1862*, in which Berkhofer explores the debate of civilization vs. Christianity in chapter 1. That the mission boards were in agreement with Schoolcraft is seen in R. Pierce Beaver, *Church, State and the American Indian: Two and a Half Centuries of Partnership in Missions Between Protestant Churches and Government*; "Church, State and the Indians: Indian Missions in the New Nation," *Journal of Church and State* 4 (May, 1962): 11–30; John F. Freeman, "The Indian Convert: Theme and Variation," *Ethnohistory* 12 (Spring, 1965): 113–28. Another article that surveys the missionaries' attitudes toward Indians is Michael C. Coleman, "Not Race, but Grace: Presbyterian Missionaries and American Indians, 1837–1893," *Journal of American History* 67 (June, 1980): 41–60.

[40] Henry R. Schoolcraft, "Mythology, Superstitions and Languages of the North American Indians," *Literary and Theological Review* 2 (March, 1835): 118.

[41] Charles Cleland to Henry R. Schoolcraft, April 18, 1832, Schoolcraft Papers, LC; Schoolcraft, *Personal Memoirs*, p. 189. The journal entry was for April 20, 1824.

[42] On Schoolcraft's disappointment on the retreat of the mission boards to expend more resources in the missionization of the Indians, see Schoolcraft, *Personal Memoirs*, pp. 578–79, 489–91, and also the letter to David Greene, pp. 506–507. At about this time Schoolcraft was active in founding the Algic Society in Detroit. The goal of this society was clearly education and mis-

At the same time that Schoolcraft increasingly viewed Indians in narrow, moralistic and pejorative terms, his opinions on Indian matters were widely sought and generally freely given. Schoolcraft basked proudly in this attention and interpreted it as just recognition of his growing scholarly reputation. He was now no longer merely an Indian agent; he was a national resource. His increased contact with eastern scholars and publishers, the recognition he received as a result of discovering the source of the Mississippi River, the experience of entertaining foreign writers and dignitaries visiting upper Michigan, and his election into American and foreign learned societies all heightened Schoolcraft's vanity and estimation of his scholarly accomplishments.[43]

Paradoxically, there was another Schoolcraft. His struggle to reach a position of social eminence left him with a respect bordering on awe for those above him in social rank and scholarly achievements. His increased reputation also left him with a tremendous sense of insecurity. No matter how solid his accomplishments, his "exile" on the frontier gave him feelings of inadequacy, frustration, and self-doubt. Power and respect in frontier communities like Sault Ste.

---

sionization and is apparent in the society's constitution. Henry R. Schoolcraft, *Constitution of the Algic Society, Instituted March 28, 1832. For Encouraging Missionary Effort in Evangelizing the North Western Tribes, and Promoting Education, Agriculture, Industry, Peace & Temperence, Among Them. To Which is Annexed an Abstract of Its Proceedings, Together with the Introductory Address by Henry R. Schoolcraft, Esq., President of the Society;* Schoolcraft, Review of *Proceedings and Fourteenth Annual Report* . . . , pp. 357–65; Henry R. Schoolcraft to Rev. A. Bingham, Jan. 6, 1832, copy, Schoolcraft Papers, LC. See also Henry R. Schoolcraft, *A Discourse Delivered on the Anniversary of the Historical Society of Michigan, June 4, 1830,* p. 44; Henry R. Schoolcraft to Rev. A. Bingham, Jan. 6, 1832, copy; Schoolcraft to Dr. Edwin James, Dec. 13, 1831, copy; Schoolcraft to Rev. W. J. Boutwell, February 14, 1832, copy; Charles Cleland to Henry R. Schoolcraft, April 18, 1832, Schoolcraft Papers, LC.

[43]Schoolcraft's earlier travel narratives previously mentioned were well received, but his *Narrative of an Expedition Through the Upper Mississippi to Itasca Lake* relating to his discovery of the source of the Mississippi River commanded instant recognition and secured his reputation as an explorer. See "Editor's Introduction," in *Schoolcraft's Expedition to Lake Itasca The Discovery of the Source of the Mississippi,* ed., Philip P. Mason, p. xxiii.

Marie and Mackinac, and a growing reputation as a scholar did not automatically translate into power and recognition at the national level. Schoolcraft's constant fawning over eastern visitors in general and political figures in particular is best explained by his driving ambition, his need for attention, and his search for notability. In pursuing these ends Schoolcraft was acutely sensitive to any personal flaw.

At this point in his career, and within this context of personal ambition and insecurity, Schoolcraft's relationship with his wife and the Johnston family took a new turn. Marriages to mixed-bloods or to Indians, commonplace at Sault Ste. Marie in the 1820s, were by the 1830s no longer socially acceptable, especially at Mackinac, where Schoolcraft had moved his agency in 1833. The more refined society in Mackinac and in Detroit, where Schoolcraft sometimes wintered, did not escape his notice. He believed that society had improved with the "accession of a few females of various European or American lineages, from educated and refined circles." [44] As the American population in Michigan increased, Indians and mixed-bloods experienced greater discrimination, not entirely the result of their generally lower economic status. Even at Sault Ste. Marie discrimination existed—children of mixed parentage were pejoratively referred to as blacks. [45]

Given the growing atmosphere of discrimination, Schoolcraft seemed increasingly sensitive about his marriage to Jane and its effect on his reputation. His association with the Johnston family, so important upon his arrival at Sault Ste. Marie, deteriorated. The Mackinac years were marked

[44] Schoolcraft, *Personal Memoirs*, p. 458. For these feelings expressed by others, see Anna B. Jameson, *Winter Studies and Summer Rambles in Canada* 3: 36; Mrs. Thomas D. Gilbert, "Memoirs of the Soo," *Michigan Pioneer and Historical Collections* 30 (1903): 629–31; Clarence E. Carter, ed. *Territorial Papers of the United States: Michigan Territory, 1820–1829* 11: 730–31.

[45] Ann Adams, "Early Days at Red River Settlement, and Fort Snelling: Reminiscences of Mrs. Ann Adams," in *Collections of the Minnesota Historical Society* 6 (1894): 75–115; see also Carter, p. 719 for discriminative attitudes in Michigan against mixed-bloods at this time.

by a growing estrangement from his wife and the whole Johnston family. This in turn deprived him of those most able to aid him in his philological studies.[46]

Although Schoolcraft continued to acknowledge the value of philology in his articles, he increasingly shifted his attention to Indian legends, a field of study in which he made his greatest contribution and on which his fame more securely rests. Schoolcraft's shift of interest to legends and Indian religious beliefs developed out of his strong suspicions that the legends reflected the operations of the Indian mind and a comprehension of the Indian mind was necessary in order to bring the Indian to Christianity. At the same time, Schoolcraft's sense of Christian duty compelled him to labor for the salvation of the Indians. The study of Indian legends also proved more congenial to his inclinations and literary studies, and perhaps lessened his reliance on the Johnston family. Public literary tastes possibly influenced his decision to pursue mythology, but they were probably not a deciding factor. The need to go beyond the resources of philology for an understanding of the workings of the Indian mind was the major factor. Philology would not tell why the Indians refused to accept Christianity.

In 1835, Schoolcraft announced that mythology was a way to approach and to comprehend Indian mentality. "The mental powers [sic] of the Indian," he wrote, "constitutes a topic which we do not design to discuss. But it must manifest, that some of their peculiarities are brought out by their systems of mythology and spirit-craft. . . . It is here

---

[46]About Schoolcraft's insecurity, see Freeman, "Religion and Personality." On Schoolcraft's wife's Indian features and evidence of the growing estrangement between Jane Schoolcraft and her husband, see Anna Jameson, 3: 36. For his son's notable Indian features, see Daniel R. Dunihue, "Journal of Daniel R. Dunihue, 1830," Mss., Dunihue Collection, Indiana State Library. An interesting account of Schoolcraft's relationship with his wife, Jane, at this time, as well as his mother's warning not to marry a mixed-blood, can be found in Mary H. Schoolcraft, *The Black Gauntlet*, pp. 467–569. Mary was Schoolcraft's second wife. Although the account is heavily biased against Jane, Schoolcraft read the book and approved it; see Chase and Stellanova Osborn, *Schoolcraft-Longfellow-Hiawatha*, p. 610.

that the Indian mind unbends itself, and reveals some of his obvious traits."[47]

Schoolcraft began collecting the oral tales of the Chippewas, Ottawas, and Potawatomis soon after becoming Indian agent. Lewis Cass, as already noted, manifested a particular interest in these tales, for he thought that through these bits of evidence the histories and migrations of Indian tribes might come to light.[48] In 1826 and 1827 these oral tales began to appear in Schoolcraft's "Literary Voyager," a manuscript journal he circulated among his friends while at Sault Ste. Marie. At that time the sole purpose of recording these tales was to entertain. Other legends appeared in later works, and there they not only amused but also served to illustrate how they reinforced Chippewa cultural values.[49] Now Schoolcraft turned to them with renewed interest, one underscored with religious fervor.[50]

Schoolcraft's initial study of the tales had elicited some facts. He discovered that the tales, with their multitude of spirits, enabled the Jossakeed, or conjurers, and Wabeno priests effectively to control the Indians' minds. "The whole mind is bowed down under these intellectual fetters, which circumscribe its volitions, and bind it, as effectually as the hooks of iron, which pierce a whirling Hindoo's flesh." In Schoolcraft's view, since the Indians drilled their children on the controlling influences these spirits possessed over life and death, it was little wonder that the Indian was, as Cass put it, a "stern and unbending fatalist," mired in moral and intellectual stagnation.[51]

With the 1839 publication of *Algic Researches*, a two-volume collection of the legends of the northern Indians, Schoolcraft's ideas assumed full-blown proportions. Here

[47] Schoolcraft, "Mythology," p. 107.

[48] Schoolcraft, *Personal Memoirs*, pp. 126, 186–87, 206–207.

[49] Henry R. Schoolcraft, *The Literary Voyager or Muzzeniegun*, ed. Philip P. Mason; Schoolcraft, *Travels*; Freeman, "Schoolcraft," pp. 194–96.

[50] Schoolcraft, *Personal Memoirs*, pp. 548–49, 585, 634; Schoolcraft, *Algic Researches, Comprising Inquiries Respecting the Mental Characteristics of North American Indians*, 1: 37–40.

[51] Schoolcraft, "Mythology," p. 103; [Cass] Review of *Documents and Proceedings . . .* , p. 74.

he presented his clearest and most succinct statement on the importance of myths for understanding the Indian. Cass earlier had posed several questions that Schoolcraft grappled with in this work. Why was the Indian so childish and impulsive? Why was he so resistant to change? Why did he seem never to employ reason? Cass attributed these defects in mentality to unknown, insurmountable obstacles that made the Indian unbending in his habits and fatalistic in his attitude toward life. Since Cass saw civilization as the product of reason, he concluded that the rejection of civilization was unreasonable. Was the Indian's mind so paralyzed that it could not reason and thus accept civilization, or was the rejection of civilization caused by something else, "an inherent difficulty, arising from the institution, character, and condition of the Indians themselves"?[52] In the context of these questions, Schoolcraft believed his study of myths and legends offered leads.

With a gratuitous bow to philology—"language constituted the initial point of inquiry . . . ."—Schoolcraft proposed mythology "as a means of acquiring an insight into [the Indians'] mode of thinking and reasoning, the sources of their fears and hopes, and the probable origin of their opinions and institutions." Mythology opened a whole new dimension in Indian studies. Wrote Schoolcraft, "Hitherto our information has related rather to their external customs and manners, their physical traits and historical peculiarities, than to what may be termed the philosophy of the Indian mind . . . Nothing in the whole inquiry has afforded so ample a clew [sic] to their opinions and thoughts, in all the great departments of life and nature, as their oral imaginative tales." Here in these "wild tales of the imagination . . . incongruous, [and] grotesque," he continued, the narrative style, the "cast of invention," and the "theory of thinking" all merge into fabulous forms, so peculiarly adaptive to a "people who wander about in woods and plains, who encounter wild beasts, believe in demons, and

---

[52][Cass] Review of *Documents and Proceedings*, pp. 67–93; Schoolcraft, *Algic Researches*, 1: 9–28.

are subject to the vicissitudes of the seasons." For School-craft these tales told in winter—where men are trans-formed into animals or winds or stars and are then trans-formed into men again; where superhuman feats of skill, bravery, and strength are woven with history and gossip; where the old becomes new and the new old—presented the "deepest insight into [Indian] character . . . and the clearest coincidences with Oriental rites and opinions." The tales illuminated "the dark cave of the Indian mind" and revealed the philosophical dimensions of Indian life.[53] Rhetorically, Schoolcraft questioned whether these compo-nents of myths and legends were clues to the Indians' ori-gins. Schoolcraft was certain that these tales indicated simi-lar "mental peculiarities" among the "Algic" tribes of the Northeast, but how extensive these "mental peculiarities" and "Oriental rites and opinions" were among the Indians of the Americas remained an important question. Were these tales used by leaders such as Manco Capac or Mon-tezuma to consolidate political power? Were they used to inspire courage in battle or console in misfortune? Do the tales inscribed in "hieroglyphic" or birch bark "bear any useful comparison with the phonetic system of Egypt, the Runic of Iceland and Norway, or with any other mode of perpetuating the knowledge of events or things known to the human race?"[54] Schoolcraft believed only future re-search would provide answers. His remarks, however, owe less to ethnological concerns or romantic orientation than to religious goals. His present endeavors were merely to il-lustrate the potential in the Indian's mind for civilization and to "infuse new energy in the cause of benevolence and awaken fresh ardour in the heart of piety" for the Indian's salvation.[55]

[53] Schoolcraft, *Algic Researches*, 1: 12, 49; Schoolcraft, *Personal Memoirs*, pp. 678–79. Schoolcraft expressed hesitancy in cutting the stories down but decided to do it for "the Indians are prolix, and attached value to many minu-tiae in the relation which not only does not help forward the denouement, but is tedious and witless to the last degree." See Schoolcraft, *Personal Mem-oirs*, p. 635.
[54] Schoolcraft, *Algic Researches*, 1: 39–40.
[55] Ibid., p. 27.

What did Schoolcraft discover that was not previously known about the Indian mind? How were missionaries to use such information? How did legends relate to Indian character, institutions, and condition? What was Schoolcraft's analysis of the tales? What theory could be propounded? Unfortunately, Schoolcraft offered neither theory nor answers. True, he pointed out that a particular legend or tale revealed a "viciousness" characteristic of a certain tribe and that other tales demonstrated moral principles to children, but there was little else. By his own admission, he was "a fact hunter," not a theoretician. He did not have "access to the Indian mind," nor could he "push his inquiries so far into their former history and mental characteristics as to clear up fully the obscurities" that still abounded. That would be the work of future researches. It was enough, Schoolcraft thought, to bring forth this manifestation of the Indian mind heretofore unstudied.[56]

Algic Researches sold well, but it is doubtful that the public bought the two-volume set for Schoolcraft's ethnological insights. The works of Sir Walter Scott and James MacPherson's supposed discovery of the wisdom of ancient Gaelic bards in the manuscripts of Ossian had fueled the public's desire for romance literature. The discovery of ancient Indian "bards" in *Algic Researches* piqued America's literary nationalism and created enthusiastic response for the work.[57]

The work's favorable reception probably cushioned for Schoolcraft the blow of removal from government service.[58] Events surrounding his dismissal are still clouded. Schoolcraft sharply denied charges of graft and misappropriation of Indian funds for his speculative adventures. Although an investigation was carried out and Schoolcraft lost the court suit, he still affirmed that he was politically hounded out of

---

[56] Ibid., pp. 27–28.

[57] G. Harrison Orians, "The Rise of Romanticism: 1805–1855," in *Transitions in American Literary History*, ed. Harry Hayden Clark, pp. 163–244; Barnett, pp. 33–43.

[58] Schoolcraft, *Personal Memoirs*, pp. 652–55 for reviews in the Detroit newspapers.

office by his enemies. In 1841 he left Michigan, setting out for New York City and a new life. Schoolcraft confided in his journal that the frontier, "however suitable it is for observation on several topics, is by no means favorable to the publication of them, while the seaboard cities possess numerous advantages of residence."[59]

With the public's reception of *Algic Researches* fresh in his mind, Schoolcraft had sanguine hopes of a literary career in New York. His luck, however, deteriorated even further. The years 1841 and 1842 proved particularly bad for him, as he later wrote in his memoirs: "I now cast myself about to publish the results of my observations on the Red Race, whom I had found, in many traits, a subject of deep interest; in some things wholly misunderstood and misrepresented; and although an object of the highest humanitarian interest. But our booksellers, or rather bookpublishers, were not yet prepared in their views to undertake anything corresponding to my ideas."[60] With New York unreceptive, Schoolcraft set off for England, where he hoped he would find some publisher more amenable to the ideas rejected in New York. England proved just as un-

---

[59]Ibid., p. 702. For a discussion of Schoolcraft's dismissal as agent, see Freeman, "Schoolcraft," pp. 215–22; Henry R. Schoolcraft to George Bancroft, June 16, 1840, Bancroft Papers, MHS, for Schoolcraft's version of his dismissal.

[60]Schoolcraft, *Personal Memoirs*, p. 703. In the reviews of *Algic Researches*, Schoolcraft was compared with the artist George Catlin. The reviewer in the *Detroit Free Press* noted that although Catlin was the "red man's painter," Schoolcraft was the Indians' "poetical historian." See Schoolcraft, *Personal Memoirs*, pp. 652–55. Schoolcraft, however, in his review of Catlin, although complimentary of Catlin's painting, did not always trust Catlin's notes. See [Henry R. Schoolcraft] Review of *Letters and Notes on the Manners, Customs, and Condition of the North American Indians* [and] *American Antiquities and Researches into the Origin and History of the Red Race* in *The North American Review* 54 (April, 1842): 283–99. In 1853, Schoolcraft was even more critical of Catlin, referring to him as a tourist who gathered his information from "retrobate" Indians who hung around frontier posts. According to Schoolcraft, Catlin's information was not reliable or useful to serious ethnologists intent on learning about the languages, customs, origins, and histories of Indian tribes. Schoolcraft also accused Catlin of distorting and "sensationalizing" the Mandan Okeepu ceremony. Henry R. Schoolcraft to George Catlin, Feb. 28, 1853, copy, Schoolcraft Papers, LC.

responsive.[61] More misfortune followed. While he was in Europe, Schoolcraft's wife died. When Schoolcraft returned to New York, he had two children to support and no position and no publishing offers. He changed his name to Colcraft, an action that one writer interpreted as a symbolic act of suicide.[62] It was a time of debt and ravenous insecurity.

From 1841 to 1847, Schoolcraft lived in New York City. These were years of both financial adversity and intellectual activity. He seemed to be searching for his proper place in the field of letters. During this period he wrote a series of articles later published in book form under the title *Oneota*, poems on Indian topics, and a revision of *Oneota* entitled *The Red Race of America*.[63]

In 1844, in an article entitled "Our Indian Policy," Schoolcraft defended the government's removal of the Indians across the Mississippi River. The article is significant not for its proremoval stand but as an expression of his growing fear that time was running out for the Indians to change their ways and for his emphasis on the role of ethnic determinism in culture. Although Schoolcraft sought to situate the whole issue of removal in the context of government Indian policy and the settlement of the nation, he also drew heavily on his belief in inherent ethnic characteristics.[64] According to Schoolcraft, both the Spaniards and the

---

[61] It is possible that the artist George Catlin, who had taken his paintings of Indians to England in 1839, had perhaps saturated English curiosity regarding the Indians. See Marjorie Halpin, "Introduction" to George Catlin, *Letters and Notes on the Manners, Customs, and Conditions of North American Indians*; Marjorie Halpin, *Catlin's Indian Gallery: The George Catlin Paintings in the United States National Museum*; Harold McCracken, *George Catlin and the Old Frontier*.

[62] Freeman, "Religion and Personality," p. 311.

[63] Henry R. Schoolcraft, *Oneota, or Characteristics of the Red Race of America: Their History, Traditions, Customs, Poetry, Picture-writings, . . .* ; Henry Rowe Schoolcraft, *Oneota, or Characteristics of the Red Races of America. From Original Notes and Manuscripts*; Henry Rowe Schoolcraft, *The Red Race of America*.

[64] Henry R. Schoolcraft, "Our Indian Policy," *Democratic Review* 14 (1844): 169–84. Schoolcraft did not always endorse Indian removal. In 1829, Schoolcraft proclaimed: "For ourselves, we are free to declare, that we have

French had done little for the Indian because they could not. The Spaniards had not developed beyond the "chivalric era" of Western civilization, and the French had remained stagnated at the "feudal period" and thus were deficient in those traits necessary to aid the Indian toward civilization. The British, on the contrary, possessed such traits. "We consider the Pilgrims as the embodiment of the true ancient Teutonic type."[65] Placed in contact with this advanced "Teutonic type," the Indian could not expect to remain untouched by civilization. For Schoolcraft the Indian and the Teutonic type were "antithetical," the "alpha and omega of the ethnological chain." Couched in cultural terms, the Indians degenerated because "civilization had more of the principles of endurance and progress than barbarism, because Christianity was superior to paganism; industry to idleness; agriculture to hunting; letters to hieroglyphics; truth to error." Schoolcraft's ringing plaudits for the Teutonic type and for civilization merely echoed the public's increasingly unsympathetic frustration with government Indian policy. Indeed, he nearly paraphrased an account of one critic who wrote in 1823 that civilization prevailed over barbarity because it was plainly better, "for if barbarity were more enduring, more permanent, more

---

no faith in the preaching to adult Indians, while they remain hunters and warriors. Consequently we deem any measures of removal, or future location, which are fitted to perpetuate their present habits, as hostile to the object." Review of *Proceedings and Fourteenth Annual Report* . . . , p. 366; see also Henry R. Schoolcraft to Andrew Jackson, Aug. 8, 1825, copy, Schoolcraft Papers, LC. By October 1829, Schoolcraft wrote to Jared Sparks: "The great question of the removal of the Indians is, as I conceive, put to rest. Time & circumstance have decided it against them. The government, & a great portion of the people have also decided it against them. It only requires the moral courage necessary to avow the principle, and to reconcile the moral feelings of the friends of the Indians, to their withdrawal under a proper system." Henry R. Schoolcraft to Jared Sparks, Oct. 13, 1829, copy, Schoolcraft Papers, LC. In the months separating these two stands, Lewis Cass, Schoolcraft's mentor on Indians, had spoken in favor of removal, and Schoolcraft apparently hastened to change his stand in acceptance of Cass's position. For Cass's change of position on this matter, see Francis Paul Prucha, *Lewis Cass and American Indian Policy*, pp. 16–17; and Freeman, "Schoolcraft," pp. 126–28.
[65] Schoolcraft, "Our Indian Policy," p. 170.

conducive to the increase and stability of population, more congenial to the human nature, . . . then it would be better than civilization."[66]

For several generations the Indian population did not pose an acute problem for Americans. By the 1830s, however, the white population was surging westward, and "the tendency of the Saxon institutions, laws, and jurisprudence, was to sweep over them." Everywhere the Indians retreated from the advance of "Saxon northmen and Huguenots." Government Indian policy, according to Schoolcraft, was the logical outgrowth of a firm belief in the impossibility of incorporating the Indians "en masse" into "our system." Not only were the Indians unable to compete, but they were an "idle, pastoral, unphilosophic, noninductive race of central Asia." The problem, as Schoolcraft saw it, was one of mental orientation. To direct their minds while they were under the often-conflicting influences of frontier whites seemed an impossible task. Removal was the only answer.[67]

Schoolcraft's racial views of Indians as products of degeneration were further stimulated by his activities and studies in New York City. His interest in history and ethnology led him to join both the New-York Historical Society and the American Ethnological Society. In the latter he came into contact with the other American ethnologists such as Samuel G. Morton, Albert Gallatin, John Stephens, John

[66] Ibid., p. 171; Review of *A Report to the Secretary of War of the U.S. on Indian Affairs* in *The North American Review* 16 (1823): 39.

[67] Schoolcraft, "Our Indian Policy," pp. 169–84; *Documents and Proceedings Relating to the Formation and Progress of a Board in the City of New York for the Emigration, Preservation, and Improvement, of the Aborigines of America, July 22, 1829.* Several historians have written extensively about the period of Indian removal. Some of the more recent works are: Prucha, *American Indian Policy,* pp. 213–49; Ronald N. Satz, *American Indian Policy in the Jacksonian Era;* Herman J. Viola, *Thomas L. McKenney: Architect of America's Early Indian Policy: 1816–1830;* Berkhofer, *The White Man's Indian,* pp. 156–67. The question of and justification for Indian removal has proved a continuing issue. For two opposing interpretations, see: Wilcomb E. Washburn, "Indian Removal Policy: Administrative, Historical and Moral Criteria for Judging Its Success or Failure," *Ethnohistory* 12 (Summer, 1965): 274–78, and Francis Paul Prucha, "Andrew Jackson's Indian Policy: A Reassessment," *Journal of American History* 56 (December, 1969): 527–39.

Bartlett, William F. Van Amringe, and others and with the more important ethnological literature. While many in America turned to George Catlin and his two-volume work *The Manners, Customs, and Condition of the North American Indian* for an impression of the American Indian, Schoolcraft turned to Alexander Bradford and his *History of the Red Race* (1841) for knowledge of early Indian history. In Bradford, Schoolcraft discovered elaborate arguments supporting his own racial interpretation of Indian history and degeneration. He believed that Bradford brought together all that was then known on the ancient Indians. It helped that Bradford's views closely paralleled his own.[68]

Bradford traced Indian origins to Asia, Europe, and Africa, and he believed that they had first settled in Central America. In his view, early migrating Indians brought with them many of the barbarous practices prevalent after the Deluge. They were not, however, totally barbarous. The wondrous cities of Central America, although in ruins, offered evidence of an advanced civilization, at least a civilization more advanced than the societies of the nomadic Indians. In time, stated Bradford, as groups split from the center of this civilization and moved north and south, they lapsed increasingly into barbarism. Bradford believed that societies did not stand still, but either progressed or degenerated, and that this was a natural course all civilizations passed through. Unlike Gallatin and others who believed that mankind slowly ascended towards civilization, Bradford believed no group of mankind ever civilized itself and that the natural course of man was to degenerate rather than advance.[69] Schoolcraft did not accept all of Bradford's

[68] Schoolcraft, *Algic Researches*, 1: 25–26; George Catlin, *The Manners, Customs, and Condition of the North American Indian*; Alexander W. Bradford, *American Antiquities and Researches into the Origin and History of the Red Race*. For Schoolcraft's view of Bradford's work, see [Henry R. Schoolcraft] Review of *Letters and Notes . . .* [and] *American Antiquities*, pp. 297–99.

[69] Bradford did not accept the Bering Strait migration thesis; he believed that the Indians came civilized and by water to Central America. From there they migrated north and south and, upon migrating, they degenerated. See Bradford, *American Antiquities*, pp. 168, 207–208. That "nearly all the aborigines appear to be of the same descent and origin; and that the barbarous

ideas, but he did agree that the Indians degenerated after the Deluge, and he applauded the scope of Bradford's study, which embraced archaeology, philology, tales, and customs in its discussion of Indian history.[70]

Despite all of Schoolcraft's reading and conversations about ethnology with the members of the American Ethnological Society, there is little evidence of his growth as an ethnological theoretician. His conceptual framework of ethnology and its goals remained the same. Pessimistic and increasingly disposed to describe the Indians in pejorative terms, he also repeatedly called for more facts and their application to what he considered the larger issue, the salvation of the Indian.

Schoolcraft's *Notes on the Iroquois* contained the kind of facts he felt should be collected. In 1845 the state of New York commissioned him to take a census of the Indian tribes within the state. He was given the liberty to include a study of Iroquois history and archaeology.[71] Unfortunately, the proposed census followed on the heels of a

tribes are the broken, scattered, and degenerated remnants of a society originally more enlightened" served to confirm for Bradford a sense of manifest destiny of the American people. As he pointed out, "the greater portion of the continent was inhabited by savage hordes; within the United States, the barbarous tribes appear to have been greatly depopulated, and the ancient and cultivated nations to have become extinct; even in Mexico and Peru the civilization of the first ages seems to have surpassed that of later times, and society generally was in a state of decadence. The old system,—its moral and social elements,—its capacity for self improvement,—had thus been fairly tried and tested; and the time had arrived when a new race, and the Christian religion, were appointed to take possession of the soil." Bradford, *American Antiquities*, pp. 430–35.

[70]Although Schoolcraft may have differed with Bradford on the usefulness of language for discovering the Indians' origins, he endorsed Bradford's contention that the Indians had migrated from the Old World and that their account of the Deluge was the same as that in the Mosaic rendition. Bradford, *American Antiquities*, pp. 228–45, 431. See also [Henry R. Schoolcraft] "Ethnological Sketch of the North American Indians," *American Quarterly Register and Magazine* 1 (May, 1848): 169.

[71]"Letter from the Secretary of State to Henry R. Schoolcraft, etc.," in Henry R. Schoolcraft, *Notes on the Iroquois*, pp. 435–37. For an account of the Ogden Land Company's dealings with the Senecas, see: Carl Resek, *Lewis Henry Morgan: American Scholar*, pp. 28–35; and William H. Armstrong, *Warrior in Two Camps: Ely S. Parker Union General and Seneca Chief*, pp. 10–11.

scheme to grab Iroquois land in western New York and to remove the Iroquois west of the Mississippi River. The scheme involved the Ogden Land Company, which in 1838 had used devious and illegal means to encourage several Seneca chiefs to sign a treaty selling the four reservations of Tonawanda, Cattaraugus, Allegheny, and Buffalo Creek. When the Senecas learned of the deal, they and local non-Indian supporters, including the Society of Friends, petitioned Congress to reject the treaty. President Van Buren, convinced that some machinations had been involved, also suggested its rejection. Congress, however, approved the treaty. The Senecas stood firm and refused to move, and public support rallied to their cause. The Ogden Land Company eventually returned two reservations and sold back a third to the Senecas. Schoolcraft was informed in his letter of commission that the Iroquois were apt to be suspicious of the census coming so soon after their troubles over the treaty of 1838. To ease their suspicions Schoolcraft was directed to assure them that the census was in no way connected to the federal government or to any land company.[72]

In *Notes on the Iroquois*, Schoolcraft collected three classes of facts that he considered basic to the promotion of sound government Indian policy: agricultural and population statistics, historical data, and legends. The facts indicated that statistically the Iroquois demonstrated progress and the acceptance of civilized ways. They were farmers engaged in both animal husbandry and agriculture. Many had also become Christians, and there were many Iroquois children in schools. Schoolcraft discovered that the Iroquois were increasing in population rather than decreasing.[73] But his primary interests lay in another direction, in the study of the origins and history of the Iroquois as a distinct people: their early wars; their archaeology; their arts, languages, and legends; and the founding of the Iroquois League, a confederacy of the Seneca, Cayuga, Onondaga, Oneida, and Mohawk nations. These data would allow a

---

[72] Schoolcraft, *Notes*, pp. 435–37.
[73] Ibid., pp. 26–27.

glimpse into the "historical mystery that shroud the Indian period, prior to 1492." Schoolcraft also believed this information vital to estimating the Indians' potential for civilization and Christianity.[74]

While Schoolcraft was at work on the Iroquois census the debate on Indian origins again assumed a certain shrillness. During the 1840s it festered as a topic of some importance, inflamed by the works of Samuel G. Morton and others. The old issue of Indian indigenousness to the Americas and its implication for polygenism again stirred the scientific community. Did separate races constitute separate species? If they did, were they inferior or unequal by nature rather than by social conditioning? The activities of the abolitionists and the discord over slavery compounded the debate over the issue of Indian origins. Schoolcraft was acutely aware of the controversy between monogenism and polygenism and its implications for both religion and the Indians' future. He could not ignore the opportunity to offer proof against polygenism and to plunge into the fray. *Notes on the Iroquois* offered him an excellent opportunity. By demonstrating through "incontrovertible" evidence that Indians had Old World origins, Schoolcraft intended to vindicate the Bible and to assure the Indians' affinity to the rest of mankind.

Schoolcraft thought language and legends were the two most useful categories of Indian culture for revealing affinities between tribes and clues to their historical origins. Too many questions still remained, however, for philology to be useful in tracing origins. Schoolcraft maintained that myths or legends were much more amenable, an argument rooted in his theory that legends contained elements or ideas traceable to other civilizations. To Schoolcraft, Iroquois tales proved especially valuable. He cited the tale of Iroquois vampires as a case in point: "Transformation and the doctrine of metempsychosis, are equally common. But hitherto, the horrid idea of the vampyre [sic] has not been noticed. It is a Greek idea, and contrary to the general

[74] Ibid., p. iv.

traits of the Indian mind, and not of an *Asiatic* cast."[75] This discovery among the Iroquois, Schoolcraft believed, indicated a Mediterranean or Phoenician contact in the New World. Character traits also tended to support such a conclusion: "If there be any tribe in the whole ample range of America, who have manifested traits of Grecian firmness and association, it is the Iroquois."[76]

But how useful were legends and tales where "reality" and fantasy mingled indiscriminately? Others had used tales that referred to a deluge, a migration from the east, or a migration from the west to support their favorite theories of Indian origins, but what of these other tales? What could be learned from them? According to Schoolcraft they served as sensitive indicators of the mind and culture of the Indian. What was related in these tales was less important than how it was related and how imagery was used. As to mind, they revealed the inability of the Indian narrator to relate "a clear, consistent chain of indisputable facts and deductions to fill up the fore ground [sic] of his history." Here in oral record was the evidence of the noninductive Oriental mind, a mind so willing to follow the mysterious and wonderful, yet so possessed of fear that it created a world filled with gods and demons that needed appeasement. The marvelous adventures of man and god played out in these legends also provided insights into the Indians' culture; the imagery "tallies admirably with their belief, at the present day, and harmonizes with itself, and with that state of proud heathendom, adventurous idolotry, and wild and roving independence, in which they lived." The imagery and wild adventures related in the oral tales told in winter found their counterparts in the frenzied war and hunting activities of Indian life and in the struggle to survive in a world where nature controlled man's destiny.[77] More proof

[75] Ibid., p. 144. His emphasis.

[76] Ibid., p. 145. Schoolcraft's analysis of the Grave Creek Stone also led him to similar conclusions of European contacts. See Henry R. Schoolcraft, "Observations Respecting the Grave Creek Mound in Western Virginia," *Transactions of the American Ethnological Society* 1 (1845): 416.

[77] Schoolcraft, *Notes*, pp. 142–45.

was required, but already the outline of Schoolcraft's Indian history was revealed.

In 1846, Schoolcraft addressed the Was-Ah-Ho-De-No-Son-Ne, or Grand Order of the Iroquois, in Aurora, New York, and called for volunteers in this grand search. Entering into the spirit of the occasion, Schoolcraft admonished the young white warriors of the Grand Order to seek out the history of the Red Man. He claimed that the antiquity of America was far more interesting and challenging than that of the Old World. Nothing should be overlooked; legends, language, ruins, and arts could all be used as keys to decipher Indian history and discover Indian origins.[78]

Schoolcraft returned to these duel themes again that year when he submitted to the board of regents of the Smithsonian Institution a plan seeking institutional support for ethnology.[79] As Schoolcraft explained, "It is proposed to consider ethnology in the most enlarged sense of which the etymology of the word admits as embracing man in his division into nations; their affinities and characteristics, mental and physical, with such proofs deduced from history, philology, antiquities, and the exact sciences, as may serve to link nation to nation, and race to race."[80] When such investigations were pursued correctly, stated Schoolcraft, the results had cosmological significance. They would provide links in the "history of the original dispersion of our species . . . and would enable us to appreciate

[78] Henry R. Schoolcraft, *An Address Delivered Before the Was-ah-Ho-de-no-son-ne, or New Confederacy of the Iroquois, August 14, 1846*, p. 5.

[79] Henry R. Schoolcraft, *Plan for the Investigation of American Ethnology* . . . (New York: Edward O. Jenkins, 1846). This plan was read before the board of regents of the Smithsonian Institution in September 1846. Twenty years later it was also published in the *Annual Report of the Board of Regents of the Smithsonian Institution, July 1885*, Part 1 (Washington: G.P.O., 1886). The editor of the annual report prefaced the publication: "The following programme, though never officially adopted by the Smithsonian Institution, embodies the result of much study of the subject by the distinguished author; and even after the lapse of forty years possesses sufficient interest and suggestiveness to justify its publication."

[80] Schoolcraft, *Plan for the Investigation*, p. 5 (pagination refers to the 1846 edition).

and understand our position on the globe."[81] Already, he believed, ethnology had determined that the Indians of both North and South America were one race. What remained was to affix their points of origin and chronology. This required employment of all the sciences: archaeology, mythology, and religious studies.

Anxious to find a position that would allow him time to pursue such researches, Schoolcraft hoped he could convince the board of regents of the Smithsonian Institution to fund such work and publication. Only such an endowed institution could financially underwrite the kind of investigation he envisioned.

> It is not an inquiry which admits of extempore results. To consider diligently the various parts of the continent which furnish aliment for the investigation, to scrutinize and collate what has been discovered and written, to collect from mounds and other sources, in various parts of the world, specimens of ancient art, and above all to embody the present and past philology of tribes and nations, is a labor requiring time and attention.[82]

These investigations, Schoolcraft explained, were beyond the resources of an individual and would not result in materials appropriate for "popular lectures." Thinking perhaps that private presses would be unable to sustain publication of these researches, he suggested that the results "be printed at a press owned and controlled by the board." Schoolcraft left the details of making a temporary or fixed appointment to facilitate the collection of these data open to consideration, but he explicitly stated "that without adequate provision for time, books, and travel incident to the inquiry, no person can be expected to enter upon effective labor in this field."[83]

A year later Schoolcraft brought essentially the same message to the New-York Historical Society. Too much mystery, he stated, remained regarding the migration of man,

[81] Ibid.
[82] Ibid.
[83] Ibid., pp. 5–6.

especially migration to the New World. Bits and pieces
of Indian culture and styles of thinking revealed ties with
the ancient Chaldeans, Phoenicians, Egyptians, Mesopo-
tamians, Persians, Copts, Zoroasters, Babylonians, Arabs,
Chinese, Japanese, and Jews. Unfortunately, Indians had
no written histories. Their history was woven into legends
and tales that had become garbled and had degenerated
into fables. Schoolcraft felt strongly that "to restore their
history from the rubbish of their traditions

> . . . to seek among the ruins, to decypher hieroglyphics, to
> unravel myths to study ancient systems of worship and as-
> tronomy, and to investigate vocabularies and theories of lan-
> guage, are the chief methods before us; and these call for
> the perseverance of Sisiphus and the clear inductive powers
> of Bacon."[84]

Although the usefulness of ethnology for religion was not
made explicit, it nevertheless was acknowledged. Ethnology would "guide the footsteps of letters, science and
piety."[85] Less modest than in his early career, Schoolcraft
was now certain that he shared the qualities of Sisiphus
and Bacon.

The opportunity for Schoolcraft to pursue such investigations arrived in 1847 when he was selected to undertake a
"national study of the Indian," not for the Smithsonian Institution but for the War Department. Several factors converged to initiate government financial support for this
work. As noted earlier, by midcentury the debate between
monogenists and polygenists, smoldering through the 1830s
and 1840s, broke out with increased virulence, and the
flames of the conflagration showed definite signs of spread-
ing. After many years of study, there were still few satisfactory answers to the many questions that revolved around
the problem of Indian origins and, by extension, their potential for civilization. If the Indians were descendants of

[84] Henry R. Schoolcraft, *Incentives to the Study of the Ancient Period of American History. An Address, Delivered Before the New York Historical Society, at its Forty-Second Anniversary, 17th November, 1846*, p. 33.
[85] Ibid., p. 17.

Adam, what was their line of descent and how and when did they reach America? Had declension from a higher level of civilization followed after their arrival? Had they always been "barbarians," and, if so, why had they remained stagnated? Were there some people exempted from the dictates of progress? These important issues held grave implications for both history and religion. The Bible's validity as an arbiter of truth and source of divine revelation was brought into question, as was the concept of progress. It was thought that a well-financed "national study" might go far toward solving these pressing questions, especially critical in the charged atmosphere of racial concerns before the Civil War.

As for the government's position, more information on the country's Indians was needed in order to devise new policy. By the 1840s most southeastern tribes were west of the Mississippi River. Some tribes still remained in the north, but the pressure from the states for their removal was mounting. Even at the time that plans were being formulated for moving midwestern tribes, the United States was increasing its domain in the Southwest, bringing still more tribes under government control. This produced a heavy strain upon the already understaffed Bureau of Indian Affairs. Settlers were moving onto tribal lands faster than tribes could be removed. By the late 1840s and early 1850s it was apparent that the government's removal policy and the idea of a permanent Indian frontier was bankrupt. Although the government pushed strenuously for new policies in its attempts to assimilate the Indians, it was stymied as to which means would be the most efficacious.[86] What the Bureau of Indian Affairs decided it needed was another

---

[86]Wilcomb E. Washburn, *The Indian in America*, pp. 165–96; Berkhofer, *The White Man's Indian*, pp. 153–66. There are several studies that explore either all or part of this period of Indian-white relations. Some are: Wilcomb E. Washburn, *Red Man's Land—White Man's Law: A Study of the Past and Present Status of the American Indian*; William T. Hagan, *American Indians*; Loring Benson Priest, *Uncle Sam's Stepchildren: The Reformation of United States Indian Policy, 1865–1887*; Edmund J. Danziger, *Indians and Bureaucrats: Administering the Reservation Policy During the Civil War*; Satz, *American Indian Policy*.

survey of Indian conditions similar to the one produced by Lewis Cass and William Clark in 1828–29.[87]

Schoolcraft's *Notes on the Iroquois* suggested a model for such a national study. It met with favorable reviews, and one review in particular called for a similar study to be carried out at the national level under the auspices of the federal government.[88] Whether this influenced Congress is difficult to say. More probable was Schoolcraft's persistent lobbying. Armed with his favorable reviews and with recommendations for such a work from the American Ethnological Society and the New-York Historical Society, Schoolcraft enlisted the aid of Senators John Calhoun and Thomas Hart Benton, Congressman Lucius Lyon, Secretary of State James Buchanan, and Commissioner of Indian Affairs William Medill. Evidently Schoolcraft was successful in promoting both his plan and himself, for when Congress subsequently passed an appropriation "to collect and digest such statistics and materials as may illustrate the history, the present condition, and the future prospects of the Indian Tribes of the United States," Schoolcraft was appointed to perform the task.[89]

Schoolcraft's private views of the project were similar to those of Congress. In a letter to a friend he confided, "The real problem of what is to become of the Race, in the United States, & what policy is best to advance their welfare, lies at the bottom of the inquiry; and furnished the principal reason, why Congress has authorized it." But he also justified the work in a way more in accord with his reli-

[87] Prucha, *American Indian Policy*, pp. 250–52. For an earlier attempt by Cass to reform government Indian affairs, see Francis Paul Prucha and Donald F. Carmony, eds., "A Memorandum of Lewis Cass: Concerning a System for the Regulation of Indian Affairs," *Wisconsin Magazine of History* 52 (Autumn, 1968): 35–50.

[88] "Administration of Indian Affairs," in *Democratic Review* 18 (May, 1846): pp. 333–36.

[89] Henry R. Schoolcraft, *Historical and Statistical Information Respecting the History, Condition, and Prospects of the Indian Tribes of the United States*, 1: v. Hereafter cited as *History*. For Schoolcraft's lobbying efforts, see Henry R. Schoolcraft to John R. Bartlett, June 23, 1846, Bartlett Papers, JCBL; Schoolcraft to Lucius Lyon, January 23, 1844, Lyon Papers, WCL; Freeman, "Schoolcraft," pp. 251–55.

gious feelings, a way which placed him in direct opposition to polygenists.

> Too long our Indian tribes have been in the hands of casual & hasty remarkers, who, struck with the interest of the subject, have done little but excite a popular taste, without, however, gratifying it. The purposes of generalization require, that they should be exhibited as one of the marked varieties of the race of man. That all we know of their history, traditions, languages, physical & mental type, etc. or can exogitate about them, should be brought to bear on this question.[90]

Although both government policy and religious considerations were combined in Schoolcraft's monumental six-volume work, the religious, antipolygenistic perspective proved paramount. His commitment to monogenism, although it had preceded his conversion to fundamental Protestantism in 1831, grew even stronger after his religious experience. He had only disgust for those who expressed a belief in polygenism.[91] Schoolcraft's repugnance became even more pronounced when theoretical differences were further exacerbated by his personality conflicts with such leading polygenists as E. G. Squier, J. C. Nott, and George Gliddon.[92] By the 1850s proponents of polygenism seemed confident that their theories would soon prevail over the entrenched forces of monogenism. Schoolcraft, staggered by the realization that some of his friends in the American Ethnological Society were flirting with the theory, recognized the alarming seriousness of the polygenist challenge.[93] He believed it his duty to rally science in defense of monogenism.

[90] Henry R. Schoolcraft to Francis Lieber, March 10, 1857, copy, Schoolcraft Papers, LC.

[91] Henry R. Schoolcraft to _____, March 14, 1851, copy, Schoolcraft Papers, LC; Freeman, "Religion and Personality," pp. 301–13.

[92] E. George Squier to Henry R. Schoolcraft, Jan. 2, 1858; W. De Haas to Henry R. Schoolcraft, Feb. 26, 1858; Henry R. Schoolcraft to E. H. Davis, April 8, 1858, copy, Schoolcraft Papers, LC; George Gliddon to E. George Squier, Sept. 21, 1847; April 16, 1851, Squier Papers, LC.

[93] Bieder and Tax, "Ethnologists to Anthropologists" in Murra, *American Anthropology*, pp. 16–18; Reginald Horsman, "Scientific Racism and the American Indian in the Mid-Nineteenth Century," *American Quarterly*

Schoolcraft's six-volume *Historical and Statistical Information Respecting the History, Condition, and Prospects of
the Indian Tribes of the United States,*[94] a massive compila-
tion of ethnographic and historical data, became his disor-
ganized and elephantine defense of monogenism. He labored on it from 1847 to 1857. Perhaps Schoolcraft believed
that the mere massing of data and its prestigious reputation as a national work supported by the government would
suffice to silence the polygenists. Whatever Schoolcraft
thought along these lines, his *History* confronted ethnological challenges that threatened to cast doubts on the salvation and civilization of the Indian. Although the *History*
contains extensive accounts of contacts between Indians
and Euro-Americans, most data included supported Schoolcraft's monogenetic perspective: his contention that Indians
originated elsewhere than in the Americas.

For example, Schoolcraft requested an article from Samuel G. Morton, principal theorist for polygenism, and another from monogenist Samuel Forrey, a medical doctor
and former editor of the *American Journal of Medicine.*
Morton's article "Physical Characteristics of the Indian" was

---

27 (May, 1975): 152–68. Horsman, I think, overstresses the polygenism case
a bit in that he sees it as the accepted paradigm in ethnology at midcentury.
This is not supported by my data although I agree it was a serious threat. See
also Horsman, *Race and Manifest Destiny.* For other treatments of the influence of polygenism at midcentury, see "From Chronology to Ethnology: J. C.
Prichard and British Anthropology, 1800–1850," in James Cowles Prichard,
Researches into the Physical History of Man, pp. xlix–lxi; William B. Cohen,
The French Encounter with Africans: White Response to Blacks, 1530–1880,
pp. 210–62; Léon Poliakov, *The Aryan Myth: A History of Racist and Na-
tionalist Ideas in Europe,* pp. 175–82; Thomas F. Gossett, *Race: The History
of an Idea in America,* pp. 54–83.
[94] Schoolcraft, *History.* Schoolcraft's *History* received mixed responses.
See Henry R. Schoolcraft to _____, March 31, 1851, Schoolcraft Papers,
LC; Henry R. Schoolcraft to R. W. Griswold, July 27, 1853, Griswold Papers,
BPL; E. Everett to Francis Bowen, April 6, 1852, Everett Papers, MHS;
Henry R. Schoolcraft to George Bancroft, July 27, 1853, Bancroft Papers,
MHS; George Gliddon to E. George Squier, April 16, 1851, Squier Papers,
LC; [Francis Bowen] Review of *Historical and Statistical Information re-
specting the History, Condition, and Prospects of the Indian Tribes of the
United States . . .* in *The North American Review* 77 (July, 1853): 243–62;
Freeman, "Schoolcraft," p. 278.

really a very mild rendition of the polygenetic argument.[95] In it he made implicit references to the autochthonous nature of the American Indian and couched his polygenetic conclusions in terms of the primordial fixity of physical varieties. He asserted that he could discern no direct or obvious links between the Americas and the rest of the world. In general the tone bespoke a diluted and ambiguous polygenism.[96]

In contrast, Forrey's article, "Considerations on the Distinctive Characteristics of American Aboriginal Tribes," rejected the primordial-fixity argument and emphasized the "accidental" or "congenital" variations in the skulls of different races of man. Forrey held that such "variations" tended to be perpetuated in offspring. If physiognomy and skin color followed the same pattern, if they were the results of accidental variation that bred true in offspring, then that might explain how races originated. Forrey believed that the shape of the skull was linked to the development of the brain, but he also pointed out that "the classification of skulls under five general heads [races] . . . is . . . entirely arbitrary, and as in every other corporeal diversity, so we find in regard to crania an imperceptible gradation among the nations of the earth, filling up the interval between the two extremes of the most perfect caucasian model and the most exaggerated Negro specimen."[97]

Along with physical anthropology, Schoolcraft utilized data from Indian religion, language, and mythology to further confirm the theory that Indians were the descendants of Shem and therefore could be fitted into the Mosaic account of man and share in the first creation. Schoolcraft cautioned that data on Indian diffusion out of Asia could be pushed only so far. It could not be made to yield the exact

[95]Schoolcraft, *History*, 2: 315–35; Morton really wanted to write on the Flathead tribe instead of on the physical characteristics of Indians, see Samuel G. Morton to Henry R. Schoolcraft, March 11, 1851, Schoolcraft Papers, LC.

[96]See P. Browne in Schoolcraft, *History*, 3: 375–93, and Henry R. Schoolcraft, "Prefatory Notes on the Unity of the Human Race," *History*, 3: 373–75.

[97]Schoolcraft, *History*, 4: 359–69.

people or tribe from which the Indians were descended, but in the absence of historical proof "the mere conjecture that these tribes are off-shoots of the Shemitic race of Asia, is important and becomes deeply interesting when it appears probable, as many of learning and genius have asserted, that their history, fate, and fortunes, can be connected with that of the Hebrew race."[98]

Both language and mythology were held up as the best examples of Indian mentality and expressions of the Oriental turn of mind. Despite Gallatin's views to the contrary, Schoolcraft found "striking principles of agreement" between grammatical structures of Indian languages and the Hebrew language. Grammar expressed the ideation of a people and carried with it the arts and ideas of a race. "Races who thought in a particular manner, or whose thoughts succeeded each other in a certain fixed train, spoke grammatically alike." In a pamphlet designed for travelers going into Indian country, written probably in the late 1840s, Schoolcraft pointed out that "no people take up, or lay down languages at will. It descends with the blood and is altered only by a process of mutation which is slow, that is wholly imperceptible at the time."[99] A knowledge of grammatical patterns, Schoolcraft asserted, was far more important in tracing Indian origins than a reliance on vocabulary. Because Indians tended to wander, they were constantly breaking off from larger groups. Over time, pronunciation of words changed and gave rise to new vocabularies. But although vocabulary changed, the way Indians thought did not.

Much in their present condition, tribal division, & manner & customs, result doubtless, from geographical phenomena. But the *mind* of the Indian—its dogmas & theories, is of a com-

[98] Schoolcraft, *History*, 5: 87, 15, 44.
[99] Henry R. Schoolcraft, *Suggestions for Travellers Visiting the Ancient Sites of Indian Occupancy in America*, p. 5. Although there is no date for this publication, its probable publication was in 1848 or 1849; see Henry R. Schoolcraft to John R. Bartlett, April 30, 1849, Bartlett Papers, JCBL, in which Schoolcraft writes that he encloses this list of words and suggestions for travellers and regrets that G. Gibbs left for Oregon without them.

paratively enduring type. The species of proof of ancient & general affiliation, which is furnished by language—by which I mean, not only the vocabulary, but the plan of thought, & method of utterance, and grammatical synthesis, is one of the most profound & important, which is connected with the subject.[100]

Likewise, examination of myths taken from a wide area revealed that "the thoughts & theories of the tribes and their plan of utterances can be traced & identified, where the sounds of the words themselves are quite lost."[101]

Embedded in Indian mythology and religion, according to Schoolcraft, were vital clues to the Indians' past that complemented linguistic study. Although sorcery, magic, and demonology among Indians presented Schoolcraft with examples of the "darkest and gloomiest picture of Indian life," he recognized that they provided scientists with insights into the Indians' past.[102] Schoolcraft discovered remnants of Persian thinking in the Indians' beliefs in gods and the powers of good and evil. In their veneration for ancestors he found survivals of Shemitic beliefs.[103] Their tales expressed more than just the Indians' hopes, beliefs, and fears; they were in a sense psychological artifacts, peopled with dwarfs, fairies, vampires, and ghosts, which constituted evidence of Asian beliefs and origins.[104]

[100] Henry R. Schoolcraft to Francis Lieber, March [?], 1857, copy, Schoolcraft Papers, LC.

[101] Schoolcraft, *History*, 1: 37; Henry R. Schoolcraft to H. Greely, Jan. 26, 1856, Schoolcraft Papers, LC.

[102] Schoolcraft, *History*, 5: 415.

[103] Ibid., pp. 406–407.

[104] Ibid., pp. 86–87, 411. Schoolcraft's obsession to establish an Asian origin for the Indians and his use of languages and legends to do so met increasing resistance. "Mr. Schoolcraft's discourse as regards the Asiatic origin of our Indians, is worth nothing to science. Indeed it does injury to science—all *facts* are against the philologie argument, and all *physical* comparisons are against the supposition of Asiatic origin." W. B. Hodgin to John R. Bartlett, Dec. 2, 1846, Bartlett Papers, JCBL. His emphasis. Even the monogenist Albert Gallatin seemed to be wary of some of Schoolcraft's reasoning and research in the area of languages and legend analysis. In attempting to find someone in Washington to gather vocabularies of visiting Indian groups, Gallatin wrote, "I have conclusive reasons for not selecting Mr. Schoolcraft for that purpose, though I may occasionally apply to him on some special

To see, as Squier did with the serpent, such thinking as an accidental similarity, independent of and parallel to the thinking of other peoples and merely indicative of mental processes at a particular stage of development, was a view Schoolcraft rejected. To him the similarities represented deeper racial patterns of thinking, inherited patterns not so much barbarian as Oriental and as such marvelous, grotesque, and unchanging. All these elements found in North American Indian mythology, Schoolcraft believed, could also be discovered in the Indian stories of Mexico and Peru.[105]

But this very fixation of mental processes that was so helpful in pointing out Indian origins to ethnologists also served to confirm Schoolcraft's growing suspicion that the Indian could not change in time. Since his religious experience in Michigan, Schoolcraft believed that the only path for the Indian to civilization was through the acceptance of Christianity. This acceptance was basically a spiritual process, "a change of heart, whereby they are brought to see their true relation to God & to their fellow creatures," and

---

points." Albert Gallatin to W. H. Emory, Oct. 20, 1847, copy, Gallatin Papers, NYHS. This remark is clarified in a letter of Schoolcraft's. "I regret to hear of Mr. Gallatin's illness, & trust he will be spared to see his last paper in print. I certainly cherish nothing but kind feelings towards him, although I have been made [?] to feel, that he has not appreciated my study of the Indian languages & antiquities. His *etymologies*, are always acute, and if he wholly underrates the Indian *mythology*, as shown by his examination of Kingsborough, his historical deductions, so far as they are *original*, are far superior to any man who has written." Henry R. Schoolcraft to John R. Bartlett, Aug. 14, 1848, Bartlett Papers, JCBL. His emphasis.

[105] Schoolcraft received further proof of his theories from one of his correspondents: "From the impressions received by me during a 5½ years' tour of duty in California, I would say that the character of the California Indians as it was before the arrival of priests among them was in no material degree different from that you give for the Indians of this valley [Mississippi]—Similar religious ceremonies—the same medicine men (the worst in the nation; the most treacherous . . .) The same dislike to tell their names—The same way of saying 'yes' to confirm a negative question—the same thoughtlessness with reference to the morrow—the same way of representing the wrath of evil spirits when one of them falls sick & similar ceremony . . . to introduce childhood to puberty—the same sweating operation for sickness." L. J. Hamilton to Henry R. Schoolcraft, Jan. 2, 1853, Schoolcraft Papers, LC.

it entailed a whole reorientation of their "moral and mental character."[106] The acceptance of Christianity required a receptive mind. Yet as Schoolcraft winnowed through his data, he slowly perceived that throughout the Americas all Indians possessed "the same indestructibility of type, the same non-progressiveness of the Indian oriental mind." It was the same nonanalytic mind that had retained the Shemitic grammars and the Asian mythology. It was a mind bound to intellectual stagnation reproducing "the same ideas in 1850 as in 1492." It was the same mind that could not change and accept Christianity and Western civilization, at least in time to prevent extinction. In Schoolcraft's opinion, as a race Indians continued in their errors as if "bound by iron fetters." Enslaved by their Oriental religion they were paralyzed in mystery, suspicion, and fear. The Indian was not a "man of anticipation"; indeed, his mind seemed always oriented toward the past. He rejected the civilization that increasingly surrounded him, and, while not really comprehending what it meant for him, he responded with stoic disdain. He did not, he could not, think like white men. Propelled by the habits of his mind, he was not progressive or inductive. Intellectually, the Indian's Oriental mind remained "incompetent" to judge the great moral truths of Christianity and civilization.[107]

At the end of his life, ill and morose, Schoolcraft absolved the white man of the Indians' demise. He felt that both government and religious organizations should continue to help the Indian, but that the Indian must be made to realize that it was not the white race but the Indian himself, with his Oriental mind and his past, who was the enemy of his own progress.

Schoolcraft's ethnology, shaped by religion, led him from philology to mythology to the collecting of facts. He was no theoretician. He saw himself as a fact collector and ethnology as the study of the Indians' past. His emphasis on

[106] Henry R. Schoolcraft to W. J. Boutwell, Feb. 14, 1832, Schoolcraft Papers, LC; Schoolcraft, *Personal Memoirs*, p. 448.

[107] Schoolcraft, *History*, 5: 32; 4: 257; 3: 22–24, 418–19, 471.

gathering bits and pieces of custom, language, legend, and artifact grew out of a cataloging mentality that envisioned a grand mosaic of history once all the pieces were supplied. The mosaic would depict the Indian diaspora out of Asia and their settlement of the Americas.

In his focus on Indian legends, Schoolcraft not only stressed the psychological over the physical but also elevated the Indian to a thinking man. To Schoolcraft, however, the Indian mind functioned differently from the white man's. Betraying its origins in a Shemitic past, the Indian mind was controlled by different sets of assumptions that over time evinced a racial caste. But it was still an Oriental mind only slightly modified by a wild and wandering life in the Americas. Whether or not the Indian could alter these sets of assumptions Schoolcraft could not say. He only knew that the Indian was part of the original Adamic creation, that he had come out of Asia, and that he did not have much time left to change.

6

Lewis Henry Morgan
and the Evolution of
an Iroquois Scholar

MANY ANTHROPOLOGISTS consider Lewis Henry Morgan
(1818–1881) the father of American anthropology and the
work of ethnologists who preceded him as prologue to his
systematic theorizing. Compared with eighteenth-century
theorists on man, Morgan's theory of social evolution seems
at once more sharply etched and more elegant than those
that came before. Viewed apart from his nineteenth-century
environment, with its wrangling disputes over ethnology,
and compared only with eighteenth-century theorists, Morgan seems revolutionary. His tremendous accomplishments
were recognizing the significance of kinship structures and
providing an evolutionary paradigm for late nineteenth-
century ethnology. It is important, however, to see these
contributions within the context of the monogenism-
polygenism controversy in which Morgan played a partisan
role. Similarly, Morgan's suggestions for an Indian policy
cannot be isolated from their day, a time when the Indian's
future, according to contemporary conceptions of society
and civilization, appeared bleak.

Like many of his contemporaries, Morgan took part in
the controversy between the polygenists and the monogenists. His efforts to trace Indian origins to Asia were made to
resolve this debate. Morgan also believed in a teleological
progress for man, and although he did not claim to see
God's guiding hand in history as strongly as did some ethnologists, such an assumption underscored his reasoning.
Indeed, given the thinking of the time on religion and science, it would be remarkable if Morgan did not hold such a
view. Unlike some others, however, he did not use science
to prove religion or religion to prove science; rather, he

offered reasoned arguments with the conviction that they did not contravene the teaching of Christianity.

Morgan began his ethnological career in the late 1840s and 1850s when the proponents of an invigorated polygenism competed strenuously with advocates of monogenism. To demolish the bulwarks of monogenism erected by Gallatin, Schoolcraft, and others seemed to the polygenists of the mid-1850s a goal within easy reach. The belief that Indians were a degenerative people who had fallen or declined from a higher level of civilization also enjoyed a swell of support. Although the Indians might be capable of progress, many believed that the preponderance of evidence—their disintegrating cultures and demographic decline—supported the opposite view. Polygenists also acknowledged this evidence and saw in it inescapable proof that the Indians could not evade the facts of their biology. Considered in this context, Morgan's support of monogenism and progress placed him squarely within the older, traditional ethnology of Albert Gallatin and the Enlightenment. Morgan wrote at a time when the restricted time frame that confined geological and biological thinking was breaking down and new theories in these fields were suggesting a longer history for man than had been before envisioned. Morgan welcomed such theories and utilized them to present his own theories on man and man's rise to civilization.

This is not to imply that Morgan's theories were derivative. Morgan was a fine thinker who provided ethnology with a theoretical model at a time when ethnologists had exhausted the tradition of gathering artifacts and noting customs without a comparative model that would allow them to draw conclusions and eventually advance knowledge. But in spite of this contribution and his later ethnological housecleaning—a task which he took on with vigor and self-righteousness—Morgan could not entirely free himself from earlier ethnological and biological assumptions and from earlier views of the Indians. In fact, Morgan lent a certain scientific respectability to earlier ethnological stereotypes of the Indian.

Born in 1818 into a well-to-do farm family near the village of Aurora in western New York, Lewis Henry Morgan
watched the sweeping events that spelled profound changes
for the state. The Erie Canal opening in 1825 seemed to
quicken the restless spirit of Yankee-Yorkers, and Morgan
watched as settlers, including two of his brothers, dissolved
family ties and headed west in search of new beginnings.
Winds of change blew over the land that only fifty years
before had supported the Iroquois. Progress and greed
seemed to coincide, as men came forth to subdue the land,
build new towns, and speculate in business. Morgan re-
joiced in farming and town building; they were communal
events in which neighbors depended on each other and
shared tasks, problems, and good times. Business speculation, especially in the larger towns, operated on different
laws, however, and Morgan grew to detest the "reserve,
distant, and pernicious" style of life that characterized such
existence. He called these businessmen the "seven per
cent gentry," and he considered them "arrogant, illiberal
and narrow minded." As a petty aristocracy they thwarted
the expression of natural laws, thwarted the economic and
social aspirations of other men, and circumscribed man's
liberty.[1]

Belief in liberty as the expression of natural law seemed
to Morgan the quintessence of the American experience.
Here neither kings nor church nor aristocracy ruled. Here
the masses were free to construct their own destiny. Morgan's study of ancient Greece, while a student in the Aurora
Academy and later at Union College, enabled him to draw
certain parallels. "We dwell with pleasure on the institutions of the Greeks," he told an audience in Aurora, "because they first proclaimed the great principles of liberty,
and sovereignty of the people."[2]

Morgan's years at Union College seemed to reinforce the
values and ideals learned in his youth in Aurora. To his con-

---

[1] Lewis H. Morgan, November 1, 1845, Manuscript Journal 1, Morgan Papers, as quoted in Carl Resek, *Lewis Henry Morgan: American Scholar*, p. 22.

[2] Lewis Henry Morgan, "Essay on the History and Genius of the Grecian
Race, Delivered before Students of Aurora Academy," November 8, 1841,
Morgan Papers, as quoted in Resek, p. 15.

Lewis Henry Morgan as a young man. Courtesy University of Rochester Library.

tinued study of ancient history he added mechanical science, mathematics, political economy, Greek, Latin, and Italian. He attended lectures given by Eliphalet Nott, a Presbyterian minister and president of Union College, who was the reigning intellectual of the institution. Nott's lectures emphasized the value of knowledge, common sense, and empiricism. According to Nott, knowledge set man apart from the animal world and made him ruler over the earth; it lifted man and propelled him forward. But this was not the knowledge of the dilettante. Less impressed with what could be learned from books than were others on his faculty, Nott pointed to the world of nature as the foremost educator of man and the greatest reservoir of useful knowledge. To Nott a practical education was far more useful than an ornamental one, and certainly one more needed by the men who would run the new nation.

Nott strove also to instill in his students an appreciation for life experience as education and an awareness for the iron laws that controlled society and progress. These laws were not to be regretted; rather, they were supremely beneficial to human beings when they recognized them and bound themselves to obey them. With François Guizot's *History of Civilization in Europe* as his text, Nott proclaimed progress and civilization to be inseparable and produced by commerce and the initiative of the middle class.

Such advice duly impressed the youthful Morgan, and in a later paper on geology he freely quoted Nott on education.[3] When Morgan studied the history of the ancient world he sought evidence of these great social laws and discovered that they were best manifested in a people's institutions, laws, religion, and government. "There is a progressive principle inherent in all civil institutions, which commencing with the monarchical, the earliest in the order of origination, as well as the simplest in form, leads onto the democratical, which constitutes their ultimate as well as most complex development."[4] In delineating this great path of progress, wars and the exploits of great men, although of interest, were not vital to an understanding of history. "To rear such an empire of Greek over Greek, re-

[3] Lewis H. Morgan, "Essay on Geology," Ms. 1841, Morgan Papers, UR.
[4] [Lewis H. Morgan] "Athenian Democracy," *The New-York Quarterly* 2 (1853): 341.

quired the rarest combination of talents; but above all, it indicated the existence of institutions eminently calculated to arouse and concentrate the national energies."[5] The origin and development of these institutions and their influence on mankind's rise to civilization, so significant in Morgan's later anthropological works, in 1853 provided him a stage on which to compare Greek and American institutions and stress the higher virtue of the latter. As a caution, however, he reminded his readers that the history of Athens was the history of the rise and eventual destruction of democratic institutions, the latter brought about through the leisure and opulence of its citizens.[6]

If famous men and sweeping events meant little to Morgan the historian, they did affect Morgan the romantic. From youth he had heard of the grand exploits of the Iroquois and of their famous men, Red Jacket and Joseph Brant. And in the woods near Aurora the young Morgan imagined "the day when the forest cast its shadow over the lake and the Indian with his bow and arrow pursued his game to the water's edge and along its winding banks; when that stillness of the wood unknown to us was unbroken even by the Indian hunter, save now and then by the twang of the bow string, the whizzing of an arrow, or the whoop indicating victory in the chase."[7] When the Gordian Knot, a secret society that he had founded based on classical Greece, gave way to the Grand Order of the Iroquois, Morgan sought to return to the splendor of Iroquois life, if only for an evening once a week in the abandoned Freemason lodge in Aurora.

Years later Morgan referred to this society as merely a frivolous social club. Indeed there was much about it that merited that description. Morgan's recording of the events of an initiation ceremony reveal a definite romantic strain.

[5] Ibid., p. 344.

[6] Ibid., pp. 361–62; Resek, pp. 10–11. See also Rush Welter, "The Idea of Progress in America," *Journal of the History of Ideas* 14 (1955): 401–15; Russel Blaine Nye, *Society and Culture in America, 1830–1860*, pp. 24–31; and the still useful John Bury, *The Idea of Progress*.

[7] Lewis H. Morgan to G. S. Riley, Dec. 12, 1845, Morgan Papers, UR.

The evening was one of universal splendor and beauty and the brave Cayugas had assembled upon a fiery [sic] spot surrounded on all sides by majestic forest for the initiation of Ossahinta. Being led to the ground the warriors marched twice around him with a heavy and solemn tred. Then having kneeled, his hands were laid upon the horns of the altar. . . . All things went smoothly on through the initiation until the administration of the oath. He not understanding the demand of the oath at first declined which caused the faces of the warriors to show some symptoms of alarm and in a moment a number of tomahawks glistened in the pale moonbeams' misty light and the twang of bow strings showed the critical situation of the hesitating warrior.[8]

For those ambitious young men from the small villages of western New York, who still were close to the revelry of college and academic life, the Grand Order of the Iroquois proved a convenient outlet for their bon vivant friendship with others of their kind.

But the order had a serious side equally attractive to Morgan and to some of his friends. In a letter to Lewis Cass making him an honorary member of the Grand Order, Morgan wrote, "We have established in New York an Indian Historical Institution. . . . Our objects are and have been not only to gather up the antiquaries of our state but to rouse a kinder feeling towards the Red Man founded upon a truer knowledge of the nature and necessities of his character."[9] Not all in the order proved capable of such a task, but there were some who, along with Morgan, exchanged their tomahawks for pens and recorded their impressions of Iroquois culture of the 1840s, impressions often written with ethnological insight and sympathy. Combing the books on Iroquois life did not long satisfy those members, and so they set off for the reservations—Tonawanda, Onondaga, and Tuscarora—to learn for themselves.[10]

[8] Lewis H. Morgan, "Grand Order of the Iroquois, Seneca Nation, Turtle Tribe, Special form of initiation, 1845," Mss. of articles, Morgan Papers, UR.

[9] Lewis H. Morgan to Lewis Cass, Dec. 30, 1845, Cass Papers, WCL.

[10] Isaac B. Hurd, "A Sketch Embracing the Doings at the Grand Council of the Iroquois held Oct., 1845," Mss. of articles; Lewis H. Morgan, Mss. Journal of Tonawanda, Oct., 1845, Morgan Papers, UR.

Morgan's desire to pattern the order on the political structure of the real Iroquois League led him to focus his investigations on the political institutions of the Iroquois. This was more than mere accident. His whole orientation toward history was rooted in the study of social institutions and in the natural laws that brought them about. As Morgan instructed his warriors in council, "We study other and ancient races as much through their institutions and governments as in their political transactions. How then shall a just estimate of the Iroquois be formed if we confine ourselves to their exploits upon the warpath and in council."[11]

From his study of the classical societies of Greece and Rome, Morgan firmly believed that their history could only be delineated from a thorough knowledge of their institutions, since the natural laws of society were best expressed through these institutions. He scorned works on the Iroquois that merely depicted the lives of war chiefs or focused only on battles. He considered these works superficial and distortions of the real nature and history of the Iroquois. As a people they were still hidden from history; their customs and institutions were still only matters of speculation. Without a knowledge of these customs and domestic and political institutions, mankind would never know the genius and character of the Iroquois.

At the Grand Order's 1845 General Council Fire of the Confederacy, Morgan spoke to his warriors of this need. All investigations needed structure, he stated, and Morgan, the young lawyer, would not hesitate to provide one. The collections of Iroquois data would be confined to five broad categories: government, people, laws, religious systems, and historical events. Because Morgan believed Iroquois history fairly obvious he did not expound upon it, but he elaborated on the others. Under government, Iroquois alliances and councils were to be examined, as were their modes of doing business and carrying out decrees. Under people, the study would involve the examination of Iro-

[11] Skenandoah [Lewis H. Morgan], "To the General Council Fire of the Confederacy At the Falls of the Genesee, 11 Gya-ong-wa [Oct.] 1845," Morgan Papers, DHS.

quois "social condition, manners and customs," as well
as their subsistence patterns, arts, games, dress, and inventions. Under laws, Morgan revealed most pointedly his
own legal background and foreshadowed his own future
ethnological concerns. Here "inquiry would necessarily
be intricate," he cautioned. As with Americans, "law was
more than usage and custom, more than a rule of action
which must be obeyed, or its violation punished. We can
however, seek their laws in relations to marriage and descent. The right of property, of personal security. The pun-
ishment of crimes. The laws of the chase. In relation to cap-
tives and to hospitality." Under religion, Morgan was less
specific. He mentioned only the study of Iroquois beliefs in
the Great Spirit, religious ceremonies, origins of evil, and
burial rites.[12]

Morgan shared in the intense search for information on
Iroquois culture that marked the activities of several of
the order's members. When his law practice permitted,
Morgan, like other members of the order, attended the ceremonies and dances at the different Iroquois reservations in
western New York State. There he listened to the speakers
who preceded the ceremonies, took notes on the dances,
interviewed the Seneca elders, collected Seneca costumes
and artifacts, and strengthened his friendship with Ely S.
Parker, a Seneca Indian whom Morgan had met in an Albany bookstore.[13] Parker, who would later become the first
Indian commissioner of Indian affairs, proved more than
just a friend to Morgan; he was a resource, who, along with
the whole Parker family, but especially Caroline and Nicholson, enlightened Morgan on Seneca customs and language.
When Morgan's pressing law practice kept him away from
ceremonies at the Tonawanda Reservation, he delegated

[12] Ibid.
[13] Morgan met Ely S. Parker in Albany where Parker was accompanying
several chiefs from Tonawanda on a visit to the governor in 1844. Parker
served as their interpreter. See Resek, p. 27; William Armstrong, *Warrior
in Two Camps: Ely S. Parker Union General and Seneca Chief*, pp. 1–3;
William N. Fenton, "Introduction," in Lewis Henry Morgan, *League of the
Iroquois*, p. x.

Ely S. Parker in 1864 when he became Grant's military secretary. From the *Life of Ely S. Parker* by Arthur C. Parker.

Caroline Parker in Seneca dress. Along with her brothers Ely and
Nicholson, Caroline provided Lewis Henry Morgan with eth-
nographic material on the Senecas. A picture of Caroline in this
Seneca dress appeared in *League of the Ho-de-no-sau-nee*, or *Iro-
quois* by Lewis Henry Morgan. Courtesy, University of Rochester
Library.

Ely Parker to record events and speeches, impressing upon him the need for exactitude.[14]

As time permitted, Morgan transposed his notes into talks and articles. For example, he incorporated his talk in 1846 before the New-York Historical Society, where Albert Gallatin presided, into his "Letters on the Iroquois Addressed to Albert Gallatin," which he published in 1847 in the *American Whig Review*. "Letters" was in sharp contrast to an article Morgan had published in 1844 in *The Knickerbocker*, titled "Vision of Karistagia, a Sachem of the Cayuga." Here Morgan had dwelled on the tragedy European civilization held for the Iroquois. In "Vision," Morgan saw civilization as a bright star rising in the East and Iroquois culture as a dim star fading in the West. But in "Letters," Morgan chose to focus on Iroquois customs and the way Iroquois once lived. The essays that comprised the "Letters" series were later brought together and expanded by Morgan and published in 1851 as the *League of the Ho-de-no-sau-nee, or Iroquois*.[15]

When Morgan began his study of the Iroquois, there were no systematic descriptions of a tribal culture. Most ethnological accounts surveyed Indians in general from the perspective of philology, religion, or physical traits. They were, in a sense, macrostudies oriented to illustrate such topics through examples drawn from many tribes. Even Schoolcraft, who compiled his data primarily from the Chippewas, considered himself a historian of all Indians. He universalized Chippewa data to illustrate Indian psychology, values, and history.

[14]Confidence in Ely S. Parker and the whole Parker family is seen in Morgan's utilization of the Parkers to check and recheck material that he collected on his field trips. See Lewis H. Morgan to Ely S. Parker, Dec. 14, 1848; Morgan to Parker, Aug. 2, 1850; Morgan to Parker, Oct. 30, ?; Lewis H. Morgan to Newton Parker, Dec. 19, 1849; Lewis H. Morgan to Caroline Parker, Feb. 28, 1847, Parker Papers, APS.

[15]Aquarius [Lewis H. Morgan], "Vision of Kar-is-ta-gi-a, a Sachem of the Cayuga," *The Knickerbocker* 24 (1844): 238–45; "Letters on the Iroquois Addressed to Albert Gallatin," *American Whig Review* 5 (1847): pp. 177–90, 242–57, 447–61; 6 (1848): 477–90, 626–33; Fenton, "Introduction," in Morgan, *League of the Iroquois*, p. xii.

This does not mean that individual accounts of tribes were nonexistent. William Prescott had published studies of the Aztecs and the Incas, but his focus was primarily on the drama of the Spanish conquest of these tribes. Less popular than Prescott's were the volumes on Iroquois leaders by William Stone. The two volumes on Joseph Brant, the Mohawk "war chief," and the volume on the famed Seneca orator Red Jacket were, according to Stone, part of a contemplated "complete history of the great Iroquois Confederacy." Through biography Stone hoped to preserve the history of the Iroquois people, but his biographies of Brant and Red Jacket did little to illustrate Iroquois culture.[16]

The works of early French explorers and Cadwallader Colden's *History of the Five Nations of Canada* were useful to Morgan as sources on Iroquois history, but they were not entirely satisfactory. Like Prescott's works, they were more concerned with the history of Indian people in their contact with Europeans or Americans than in Indian culture per se. Although James Adair's *History of the Indians* did not deal with the Iroquois, it proved objectionable to Morgan because it focused more on a theory of Indian origin than on Indians themselves.[17]

It was difficult in the nineteenth century to conceive of Indian history in terms other than the history of Indian-white relations. History depended upon written documents, and, since Indians did not write, they could provide little that could be considered valid history. They were regarded as primitive peoples who lived outside history. This had exasperated Schoolcraft, who lamented that Indians had no history because they had no historians; they had no

---

[16] William L. Stone, *The Life and Times of Red Jacket, or Sa-Go-Ye-Wat-Ha; Being the Sequel to the History of the Six Nations; Life of Joseph Brant-Thayendanegea . . . .* Morgan found Stone's works quite useless for revealing any information on the political structure or on the institutions of the Iroquois. See Resek, pp. 24–25.

[17] John Adair, *The History of the American Indians . . .*; see Charles Hudson, "James Adair As Anthropologist," *Ethnohistory* 24 (Fall, 1977): 311–28, for a favorable appraisal of the ethnological importance of Adair's work.

records that could throw light upon their past before European contact. Schoolcraft considered their legends too fabulous and their picture writing insufficient for constructing real histories. Although Schoolcraft recorded Iroquois customs, legends, religious beliefs, and history in his *Notes on the Iroquois* (1847),[18] the real purpose of his work was to enumerate New York State's Indian population and to assess advances in agriculture and manufacturing. Aspects of Iroquois culture were accented, but, in general, *Notes* was predominantly the history of Iroquois-white relations.

Although Morgan drew upon the works of French writer Charlevoix and the descriptions of the De Nonville expedition, he did not utilize nor seem to know about the eighteenth-century description of Huron-Iroquois culture by the French Jesuit priest Joseph François Lafitau or of the *Jesuit Relations*. Morgan was familiar with the speech of Cayuga chief Peter Wilson before the New-York Historical Society, but he failed to note the work of another Iroquois historian, David Cusick, a Tuscarora Indian. Despite his extensive search, Morgan was disappointed by the extant literature on the Iroquois, and he perceived a need for a more comprehensive account of Iroquois culture. He set about to fill this void by approaching the task through an analysis of Iroquois social institutions. To these ends Morgan and the members of the Grand Order of the Iroquois devoted their efforts.[19]

Morgan's attempt to discover the government organization of the Iroquois Confederacy for his own Grand Order

[18] Henry R. Schoolcraft, *Notes on the Iroquois.*

[19] Both Resek, p. 70 and William N. Fenton attest that Morgan did not know about Lafitau's work. For Fenton, see his "Introduction" in Joseph François Lafitau, *Customs of the American Indians Compared with the Customs of Primitive Times,* p. cvii. The work of David Cusick was his *Sketches of ancient history of the Six nations,* published in 1827. This work was also republished in 1848 by Turner and McCullum of Lockport, New York. Gallatin in "Synopsis" made observations on Indian social organization, including a brief mention of the concept of totem, but they were tucked in a chapter more as an aside than as a topic worthy of more extended discussion. See Albert Gallatin, "Synopsis of the Indian Tribes of North America," *Transactions of the American Antiquarian Society* 2 (1836): 109–14.

led him to do "field work."[20] Accompanying him to the Tonawanda and Onondaga reservations, and perhaps to the Six Nations reserve in Canada, were others of the Grand Order who also engaged in fieldwork and who amassed data on Iroquois kinship relations, dances, political organization, and funeral and religious customs. They, too, shared Morgan's concern that Iroquois culture was rapidly disintegrating and passing from the scene forever.

Some members of the Grand Order shared the views of many Americans, especially those of Schoolcraft, that although Indians were still "savages" they would in time embrace civilization. One member, Clinton Rogers, expressed it well when he spoke before the Grand Order, denying the validity of many current theories of Indian origins and, particularly, concepts of Indian character. He observed that Indians were not like white men; they possessed no "love of approbation." They sought neither fame nor material goods. Their craftiness in war resulted from the kinds of weapons they used and their Indian mentality. "Their peculiar frame of mind prohibits any enlarged sphere of action they can only reason from leaves and running brooks . . . they cannot discern the majuestual [sic] they cannot reason *philosophically.*" Yet Rogers was sanguine that their destiny would not be extinction, but that they would be convinced of the benefits of American civilization and elect to follow a new road.[21]

Another member, James S. Bush, agreed. He called for Indian citizenship along with its incumbent duty of paying

[20] As one of Morgan's biographers wryly put it, in taking issue with a Morgan disciple, "Morgan was not, . . . a 'born ethnologist,' as his friend and coworker, Adolph Bandelier, characterized him, but was made one by a secret society." Bernard J. Stern, *Lewis Henry Morgan, Social Evolutionist,* p. 16. The "secret society" was, of course, the Grand Order of the Iroquois. See Fenton, "Introduction," in Morgan, *League of the Iroquois,* p. ix; Resek, pp. 21–44; John Wesley Powell, "Sketch of Lewis Henry Morgan," *Popular Science Monthly* 18 (1880): 114; Frederick Ward Putnam, "Sketch of Hon. Lewis H. Morgan," *Proceedings of the American Academy of Arts and Sciences* 17 (May, 1882): 430.

[21] Clinton Rogers, "Paper read December 10, 1846," Mss. p. B684, Morgan Papers, UR.

taxes. These two factors alone would change their society and personality.

> A change in their political condition must of necessity react upon their social and moral nature, and divest them entirely of those peculiarities by which they are now distinguished. Under the elective franchise, the extermination of the Indian race, though rendered certain by 'the inevitable laws of population,' will be gradual and imperceptible; occasioned not by the degrading vices incident to a barbarous state, nor by the oppression and contaminating evils, which too often attend civilization, but by assimilating the inferior race to the superior, by merging the former into the latter, with a temporary benefit to one, and without injury to the other.[22]

These comments not only mirrored popular thinking on Indians in the 1840s but, in substance, found expression in the ethnological writings of the day.[23]

The papers of another member, Isaac Hurd, reveal the completely different tack he took in his investigations. An inquisitive researcher and sharp observer, Hurd would spend several days at a time engaged in fieldwork. Like Morgan, he was at Tonawanda Reservation in October 1845 to observe a condolence ceremony, so called to recognize the passing of several sachems and to raise up new sachems in the Iroquois confederacy. In 1846 he traveled to Onondaga reservation to witness a midwinter ceremony. The care Hurd expended in recording his observations and interviews led him to think about the pursuit of fieldwork. He observed to his fellow Grand Order members:

> In the investigation of the Political fabric and history of the Six Nations it behooves us to exercise great care and caution, in the manner of conducting our researches, and the means ap-

[22]James S. Bush, "Should the Elective Franchise Be Extended to Our Indian Population?" Mss. July 9, 1846, p. B642, Morgan Papers, UR.

[23]For similar sentiments, see Henry R. Schoolcraft, *Personal Memoirs of a Residence of Thirty Years with the Indian Tribes on the American Frontiers*, pp. 318–19. Both Robert Winston Mardock in *The Reformers and the American Indian* and Linda K. Kerber, "The Abolitionist Perception of the Indian," *Journal of American History* 62 (September, 1975): 271–95, touch on some of these reform measures as they relate to the Indian.

plied to ferret out and bring to light the peculiar and complicated machinery of their government. Those who are conversant with the history and laws of the old Confederacy, in
consequence of their limited knowledge of the English language, find it very difficult to express themselves clearly, or
comprehending accurately the questions propounded, have
for their object the elucidation of their Confederate organization—it is almost impossible for them to catch your design the
first time, and therefore it . . . is imposed upon the inquirer to
make his questions simple, yet comprehensive, brief, yet embracing all the important points necessary to be known. It will
not do to ask questions, and then answer them, as best suits
the fancy of the investigator, for in that case the facts which he
supposed he had luckily obtained, are not facts, but a specious
decoction of his own brain.[24]

The pioneering efforts in ethnology by members of the
Grand Order under Morgan's direction were truly remarkable, considering the youth and inexperience of the members. At a time when the American Ethnological Society
was beginning its slow decline, in the countryside of western New York groups of men were pursuing the study of
ethnology with a zeal the savants in New York City could
not match. The ceremonies of the Grand Order of the Iroquois provoked not only a certain enthusiasm for gathering
ethnological data, but also imbued the search with a rich-
ness and excitement that more professional organizations
could not hope to equal. The mission of the Grand Order
was marked not only with a certain zest, but also with the
exuberance of youth.

Several authors have viewed Morgan's Grand Order as
the impetus that launched him on his career as an ethnologist.[25] As Morgan admitted late in life, "Whatever interest I have since taken in Indian studies was awakened
through my connection with this Indian fraternity."[26] Mor-

[24]Isaac Hurd, "The Onondaga Reservation," Mss., n.d., Morgan Papers, UR.
[25]See, for example, Powell, p. 114; Putnam, p. 430.
[26]Quoted in Leslie A. White, "How Morgan Came to Write Systems of
Consanguinity and Affinity," *Papers of the Michigan Academy of Science,
Arts and Letters* 42 (1957): 261–62. See also Lewis Henry Morgan, *The Indian Journals 1859–62*, ed. Leslie A. White, p. 4.

gan's subsequent work, *League of the Iroquois*, grew out of his own observations and interests stimulated by Ely S. Parker and field trips. These interests, however, were complemented and supported by coworkers in early ethnology such as Isaac Hurd and fellow members of the Grand Order who "played" at being Indian but who nevertheless took time to record aspects of a culture that was disappearing.[27]

Morgan wrote the *League of the Iroquois* in six months, accomplishing the task by incorporating new materials into his earlier articles on the Iroquois.[28] With this publication Morgan fulfilled the task he had placed before the Grand Order: "Our objects are and have been not only to gather up the antiquities of our state but to rouse a kinder feeling towards the Red Man founded upon a truer knowledge of the motives and necessities of his character."[29] The opening lines of the *League of the Iroquois* are very similar: "To encourage a kinder feeling towards the Indian, founded upon a truer knowledge of his civil and domestic institutions, and of his capabilities for future elevation, is the motive in which this work originated."[30] In the latter quote the phrase "civil and domestic institutions" betrays Morgan's preoccupation with social structure and the legal fabric of a society as a means of determining its history, thus signaling a more legalistic approach to the study of culture.

Young lawyer Morgan felt that the public's perception of the Iroquois derived only from a knowledge of their military activities and alliances with European and American governments, not from those social ties that bound them together and the laws and institutions that gave meaning to their existence and shaped their minds.[31] He believed the

[27] See Robert E. Bieder, "The Grand Order of the Iroquois: Influences on Lewis Henry Morgan's Ethnology," *Ethnohistory* 27 (Fall, 1980): 349–61 and Elisabeth Tooker, "Isaac N. Hurd's Ethnographic Studies of the Iroquois: Their Significance and Ethnographic Value," *Ethnohistory* 27 (Fall, 1980): 363–69.

[28] Fenton, "Introduction" in Morgan, *League of the Iroquois*, p. xii; Resek, p. 41.

[29] Lewis H. Morgan to Lewis Cass, Dec. 30, 1845, Cass Papers, WCL.

[30] Morgan, *League of the Iroquois*, p. ix.

[31] Ibid., pp. 56–57.

public's skewed vision resulted from the absence of information upon which to form a just appraisal of Iroquois history. Despite the ravages Iroquois culture suffered in its contact with American society—despite the poverty and loss of social control—their system of confederate government, the league, continued. "The League of the Iroquois, dismembered and in fragments, still clings together in the twilight of its existence, by the shreds of that moral faith, which no political misfortune could loosen, and no lapse of years could rend asunder."[32] Morgan was not interested in charting the league's decline, which he believed inevitable. Rather he was fascinated by how the league could keep operating for so long. This, he pointed out, had never been a subject of inquiry. The answer, he believed, must lie in Iroquois laws and institutions, which acted upon the Iroquois mind. And so, besides a "kinder feeling" toward the Indian, Morgan's goal was "to inquire into the structure and spirit of the government, and the nature of the institutions, under and through which these historical results were produced."[33]

According to Morgan, a people's social relations and governmental structures resulted from a hierarchy of institutions that shaped their minds and guided their history. Morgan theorized that a complex reciprocity existed between the mind and these institutions; the mind shaped institutions and, in turn, was shaped by institutions. He pointed to this psychological phenomenon when he reminded his readers of the civilizing function of society: "By the formation of societies and governments, mankind are brought under the influence of the social relations, and their progress has been found to be in proportions to the wisdom of the *institutions under which their minds were developed.*"[34]

Regarding the Iroquois, Morgan felt their government and social relationships resulted from the hunting life. Hunting was a "passion" too deeply seated in Iroquois men-

[32] Ibid.
[33] Ibid.
[34] Ibid., my emphasis.

tality to be altered by legislation, and Iroquois government had to conform to "this irresistible tendency of his mind, this inborn sentiment; otherwise it would have been disregarded." This mental set—Morgan termed it a "powerful principle"—the Iroquois had inherited from untold generations. It enchained them; indeed, it enchained all Indians to a "primitive state." Here lay the true cause, Morgan thought, for "why the red race has never risen, or can rise above its present level." The hunting life proved to be the catalyst that prompted Indians to divide into small bands and that propelled them into a life of incessant migration. Although this observation was not new, Morgan did not attach to it claims of degeneration as others had done.[35]

For Morgan the Iroquois were both unique and representative. Although Iroquois "institutions contain the sum and substance of those of the whole Indian family," the Iroquois's greater intelligence had comprehended the divisive effect of such a life on their society, and they moved to reshape it along new lines. By this intellectual act Morgan believed the Iroquois not only proved their genius but also progressed further than any people in North America, except the Aztecs, toward eventual civilization.[36] Morgan held that the organization of the league constituted the finest example of the mental capability of the Iroquois, and the league served as the lens through which he interpreted Iroquois religion, arts, games, and society.

After Morgan published the *League of the Iroquois* in 1851, he fully believed he had devoted enough time to Indian studies. In this, however, he greatly underestimated the attraction such studies would subsequently have on him. What brought him back to this subject can probably be attributed to several influences. It is difficult to give a priority to any one of them.

Certainly Morgan possessed an active and inquisitive mind that enjoyed grappling with the large intellectual

[35] Ibid., p. 57. As an example of only one such view, see Alexander W. Bradford, *American Antiquities and Researches into the Origin and History of the Red Race.*

[36] Morgan, *League of the Iroquois*, pp. 58–59.

problems of the day. This probably proved the dominant reason for gathering in his home in 1854 a group of friends— public-spirited intellectuals enthused with the progressive nature of American society—who would meet monthly to share ideas. This gathering, later called the Pundit Club, served as a vehicle for delivering papers on various topics ranging from intellectual and theoretical essays, such as "On the Theories of Perception from Democritus to the Present Time" and "On the Theories of Insanity: With an Exposition of the Doctrine of Moral Insanity," to very practical essays, such as "On Cotton, Its Production, Manufacture and Consumption" and "On the Rise, Progress and Present Condition of the Railroad System of Europe and the United States."[37] When Morgan's turn to address the club came, he generally spoke on Indian ethnography.[38]

It was, perhaps, this continuing interest in intellectual affairs, particularly science, that led Morgan in 1856 to attend the Albany meeting of the recently formed American Association for the Advancement of Science. There, according to Carl Resek, Morgan was impressed with the scientific theories put forth and the rigor of scholarship that they entailed. He returned to Rochester with plans to attend the AAAS the following year. In 1857, Morgan again attended the AAAS, but this time to read a paper on "The Laws of Descent of the Iroquois."[39] Morgan described the way Iroquois considered descent, a system totally different

[37] See Lewis H. Morgan, "List of Papers Read From October 1858," Mss. Morgan Papers, UR.

[38] Morgan also spoke on animal psychology, another topic in which he was interested. See Lewis H. Morgan, *The American Beaver and His Works*; Lewis H. Morgan, "Animal Psychology," Mss. read before the club, April 7, 1857, Morgan Papers, UR; Lewis H. Morgan, "Instinct: Its Office in the Animal Kingdom," *Nation* 14 (1872): pp. 291–92. Morgan sought in these works to diminish the gap that eighteenth-century man saw between man and the lower animals. This move to demote man from his place of eminence in the animal kingdom and to see animals in anthropomorphic terms in the nineteenth century is one of the themes explored in James W. Turner's *Reckoning with the Beast: Animals, Pain and Humanity in the Victorian Mind*.

[39] Resek, pp. 69–70; Lewis H. Morgan, "Laws of Descent of the Iroquois," *American Association for the Advancement of Science, Proceedings* 11 (1858): 132–48.

from others in Western civilization. Property and offices were not inherited in the male line but rather descended in the female line. Furthermore, collateral relations, such as uncles, cousins, and nephews, were designated as fathers, brothers, and sons. Morgan observed that the institution of the family and the laws of descent inherent in this institution furnished "a singular illustration of the cast of the Indian intellect." He questioned, "Can their code of descent, or any other original, well-defined, Indian institution, be used as a test of the truthfulness of history? . . . Can it be employed as an instrument in the attempt to solve the great problem of the origin of our Indian races?"[40]

The question, never an idle one, certainly was important in the 1850s, a decade that saw both rhetoric and politics increasingly focused on the problem of race. A certain urgency prevailed in the shaping of attitudes, both positive and negative, on race and especially on the position and capabilities of blacks in America. An ambivalence marked Morgan's reaction to this growing national controversy that was already beginning to shake the nation's political foundations. Although he did not sanction slavery and believed the annexation of Texas a political affront to the North, Morgan opposed any steps that would divide the Union. In fact he felt that if war did come "the damned abolitionists ought to be enlisted to a man. . . ."[41] Morgan was never guilty of advocating an enlightened policy toward the slaves or of being optimistic about their future in America. As he pointed out to Senator William Henry Seward in 1850, "The black population has no independent vitality among us. . . . It is too thin a race intellectually to be fit to propagate and I am perfectly satisfied from reflections the feeling towards this race is one of hostility throughout the north. We have no respect for them whatever."[42]

Yet America's growing concern over race and slavery af-

[40]Morgan, "Laws of Descent," pp. 139–40.
[41]Lewis H. Morgan to William Allen, March 4, 1845, Morgan Papers, NYHS, quoted in Resek, p. 54.
[42]Lewis H. Morgan to William H. Seward, Feb. 2, 1850, Seward Mss., quoted in Resek, p. 63.

fected Morgan and led him to examine the racial question as then posed in science: were the various races of man the product of separate creation? Morgan balked at accepting the theory that nonwhites constituted a separate species or had separate centers of origin. Louis Agassiz, who lectured in Rochester in 1854, firmly believed that biological variations were the result of separate creations, that each organism was created for a specific zoological province. Agassiz's academic position at Harvard and his immense reputation as one of the world's foremost biologists went far to establish this theory as truth. Yet Morgan and his friends in the Pundit Club were not convinced by the professor's reasoning. If blacks by this theory were set adrift from the human race, so too would be the Indians; this Morgan could not accept. Not only might the importance of Indian education be undercut by the general acceptance of polygenism, but the extension of human nature to the Indian might also be placed in doubt. Morgan proclaimed in the *League of the Iroquois* that there were only "two means of rescuing the Indian . . . these are education and Christianity." But this view depended on the assumption that Indian ratiocination was the same as that of white men, and polygenism cast this into doubt.[43]

Morgan knew that Agassiz's arguments in support of polygenism would not be destroyed by emotional denials; only firm, solid, scientific evidence could disprove the theory. The members of the Pundit Club followed Morgan's lead and accepted the challenge of confronting the great Agassiz and his friends J. A. Nott, George Glidden, and other polygenists. Morgan's good friend Rev. Josiah Hall McIlvaine sought to disprove the theory through linguistic analysis; another friend, Dr. Edward Mott Moore, a physician, believed that an analysis of blood samples from around the world would definitely destroy the theory of polygenism.[44] Morgan turned to ethnology to prove the unity of man. In a paper before the Pundits, Morgan claimed:

[43] Morgan, *League of the Iroquois*, p. 447.
[44] Resek, p. 63. Another paper read before the club at this time, circa 1854, on the same subject was Martin B. Anderson's "On the Objections Urged Against the Unity of the Human Race," Morgan Papers, UR.

It is not a little singular that while zoology and palaeontology were gradually preparing the way for the introduction of the theory of the diverse origins of the human race, the new science of Ethnology should have come into existence, and with the avowed object of making herself the champion of the old theory of Unity of Origin. The youngest, but not the least important of the sciences, is substantially committed to this as her special question, and such is her confidence in the material already gathered, and in the results already reached that she fully expects to furnish a solution of this momentous problem on purely scientific grounds.[45]

Already, Morgan proclaimed, through ethnology "the Asiatic origins of most of the primitive stocks has been established." Only lacking was absolute proof. If this were acquired, "it would explode the new doctrine of many zoological provinces by reducing them to one if it did not furnish a convincing and unanswerable argument in favor of Unity of Origin."[46] Morgan elected to discover confirming data, which were to prove very difficult and expensive to accumulate.

When Morgan presented his paper on Iroquois descent before the AAAS in 1857, he thought the Iroquois system of descent might be universal among American Indians because it fit so well with their hunting life.[47] Descent in the female line, he believed, would ensure the individual freedom on which the hunting stage depended. Since Morgan believed all Indians were hunters or in the hunter stage, and since matrilineal descent fit so well the exigencies of a hunter society, Morgan reasoned that matrilineal descent would be widespread. But how similar the Iroquois system was to that of other tribes still remained a question. He could only speculate until a business venture took him to Michigan in 1858 and threw him into contact with some

[45]Lewis H. Morgan, "Agassiz's Theory of the diverse origin of the human race," read before the club, May 16, 1859, pp. 22–23, Morgan Papers, UR.

[46]Ibid., pp. 23–24.

[47]Morgan, "Laws of Descent," p. 148. See also White, "How Morgan Came to Write Systems." White quotes Morgan, "at this time [1856] I did not know that the system extended beyond the Iroquois, although I surmised its probability." Morgan read this paper before the club on Feb. 23, 1858, p. 263.

Sioux Indians on a train and with Ojibwa Indians in upper Michigan. Although his attempt to elicit information from the Sioux on their kinship system proved less than successful, this was not the case with the Ojibwas.[48]

> To my surprise somewhat, and not a little to my delight, I found their system was substantially the same as that of the Iroquois; thus by including a second stock language, extending very greatly the area of its distribution. From this time I began to be sensitive to the important uses which such a primary institution as this must have in its bearing upon the question of the genetic connection of the American Indian nations not only, but also upon the still more important question of their Asiatic origin.[49]

Upon his return home Morgan checked in the *Grammar and Dictionary of the Dakota Languages* by Rev. Stephen R. Riggs. He noted clues that indicated the Sioux followed a similar system. This prompted him to draw up and print a "schedule" for recording kinship systems, which he proceeded to send out to missionaries and Indian agents, hoping their replies would confirm his theory that Indian kinship systems were all alike.[50]

Unfortunately, the response from these mailings proved disappointing. Few were returned, and many of those that were indicated the schedule had been misunderstood.[51]

[48] White, "How Morgan Came to Write Systems," p. 263.

[49] Morgan quoted in White, "How Morgan Came to Write Systems," p. 263. See also Josiah Hall McIlvaine, *The Life and Work of Lewis Henry Morgan: An Address at His Funeral* (Rochester: n.p., 1882), pp. 11–12, reprinted in *Rochester Historical Society Publications* 2 (1923): 47–60. Pages cited are to the 1882 publication.

[50] Resek, pp. 73–74.

[51] Lewis H. Morgan, *Circular Letter in Regard to the Possibility of Identifying the Systems of Consanguinity of the North American Indians with That of Certain Peoples of Asia.* Gathering ethnological information through questionnaires was a common practice in the nineteenth century. It also proved an unreliable way to gather information as Gallatin, Cass, and others discovered. See Don Fowler, "Notes on Inquiries in Anthropology: A Bibliographic Essay," in Timothy H. H. Thoreson, *Toward a Science of Man. Essays in the History of Anthropology*, pp. 15–32. See also William N. Fenton, "Answers to Governor Cass's Questions by Jacob Jameson, A Seneca [ca. 1821–1825]," *Ethnohistory* 16 (Spring, 1969): 113–39; Curtis M. Hinsley, Jr., *Savages and Scientists: The Smithsonian Institution and the Development of American Anthropology 1846–1910*, pp. 47–48.

Thus in the summer of 1859 Morgan packed his bags for a field trip to the West to determine for himself the intricacies of Indian kinship systems.

Between 1859 and 1869 Morgan traveled west four times and continued his trips to upper Michigan. He went primarily to gather data on kinship systems, but he also discovered other things about Indians that piqued his interest. His journals were crammed with accounts of their behavior, customs, and physical appearance. He focused especially on their "advances" in acculturation (or, as he noted, civilization), along with observations on mission schools and government Indian policy. Although Morgan's kinship studies are of primary significance for the development of his anthropological theory and constitute his major contribution to the field of anthropology, it is the latter area, his notes on Indian customs, behavior, and physical appearance, that is most important for comprehending his views on Indians and their potential for living in American society.

As a result of what he saw in Kansas and Nebraska, Morgan altered his position on intermarriage between whites and Indians, an act he had earlier viewed in pejorative terms.[52] He now attributed advances in acculturation and mental development not to the length of time a tribe had had contact with whites, but to the degree a tribe had intermarried with whites.

On his first trip to Kansas and Nebraska, where he visited the Kaws, Shawnees, Ottawas, Potawatomis, Sacs, Foxes, and Delawares, Morgan observed perspicaciously the degree of Indian-white mixtures in the West: "The color of the Indian women is quite uniform, and is light. It shows that white blood infused into them in the East has been well diffused throughout. The next cross will make a pretty white child."[53] The "amalgamation" Morgan thought beneficial for both races. Heretofore union was with only the lowest Americans and most base of frontier society, but now in Kansas the "first honest and regular experiment"

[52][Lewis H. Morgan] "Publisher's Note," in *Life of Mary Jemison: Deh-he-wa-mis,* ed. J. E. Seaver, p. 7.
    [53]Morgan, *Indian Journals,* p. 50.

will take place.[54] Morgan believed that whites would certainly find economic motivation to marry Indian women, for, as he noted, they "marry Indian wives and get adopted into the tribes and thus some few have gained farms, or the possession at least of valuable land."[55] To that end Indian women "are interfered with a good deal by the whites," but the women also seemed "quick to marry white husbands," regarding it as "advancing." Morgan noted, perhaps a bit sardonically, that this move upward would be true "were their husbands respectable." But with more optimism Morgan believed that as Indians and mixed-bloods alike became wealthy farmers

> their children will intermarry respectably with our white people and thus the children will become respectable and, if educated, in the second and third generations will become beautiful and attractive. This is to be the end of the Indian absorption of a small portion, which will improve and toughen our race, and the residue [will be] run out or forced into the regions of the mountains.[56]

Morgan's professed optimism was tempered, however, by the many "base white men" who frequented the payment of annuities. "There were more white men around today than looked well for the Indian women."[57] This was not just a mere expression of Victorian morality. Morgan seemed astonished to learn that although the women "looked strong, literally cleanly and healthy, . . . I am told . . . that syphilis is among their women to an alarming extent. Their faces would not lead to such a suspicion."[58]

Morgan favored Indian ownership of individual farms. The old "wild and thriftless state" certainly could not and ought not be preserved. Those who persisted in this illusion and refused to adjust to the demands of a new time "must fade away." The Indians' longing for their old homes and old ways, although painful to hear, could not alter the

[54] Ibid.
[55] Ibid., p. 28.
[56] Ibid., p. 55.
[57] Ibid., p. 51.
[58] Ibid., p. 50.

situation. Eventually, "He must become a farmer and make money and throw off the Indian past. Those alone who do this will be able to save themselves and ultimately will be absorbed in our race."[59] But were they ready for this step?

Morgan recognized the inevitable changes that the restless course of westward pioneers forced upon the Indians, but he wondered if there were time enough for Indians to adjust. Some individuals and some tribes surprised Morgan by the steps they had already taken in the direction of farming and management of individual farm holdings. He held less optimism for others. Wary of the pioneers' avarice for good land, Morgan hoped the government would protect the farms of individual Indians by prohibiting them from selling their lands except with the permission of the tribal council. Both the Ottawas and the Shawnees were anxious to move toward private land ownership. The Ottawas had even chosen to defy the government; some "have had their land surveyed and agreed to make a division among themselves with out the aid of [the] government." The Shawnees closely followed in this "great and dangerous experiment."[60] Morgan speculated about the timing and the wisdom of their actions and wondered if they were mentally prepared for such a step. Nevertheless, he wished them well.[61]

In 1859, after returning from his first trip west, Morgan learned to his great delight from a correspondent that the kinship of the Tamil of India paralleled that of the Iroquois. This was not entirely unexpected. On one occasion he told his friend McIlvaine, "I shall find it, I shall find it among the Tamil people and Dravidian tribes of Southern India." McIlvaine, who was doubtful, urged Morgan to concentrate on the tribes of the Americas and to forget about the Old World. According to McIlvaine, Morgan replied, "I can not do it—I can not do it—I must go on, for I am sure I shall find it there."[62]

[59]Ibid., p. 36.
[60]Ibid., pp. 37, 44.
[61]Ibid., pp. 37, 48.
[62]McIlvaine, p. 12.

This discovery truly excited Morgan, for here was proof that the Indians were distantly related to Asians. Further trips west were now necessary to gather additional proof to confirm his theory. On his subsequent trips—to Kansas and Nebraska again in 1860, through Minnesota to Pembina in 1861, and up the Missouri River to the Yellowstone in 1862—Morgan continued his observations of Indian customs, government policy, and, above all, kinship systems.

Recording Indian customs now assumed additional significance. To Morgan, the singularity of some customs shared between peoples indicated additional proof of genetic ties. Were there any customs of Asian peoples that could be found among the Indians to further support the theory of the Indians' Asian connection? Morgan thought there were. When he first encountered the Plains Indians' custom of sleeping nude, he realized that it might be useful as an index for both Asian relatedness and for Indian migration. The same was true of an item of clothing, the breechcloth. "There is no doubt, I think, that it prevailed from the Eskimo inclusive to Mexico, and probably to Patagonia."[63] Knowing that the Eskimo both wore the breechcloth and slept nude, Morgan was certain that, contrary to the findings of Samuel G. Morton, the Eskimo and the Indian were one people.

Sleeping in the nude appeared an extraordinary custom for a polar people, and Morgan felt constrained to explain its occurrence in Eskimo culture. It seemed obvious to him that the Eskimos once inhabited a milder country and were forced northward either through war or population pressure. Once in the Arctic they acclimated and adapted themselves to the northern region and then migrated along latitudinal lines. Customs such as sleeping nude, although originating in warmer regions, were inherited and proved immune to environmental change. This assumption led Morgan to observe, "It has only come into my mind that the existence of this custom among the Eskimo and our Indians carries with it some evidence of a common origin."[64]

[63] Morgan, *Indian Journals*, p. 86.
[64] Ibid.

Later Morgan would expand upon this conjecture. After learning that people in southern India also slept nude and wore breechcloths, Morgan affirmed that these customs were not merely handed down but were literally passed through the blood.[65] Here was Morgan as biological determinist.

Using blood as a means to explain inheritance was no mere metaphorical device for Morgan. To him it became the controlling or limiting factor in the transmission of culture. With no knowledge of genetics and little appreciation of man's malleable nature and ability to respond to changing stimuli, Morgan viewed the tenacious hold of certain customs in terms of innate causes. Even the Indians' "customs" of music and dance were biologically determined. "The dance, the song, the music, and the step among all our Indians came out of one brain."[66]

Morgan elaborated on the full impact of these inherited customs in an 1861 address given in memory of his friend Calvin Huson.

Nations, willingly or unwillingly, live under the absolute control of fundamental ideas and principles, which work out their results with certainty and uniformity of physical laws. Our institutions are not created by an arbitrary exercise of intelligence, but they are developed, by the [utility?] of national logic, from primary ideas which are wrought into the brains of the race in the infancy of its existence. Hence as logical sequences they are self supporting and homogeneous. It is impossible to put an alien institution upon any race in the vigor of its life and maintain it permanently. The ethnic life of the people must be first subdued, otherwise it will cast it out as certainly as it continues to raise itself into a position of influence or encroachment. The institutions of a people, therefore, must be germane to their primary ideas, and consequently homogeneous, or the current of public feeling will be in a constant state of abrasion. Experience teaches us that no institu-

[65] Lewis H. Morgan, *Systems of Consanguinity and Affinity of the Human Family*, p. 274; Morgan, *Indian Journals*, pp. 78, 82, 86, 96, 115, 172.

[66] Morgan, *Indian Journals*, p. 163. In another passage Morgan states: "The music and dance of all our Indians are *sui generis*. They came out of the same brain and temper of mind." p. 148.

tion can spring up and florish with vigor which is not deeply rooted in the sentiments of the people.[67]

Huson had died in a Confederate prison camp. Although Morgan condemned the "folly" of the Southern cause, he also used his address as the occasion to stress the innateness of fundamental ideas or principles that evolve in a people and determine their destiny. In this particular case he referred to American society and slavery, but the argument served as well for his interpretation of Indian mental processes and the development of Indian society.

This biological determinism extended to Morgan's consideration of Indian women. The evolution of his thoughts can be seen in his reports on his western trips. On his first trip to the West not only the comportment and dress of the women attracted his attention, but also their morals. Delaware women, he noted with approval, had ceased wearing the Indian skirt and instead were wearing long dresses in imitation of white women. Although the overall effect struck Morgan as "fantastic and ludicrous," he nevertheless considered the long gown "a move in the right direction."[68]

On Morgan's second trip in 1860, dress and morals were less important than inquiries about the passion and behavior of Indian women.[69] He encountered trappers and

[67] Lewis H. Morgan, "Memoir of Calvin Huson, Jr.," read before the club, Nov. 5, 1861, Morgan Papers, UR. Morgan generally used the term "primary" rather than "fundamental."

[68] In comparison the outfits of the males appeared to Morgan as gross and gaudy. "Their fancy dresses were cheap and absurd, rendering their general appearance ridiculous." Some men still painted their faces, which, to Morgan, gave them a "low appearance." Morgan, *Indian Journals*, p. 50.

[69] Ibid., p. 66. The Pawnees in 1859, when Morgan saw them in Omaha, had recently passed through a reversal of fortunes. In 1839 they were one of the most powerful tribes on the northern Plains, but smallpox, cholera, and battle losses to the Sioux had reduced their numbers in roughly fifty years to about half, with women outnumbering men two to one. The Sioux at midcentury, faced with a population explosion, were expanding to the south, west, and north. The Pawnees, caught between an aggressively expanding white population and the Sioux to the north, suffered severely and by 1859 were a defeated and nearly landless people. Although Morgan notes that they were a demoralized people, he probably did not realize just how tragic their situation was nor how demoralized they actually were. For an excellent inter-

traders who had taken Indian women as wives, and this presented him with the opportunity to question these men about their domestic relationships and their wives' sexual responses. Although most of the men seemed eager to offer their opinions on the matter, Morgan out of delicacy hesitated to take down all the information. From American Fur Company trader Charles Martin he learned much. "Martin has had a large experience with Indian women and mentioned to me many facts which it would be perhaps injudicious to note down, although I sought them and wished to know." According to Martin, Indian women were "universally industrious" but "know nothing of love, and cannot be made to manifest passion. They are always the same passive and passionless creatures, but acknowledging the principle of obedience."[70] Drawing upon his own observations, Morgan agreed. "Martin confirms my former position that the Indian woman has no passion, no love in our sense. She is quiescent and submissive to her husband from duty, but without active passion."[71] To Morgan, this deficiency of passion, like sleeping nude, proved not a matter of culture or education but of biological inheritance.

To instill "active passion" in areas beyond that of affection and to bring the Indian around to civilization, Morgan began to accept the view expressed by some frontier men that Indians were like wolves: there was no way to tame them if they remained Indians—"the only way to tame him is to put in the white blood." Morgan duly noted in his journal:

> I think a most important idea lies in here and it is one which has occurred to me before; and that is, whether after all it is not in virtue of the white blood already taken up and distributed among the emigrant nations the improvement we see

---

pretation of Pawnee history at this period, see Richard White, "The Winning of the West: The Expansion of the Western Sioux in the Eighteenth and Nineteenth Centuries," *Journal of American History* 65 (1978): 319–43.

[70] Morgan, *Indian Journals*, pp. 100–101. Note also Major Culbertson's remark to Morgan on his trip up the Missouri River in 1862, "The women know nothing of this passion [love] in our sense, or the men." p. 145.

[71] Ibid., p. 100.

among them has come to pass; and that but for this blood all efforts would have been unavailing to introduce agriculture among them. I can hardly think this is true and yet it may be.[72]

In 1863 at a stop at Sugar Island, Michigan, where S.P. Church provided jobs for an Ojibwa community, Morgan believed his suspicions were confirmed regarding the beneficial effects of white blood. Church had acquired a modest fortune employing Indians in his timber and jam-making industries, and the Indians who worked for him seemed to Morgan industrious and materially better off than other Indians in Michigan. Although Morgan strongly advocated just such a "factory system" for other Indians and saw it as a chance to reform government Indian policy, he cautioned, "It must not be forgotten, however, that much of the success of Mr. Church's experiment is due to the white blood in the veins of the Chippewas . . . and just in the proportion as it is found among the western nations will the chance of success of the same experiment among them be increased."[73] The emphasis on blood and its use as a vehicle of inheritance of traits, along with advocacy of miscegenation, continued to be an important theme in Morgan's subsequent writings on Indians and especially in his next anthropological work, *Systems of Consanguinity and Affinity.*[74]

Morgan poured into *Systems* the distillation of his years of research on the Iroquois and the data gathered on his four arduous field trips to the West. This was Morgan's great work of refutation to the polygenists. As he pointed out to his friend Francis Parkman, "If I am not mistaken I have shown the Unity of origin of the American aborigines . . . and also the Asiatic origin of the Indian family. Upon this

[72] Ibid., p. 94.

[73] Lewis H. Morgan, Manuscript Journal VI, pp. 92–112, Morgan Papers, UR. That this view continued into the twentieth century, see Robert Sterling Yard, *Our Federal Lands: A Romance of American Development*, who states, "It is the belief of experienced observers that, in spite of a good education, the Indian will never much improve in those respects which make for competitive success except by intermixture of white blood. This has often yielded excellent results. Crossing [Indians] with Asiatic and African stock, which happens extensively in Oklahoma, works no improvement." p. 204.

[74] Morgan, *Systems of Consanguinity and Affinity.*

last point the evidence seems to me to be decisive; but it may fail of convincing others."[75] Morgan was more confident of the proof of his labors in a letter to Joseph Henry of the Smithsonian Institution.

You will remember that I told you this singular research would either lead to my important result or prove a total failure:— that it would furnish a new instrument for the prosecution of ethnological investigations, more efficient than the grammatical structure of language, or come to nothing. For a long time I did not know where my facts would lead me, but I am now satisfied I have found solid ground to stand upon. I think I am safe in saying that the Asiatic origin of the Indian family as well as the unity of origin of all of the Indian nations represented in the Tables—are demonstrated by   proofs sufficient to satisfy the most exacting.[76]

Systems of Consanguinity and Affinity, finished in 1865 and published in 1871 by the Smithsonian Institution, assured Morgan a prominent position among social evolutionists.[77] According to one anthropologist, "Morgan's great contribution was his virtual discovery of the variety of kinship terminologies" and their connection with social

[75]Lewis H. Morgan to Francis Parkman, June 5, 1867, Parkman Papers, MHS.

[76]Lewis H. Morgan to Joseph Henry, March 13, 1865, copy, Morgan Papers, UR.

[77]Others were Henry Maine with *Ancient Law* (1861), J. J. Bachofen with *Das Mutterrecht* (1861), and John F. McLennan with *Primitive Marriage* (1865). A recent excellent study that surveys the works of Bachofen, McLennan, and Morgan is Hans-Jürgen Hildebrandt, "Der Evolutionismus in der Familienforschung des 19. Jahrhunderts. Ansätze einer allgemeinen, historisch orientierten Theorie der Familie bei Johann Jakob Bachofen, John Ferguson McLennan und Lewis Henry Morgan" (Ph.D. diss., Mainz: Johannes Gutenberg Universität, 1981). The history of the publication of *Systems* and the encouragement and support Morgan received from Joseph Henry, secretary of the Smithsonian Institution, has been well told by others. See Resek, pp. 90–100 and Leslie A. White, "The Correspondence between Lewis Henry Morgan and Joseph Henry," *The University of Rochester Library Bulletin* 12 (Winter, 1957): 17–22. Through *Systems* Morgan established a lasting friendship with Joseph Henry, who had proved a friend to earlier ethnologists E. George Squier and Henry R. Schoolcraft. Indeed, it was Henry and the Smithsonian that did so much to augment Morgan's international reputation as an ethnologist and social evolutionist.

systems.[78] Morgan, too, seemed aware of the momentous significance of his discovery and what it meant for the eventual discovery of the Indians' origins. In a letter to Parkman he pointed out: "Indians, excluding the Eskimo are one stock in blood and lineage . . . whatever civilization has been found on either continent was indigenous. If these propositions are true, then our chief study as I conceive should be their domestic institutions. Greater and more reliable results can be reached from this source I believe than from language."[79]

Morgan theorized in *Systems* an Asian origin for the American Indian based on these "domestic institutions." Even more significant for Morgan than finding that the kinship system of the American Indian—which he termed the "classificatory system"—resembled systems in Asia, was his conception that the Indians brought these systems with them upon emigrating, transmitting them from one

[78] Sol Tax, "From Lafitau to Radcliff-Brown: A Short History of the Study of Social Organization," in *Social Anthropology of North American Tribes*, ed. Fred Eggan, pp. 445–81; Fred Eggan, "Lewis Henry Morgan in Kinship Perspective," in *Essays in the Science of Culture in Honor of Leslie A. White*, eds. G. E. Dole and R. L. Carneiro, pp. 178–201; Fred Eggan, *The American Indian: Perspectives for the Study of Social Change*, pp. 1–14; Meyer Fortes, *Kinship and the Social Order: The Legacy of Lewis Henry Morgan*, chaps. 1, 2. For a provocative discussion between Fortes and other scholars on Morgan's influence, see also Meyer Fortes, "Kinship and the Social Order: The Legacy of L. H. Morgan," *Current Anthropology* 13 (April, 1972): 285–96; and Fred Eggan, "Lewis Henry Morgan's Systems: A Reevaluation," in *Kinship Studies in the Morgan Centennial Year*, ed. Priscilla Reining, pp. 1–16. Several Marxist anthropologists have also appraised Morgan's contributions to anthropology, including Maurice Godelier, "Lewis Henry Morgan (1818–1881)," in *Horizon: Trajets marxistes en anthropologie*, pp. 174–82 and Emmanuel Terray, "Morgan and Contemporary Anthropology," in *Marxism and "Primitive" Societies*, trans. Mary Klopper, pp. 5–92. See also P. Tolstoy, "Morgan and Soviet Anthropological Thought," *American Anthropologist* 54 n.s. (January-March, 1952): 8–17 and I. I. Semenov, "The Doctrine of Morgan, Marxism and Contemporary Ethnography," *Soviet Anthropology and Archaeology* 4 (1965): 3–15. A recent study of Morgan's ideas is Elman R. Service, "The Mind of Lewis H. Morgan," *Current Anthropology* 22 (February, 1981): 25–43.

[79] Lewis H. Morgan to Francis Parkman, June 5, 1867, Parkman Papers, MHS.

generation to another. Morgan could not accept the possibility that such classificatory systems were the result of the operation of similar institutions in separate societies. For Morgan, too many factors mitigated against such a possibility. Classificatory systems were too intricate, Morgan believed, to ever evolve by chance. They had to be passed from one people to another, which indicated a historical connection. In addition, Morgan believed that domestic institutions did not change easily but remained relatively stable over time because they "exist by usage rather than legal enactment. . . . Their use and preservation are entrusted to every person who speaks the common language, and their channel to transmission is the blood."[80] Not only did kinship systems descend "with streams of the blood" but so too did racial mentalities and customs like breechcloths and sleeping nude. "There are some customs of such a strikingly personal character that they may, in a pre-eminent degree, be regarded as customs of the blood," he wrote, and as such, he believed, they were immune to both changes in the environment and behavioral conditions.[81]

Because Indians were all one race and of common blood, Morgan believed he could extrapolate for them a common "intellectual life." Whereas in the *League of the Iroquois* he had used the Iroquois as a cultural model for all Indians, now he generalized again and claimed that by virtue of a common blood, Indians possessed a common mind. To Morgan this was evident in all their works. "The marks of the uniform operation of minds . . . inherited from common ancestors can be successfully traced through periods of time." As examples of this Morgan pointed to Indian ar-

[80]Morgan, *Systems*, pp. 4–5, 14–15; Tax, "Lafitau" in Eggan, *Social Anthropology*, pp. 460–61; Schoolcraft held a similar interpretation, feeling that writing systems were transmitted by blood. See Henry R. Schoolcraft, *Suggestions for Travellers Visiting the Ancient Sites of Indian Occupancy in America*, p. 5.

[81]Morgan, *Systems*, p. 166. In the example of the breechcloths, Morgan pointed out, "It illustrates the difficulty of casting off, under changed conditions, these blood or hereditary usages." pp. 274–75, footnote 1.

chitecture, tribal organization, dances, burial customs, and systems of relationship. In all of these "the same mental characteristics are constantly revealed."[82]

Given such thinking, it is not surprising to find Morgan's attention drawn to the Red River settlement near Lake Winnipeg, Canada, where a large mixed-blood population resided. How would the extensive intermixing of the white and Indian races affect his theories on the enduring qualities produced by a "common mind"?

Although Morgan's interests in this community were ethnological, his rendering of this "great experiment" seems more biological than ethnological. Like many ethnologists, Morgan wondered if the "new stock" produced at the Red River would be "able to perpetuate itself." Still fresh in his mind were memories of the Delawares in Kansas, the effect intermarriage with whites had produced in that community, and the words of Charles Martin. The situation at the Red River settlement, however, appeared more ambiguous. There were adverse signs and the verdict was still out when he wrote in *Systems*:

> There is a purely physiological principle involved, which connects itself directly with this experiment. The Indian and European are at opposite poles in their physiological conditions. In the former there is very little animal passion, which with the latter it is superabundant. A pure-blooded Indian has very little animal passion, but in the half blood it is sensibly augmented; and when the second generation is reached with a cross giving three-fourths white blood, it becomes excessive, and tends to indiscriminate licentiousness. If this be true in fact, it is a potent adverse element leading to demoralization and decay, which it will be extremely difficult to overmaster and finally escape. . . . Whether this abnormal or disturbed state of the animal passions will finally subside into a proper equilibrium, is one of the questions involved.[83]

Unlike Buffon a century earlier, Morgan did not see this lack of passion as an explicit sign of degeneration or in-

[82] Ibid., p. 257.
[83] Ibid., p. 207.

feriority; rather, he placed the whole matter in a genetic context. If the Indian "in his native state . . . is below the passion of love," it resulted from physiological causes that were genetic or transmitted by the blood. How such a characteristic came about did not concern him.[84]

Others had also expressed interest in this "experiment" of miscegenation. Morgan's friend Daniel Wilson, noted for his works on Scottish prehistory, wrote to Morgan in 1859 that the Hurons were no longer pure bloods but now merely "wretched relics." In 1863, Wilson wrote to Morgan asking about the Red River settlement. He wondered how large the mixed-blood population was and how the mixed-bloods differed physically, mentally, and morally from the parent stocks. More importantly, he asked if the mixed stock could survive if left alone.[85]

Although most so-called Indian reformers of the day steered away from suggesting miscegenation as a means of "improving" the Indian, Morgan felt that it held a certain utilitarian value. Through selective breeding, Morgan thought, Indians could be absorbed into the white population with little or no negative effects to the general white population. Morgan concluded from his observations that the half blood was inferior to the pureblood Indian both physically and mentally, "but the second cross, giving three-quarters Indian, is an advance upon the native; and giving three fourths white is still a greater advance" resulting in near equality with the white ancestor. "With the white carried still further, full equality is reached, tending to show that Indian blood can be taken up without physical or intellectual detriment."[86]

[84] In the late nineteenth century the subject of "animal passions," or sex, remained a delicate subject although one not without "scientific" interest for Morgan. His "proof" for the Indian's lack of passion came not only from trappers and traders, but also from his own observation, for as he noted in his journal, their lack of passion "is sufficiently proved by the universal prevalence of the custom of disposing of the females in marriage without their knowledge or participation in the arrangement." Ibid., p. 207.

[85] Daniel Wilson to Lewis Henry Morgan, May 9, 1859, Jan. 21, 1863, Morgan Papers, UR.

[86] Morgan, *Systems*, p. 207.

Morgan's comments on physiology should not be equated with similar terms used by Samuel G. Morton.[87] Both men saw Indians as racially inferior to Caucasians, but the connotations of Morgan's remarks, although disparaging, were different from those of the Philadelphia physician. Morton perceived Indians both in polygenetic terms and in relatively static terms; Indians were as they were because they were created that way and could not possibly change. Morgan, however, viewed Indians in monogenetic terms and felt that their capacity for change was open-ended. Intermarriage merely speeded up an extremely slow process of mental and physical development in the race. This emphasis on change becomes even more evident in Morgan's later works, in which he stressed the slow movement of man toward civilization.

Morgan's concept of "selective breeding" did not result solely from his understanding of biological evolution or from his observations of mixed-bloods in the West. It is quite likely that his views were molded by contemporary social theories that looked to breeding (although generally excluding blacks and Indians) as the logical progressive and scientific step toward a better society. From religious revivals that heightened man's spiritual health, it was a logical step to "perfecting the race" through diets and selective breeding or, as one recent historian has noted, to devising ways so that "human beings could breed for progress." Charles Darwin in his *Origin of Species* provided a certain impetus for this rationale. In the United States, the founder of the Oneida Colony, John Humphrey Noyes, saw that although Darwin's "object was to establish a theory looking backward to the origin of species, . . . the practical result of his labors has been to establish a theory looking forward to the duty of scientific propagation." For Noyes, "the foundations of scientific society are to be laid in scien-

---

[87] Leslie A. White, who claimed that Morgan's remarks were similar to those of Samuel G. Morton's, did so in an attempt to see Morgan as a product of his age. This comparison, I believe, is a mistake. In contrast to Morton, Morgan believed in a kind of racial progress brought about by miscegenation. See Leslie A. White in Morgan, *Indian Journals*, pp. 214–15, footnote 6.

tific propagation of human beings." Phrenologists were only one group seeking to improve society through strict adherence to the careful selection of marriage partners for qualities of intelligence and health. Noyes claimed scientific propagation had long remained the goal not only of phrenologists but also of popular physiologists and reformers; indeed, "it is remarkable how common it has become for books and newspapers to acknowledge the duty of scientific propagation." Noyes pointed out that Francis Galton (not unlike Morgan) had demonstrated that "the physical qualities of individuals and races, . . . their artistic, and moral characteristics, and even their spiritual proclivities, are as transmissible as the speed of horses."[88] By the end of the nineteenth century, the eugenics movement would further elaborate these arguments. But for Morgan in the 1870s progress through miscegenation seemed to make sense.

If Morgan believed culture was hereditary, what chance was there for change and for progress other than through miscegenation? Morgan's answer, although he admitted it was slower than miscegenation, lay in his concept of evolution. Morgan's scheme for social evolution was not biological, but rather reflected his somewhat romantic-idealistic con-

[88] Ronald G. Walters, *Primers for Prudery*, p. 148; Noyes quoted in Walters, p. 149, but see also chap. 9. In his chapter "Heredity, Disease and Society Thought," Charles Rosenberg asserts that hereditarian explanations devised in the 1840s continued almost unchanged but increased in explanatory force for decades. "The vast majority of the publicists, social thinkers, and physicians who popularized hereditarian ideas never questioned their truth or adequacy; they simply used them more frequently, more deterministically, and in increasingly social contexts." Charles E. Rosenberg, *No Other Gods: On Science and American Social Thought*, p. 34. See also Ronald G. Walters, *American Reformers, 1815–1860*, chap. 7. For works on phrenology, see John D. Davies, *Phrenology: Fad and Science. A 19th-Century American Crusade*; George Lanteri-Laura, *Histoire de la Phrenologie*; David de Giustino, *Conquest of Mind: Phrenology and Victorian Social Thought*; Madelein B. Stern, *Heads and Headlines: The Phrenological Fowlers*. The importance of phrenology for ethnology in Britain at this time is discussed in Robert M. Young, "The Role of Psychology in the Nineteenth-Century Evolution Debate," in Mary Henle, Julian Jayness, and John J. Sullivan, eds., *Historical Conceptions of Psychology*, pp. 180–204, and Robert M. Young, *Mind, Brain and Adaptation in the Nineteenth Century: Cerebral Localization and Its Biological Context from Gall to Ferrier*.

cept of mental or psychological development. According to Morgan, all men were capable of progress because all men possessed the "germ" or "germs" of civilization. Implanted in the "primitive ages of man," these germs constituted part of human mental endowment and, once given the chance, they would eventually ripen to maturity. Those germs, or ideas, behaved in an organic way and were controlled by natural law. Just how these laws operated Morgan never specified, but he did think "germination" could be accelerated through environmental conditions. In regard to the Indian, Morgan believed that Americans should help create a receptive environment to prod the germination of these innate "ideas."[89]

Morgan explored these thoughts more fully in his *Ancient Society* (1877), a book that may have reflected his reading of Charles Darwin's *Origin of Species*. As Morgan pointed out to a friend,

> When Darwin's great work on the Origin of Species appeared I resisted his theory, and was inclined to adopt Agassiz's views of the permanence of species. For some years I stood in this posi-

---

[89] Maurice Mandelbaum's contention that the works on social evolution that were published shortly after Darwin's *Origin of Species* were devoid of either Darwin's theory or any earlier biological theory of evolution. Mandelbaum, given his concept of evolutionary theory in biology, is correct. See Maurice Mandelbaum, *History, Man, & Reason: A Study in Nineteenth-Century Thought*, pp. 78, 93–94. Morgan used terms and phrases such as "organic," "plant the roots," "ripen," and "germ" (the latter carries a heavy burden of meaning in his works), but they were not conceived of in evolutionary terms. At the time Morgan wrote *Systems*, his primary interest was in the historical reconstruction and comparison of social organizations horizontally rather than vertically through time. See Morgan, *Systems*, pp. 172, 479, 494, 497, 500–506. Morgan also used these terms in *Ancient Society, or Researches in the Lines of Human Progress from Savagery through Barbarism to Civilization*, ed. Eleanor Burke Leacock. Philip Howard Gray in "The Early Animal Behaviorists: Prolegomenon to Ethnology," *Isis* 59 (Winter, 1968): 383, also notes that Morgan was not an evolutionist in the biological sense. Morgan's emphasis on "germs" or ideas that germinate and unfold under proper environmental conditions departs from the more traditional empiricism of an earlier ethnology and borders upon an ethnology that George W. Stocking sees at once as more romantic and idealistic. See George W. Stocking, "Some Problems in the Understanding of Nineteenth Century Cultural Evolutionism," in *Readings in the History of Anthropology*, ed. Regna Darnell, pp. 407–408, 420–22.

tion. After working up the results from consanguinity, I was compelled to change them, and to adopt the conclusions that "man commenced at the bottom of the scale" from which he worked himself up to his present status.[90]

Utilizing the traditional three-stage theory of progress—savagism, barbarism, and civilization—Morgan expanded upon it, adding substages at each level. Both stages and substages were arranged according to a conjectured scheme where a hierarchy of inventions and discoveries was situated parallel to a hierarchy of social, economic, and political institutions. For Morgan there was a relationship between an advance in inventions and discoveries and the unfolding of social, economic, and political institutions, and both constituted a record of progress and the gradual development of the human mind.

Morgan's repeated observations of Indian life led him to place Indians firmly in the several levels of barbarism. The similarity of their institutions and artifacts denoted a common mind, and, although discrepancies between Indian groups existed, these discrepancies were not of a magnitude to raise any Indian groups out of barbarism. Thus Morgan took issue with those who claimed that some In-

[90]Lewis H. Morgan to Lorimer Fison, Sept. 20, 1872, copy, Morgan Papers, UR. Morgan's statement should be contrasted with a letter to Morgan from Rev. Josiah Hall McIlvaine: "I think it [*Ancient Society*] a great work, and decidedly the strongest argument against the Darwinians, and in favor of the permanence of species, that has ever been given to the world. You demonstrate that man has been of one species, ever since he has been on the earth—say 3 or 400,000 years. If a new species cannot be formed in that length of time we may well doubt whether it ever could be, and we may be sure that the formation of a new species will never be demonstrated." Josiah Hall McIlvaine to Lewis H. Morgan, June 18, 1877, Morgan Papers, UR. The question of Darwin's influence on Morgan is still disputed. Leslie A. White claims that Morgan arrived at his ideas of cultural evolution independently while working up his material for *Systems*. See Leslie A. White, "The Concept of Evolution in Cultural Anthropology," in *Evolution and Anthropology: A Centennial Appraisal*, ed. Betty J. Meggers, pp. 123–24. Carl Resek claims that McIlvaine suggested the evolution hypothesis. Resek, p. 97. Although Morgan in his reading of early nineteenth-century ethnologists had ample sources to draw upon for his "evolutionary" views of society, his letter to Fison suggests that Darwin may have played a role in directing him along an evolutionary path of thought or that Darwin at least urged him along a path he was already on.

dian groups had formerly enjoyed an advanced civilization with governmental institutions similar to Europeans.

Morgan's perception of the uniformity of Indian civil organization led him to attack the prevalent assumption in American ethnology that Central and South American Indians were more advanced than North American Indians. In a letter to archaeologist Frederick Ward Putnam in 1876, Morgan called attention to the strong interest then expressed in Indian studies. He noted unhappily that most of these studies were carried out by amateurs. "Inflation and imaginary magnificance is the bane that infests all their efforts." The truth was, he complained, "at this moment we have no science of American Ethnology." The main difficulty lay with certain widely held assumptions.

> It has been my aim and object for years to get investigations started in the right direction. If we can but do that—results that will come at the end of a few years will be splendid. They will be immense for the necessity of doing over European Ethnology for the Middle & for the Upper Status of barbarism will be demonstrated.
>
> Our first dead weight to be got rid off [sic] is the Aztec Monarchy and the Aztec romance. The institutions of the Indian tribes, including the Aztec tribe, are essentially democratical and the whole series of Spanish and American histories are delusive and fictitious, so far as Indian society and government are concerned I have felt the dead weight of these accounts for [years?] and have made a number of gentle remonstrances against it: but regard for the memory of Prescott has restrained my hand. The publication of Bancroft's Native Races alters this question. . . . This work and the commendations it is receiving is nothing less than a crime against Ethnological Science. Every way it is lamentable: but it can be made an occasion for a rising against the entire humbug and thus good may come of it.[91]

[91] Lewis H. Morgan to Frederick Ward Putnam, Jan. 29, 1876, copy; Lewis H. Morgan to Eben Horsford, March 22, 1876, copy; Lewis H. Morgan to Samuel Haven, Feb. 22, 1877, copy, Morgan Papers, UR; Lewis H. Morgan to Francis Parkman, June 5, 1867, Parkman Papers, MHS; Lewis H. Morgan to Charles Deane, Jan. 27, 1869, Deane Papers, MHS. Morgan also expressed these views in several articles he wrote about this time. See "The

At first Morgan declined to review *Native Races* for *The Nation*, but upon examining it he felt it his duty. His review, entitled "Montezuma's Dinner," he believed perhaps too harsh, "too pronounced for the review," but the cure had to be as strong as the disease. Morgan asked Putnam to read the work for "it contains some general suggestions upon what must be done if we would make a scientific exposition of the social organization, usages & customs and plan of life of the Indian Tribe."[92]

In his review Morgan repeated most of his comments to Putnam. He refined his concept of ethnology and accused Americans of lacking any interest in pursuing ethnology in a scientific manner. "The question still before us, as a Nation, whether we will undertake the work of furnishing to the world a scientific exposition of Indian society, or leave it as it now appears, crude, unmeaning, unintelligible, a chaos of contradictions and puerile absurdities."[93]

In "Montezuma's Dinner" Morgan sought to present the world with an example of how ethnology could rewrite history. Using such "facts" as he could find in Spanish accounts, comparing them to what was known of other Indian societies, and incorporating all these data into his overarching theory of social evolution, Morgan found the Aztecs to be merely a confederacy of three tribes, not unlike other Indian confederacies. Their inventions and institutions

'Seven Cities of Cibola,'" in *The North American Review* 108 (April, 1869): 498; "Architecture of the American Aborigines," in *Johnson's New Universal Cyclopedia*, pp. 217–29; "On the Ruins of a Stone Pueblo on the Animas River in New Mexico; with a Ground Plan," *Peabody Museum of American Archaeology and Ethnology, 12th Annual Report* 2 (1880): 536–56; "A Study of the Houses of the American Aborigines; with suggestions for the exploration of the Ruins in New Mexico, Arizona, the Valley of the San Juan, and in Yucatan and Central America," *Archaeological Institute of America, 1st Annual Report of the Executive Committee* (1880): 29–80. Parts of all these articles were incorporated in Lewis Henry Morgan, *Houses and House Life of the American Aborigines.*

[92] Lewis H. Morgan to Frederick Ward Putnam, Jan. 29, 1876, copy, Morgan Papers, UR.

[93] Lewis H. Morgan, "Montezuma's Dinner," *The North American Review* 122 (1876): 269.

were those of barbarism. Like other Indian societies, the Aztecs were communal and lived without kings and palaces. "They were still a breech-cloth people, wearing this rag of barbarism as the unmistakable evidence of their condition; and the family was in the syndyasmian or pairing form, with separation at any moment at the option of either party."[94] The view of the Aztecs as an advanced people with large cities, royalty, and banquet halls merely reflected the fantastic imagination of the conquistadors. Historians without seeking the truth of the matter had accepted the image. Indian society had "very little in common with European society. . . . Its institutions, inventions, and customs find no analogues in those of civilized nations, and cannot be explained in terms adapted to such a society." To do so only produced a skewed interpretation of the Aztecs and the failure of observers to realize that Indian society was everywhere the same.[95] Because Indian society differed so markedly from Western civilized society, more careful collection of data was necessary for its description.

This difference between Indian and Western societies did not carry with it the implication that the former was static and the latter progressive. Rather, Indian society's rate of progress merely was slower. Morgan's theory of social evolution contravened degeneration theory through its recognition of the vast time period of man's existence and by demonstration of how discoveries, inventions, social systems, and governments progressed by slow increments. Although he admitted he might be wrong with respect to which inventions were significant for a society's prog-

[94] Ibid., p. 293. In writing "Montezuma's Dinner," Morgan had the help of Adolph F. Bandelier, who found and translated pertinent passages from the Spanish sources. See Leslie A. White, ed., *Pioneers in American Anthropology: The Bandelier-Morgan Letters 1873–1883,* 1: 242–61 and passim. After "Montezuma's Dinner" appeared, Bandelier sent to Morgan a list of errors he found in the text and pointed out that Morgan had not perhaps read his earlier letters carefully enough. pp. 265–71.

[95] Ibid., p. 269 and passim. See also Charles Gibson, "Lewis Henry Morgan and the Aztec 'Monarchy,'" *Southwestern Journal of Anthropology* 35 (Spring, 1947): 78–84, and Benjamin Keen, *The Aztec Image,* pp. 380–410, for interesting discussions of Morgan's views on the Aztecs.

ress, Morgan nevertheless believed his approach theoretically sound.[96]

According to Morgan, all mankind was endowed with equal capacity for progress. All moved forward toward civilization, but the pace was uneven, and some stopped or delayed their march. A people's progress was slowed or accelerated by the experiences and the institutions under which they lived. Another factor that contributed to a people's progress was their intelligence. It helped shape these institutions, and, in turn, intelligence was influenced by these institutions. Thus to Morgan's reasoning, a people's brain size corresponded to its position on the social evolutionary scale; the smaller the brain the more primitive the people.[97] Morgan stressed this point in a letter to John Wesley Powell, director of the Bureau of American Ethnology.

> Our first thing, as you state, is to come down to the infantile condition of the Indian mind in its apprehension of the supernatural. The imagination among them is undisciplined as well as in powerful action, and their knowledge of physical phenomena nearly zero. Their myths and fables are not only credited by children, but completely credited by adults. It presents a curious phase in the development of the mental principle.[98]

He elaborated upon this theory in three articles critical of the government's Indian policy: "The Hue and Cry against the Indian" (1876), "Factory System for the Indian" (1876), and "The Indian Question" (1878).[99]

Morgan, more than any other ethnologist of his day except Schoolcraft, repeatedly tried to influence government Indian policy. He tried unsuccessfully in 1861 to obtain the office of commissioner of Indian affairs in the Lincoln ad-

[96] Lewis H. Morgan to Joseph Henry, Nov. 28, 1876, copy, Morgan Papers, UR.
[97] Morgan, *Ancient Society*, pp. 513–15.
[98] Lewis H. Morgan to John W. Powell, Feb. 19, 1877, copy, Morgan Papers, UR.
[99] Lewis H. Morgan, "Factory System for Indian Reservations," *The Nation* 23 (July 27, 1876): 58–59; "The Hue and Cry Against the Indians. Letter on the Custer Massacre," *The Nation* 23 (July 20, 1876): 40–41; "The Indian Question in 1878," *The Nation* 27 (Nov. 28, 1878): 332–33.

ministration. When he served in the New York State Assembly he was named chairman of the Committee of Indian
Affairs in 1861.[100] Years earlier, as a member of the Grand
Order of the Iroquois, Morgan had helped the Senecas in
their case against the Ogden Land Company and carried a
petition in defense of the Senecas to Washington. But what
he saw on his trips to Michigan and to the West unleashed
his indignation at the cruel and wasteful way the government treated the Indians. With acerbity he attacked the
caliber of government agents, their callous attitude, and
the fraud, greed, general debasement, and immorality they
exhibited toward their charges. Yet, he pointed out, such
agents passed for honest men. The army, the American Fur
Company, and the missionaries each received a share of his
bitter indictment. The military, Morgan said, must have
their Indian women and the result was debauchery and de-
moralization among the Indians. The American Fur Company made pawns of the Indian agents and in this way not
only corrupted them but engaged them in conspiracies to
rob and cheat the Indians of what little they had left. Even
missionary schools pocketed government money sent for
the Indians without really educating the children or even
providing clean and wholesome living conditions at the
school. Morgan regarded the agency system a failure, and
he concluded in 1860, "It is impossible to escape all abuses,
or to make the affairs of the Red men easy of management,
but if the complaints which any man may hear on the Missouri and west of it are one quarter of them true, it is time
the whole system was overturned and reformed."[101]

Although Morgan's feelings simmered for several years, it
took the public's reaction to the death of General Custer
and his men in 1876 at the hands of the Sioux and the
Cheyennes to force Morgan to speak. Custer's defeat agi-
tated the public and evoked its wrath against the Indian.
Morgan sought to place the incident in a larger context in
order to shed light on what prompted the Sioux and the

[100] Resek, pp. 82–83.
[101] Morgan, *Indian Journals*, p. 97; note also pp. 37, 101, 138–42, 148,
151–52.

Cheyennes to fight. In Morgan's opinion, the government was clearly in the wrong in this war, but that was not the real issue. More grave was "the absence of intelligence and judgement in the management of our Indian affairs." The administration of Indian affairs proved a national disgrace and reflected on the reputation of the American people before the world. What was needed, stated Morgan, was a cabinet-level department of Indian affairs staffed with "the first men of the nation." [102]

In reality, the government's Indian policy was changing. Many advocated allotment, that is dividing the reservations into farms, one for each Indian family, as a way to save the Indians from extinction. It was hoped that allotment would teach the Indians the concept of private property necessary for survival in American society and also remove the responsibility for the Indians from government. In addition, as Indians became farmers they would begin to become part of the general population. In the 1880s, first with the Omaha Allotment Act (1882) and the Dawes Severalty Act (1887), Congress sought to speed the Indians toward this goal. These were not the first attempts to settle Indians on individual homesteads. Allotment had been official government policy for some Indians as early as 1830. [103]

Although Morgan called for change, the allotment of Indian land was not what he envisioned, and had he lived he likely would have vehemently opposed it. [104] Morgan believed that Indian policy ought to be rational and built on the science of ethnology. The fruits of civilization were acquired only after a long, slow ripening period. Man could not be civilized overnight or even in one generation. Throwing the Indians on reservations abruptly changed their lives, and they lacked the experience to deal with the problems that such a life generated. Drawing on his findings in ethnology Morgan proclaimed: "They have the skulls and brains of bar-

[102] Morgan, "Factory System"; "Hue and Cry"; and "The Indian Question."
[103] Robert F. Berkhofer, Jr., *The White Man's Indian: Images of the American Indian from Columbus to the Present*, pp. 156–57; Francis Paul Prucha, *American Indian Policy in Crisis: Christian Reformers and the Indian, 1865–1900*, pp. 228–33; Mardock, p. 211.
[104] Prucha, pp. 156–57.

barians, and must grow toward civilization as all mankind have done who attained it by a progressive experience."[105] This would all take time. "In relative progress they are now precisely where our own barbarous ancestors were when, by the domestication of animals, they passed from a similar into a higher condition of barbarism, though still two ethnical periods below civilization." The road from barbarism to civilization would take time. "We wonder that our Indians cannot civilize but how could they, anymore than our own remote barbarous ancestors, jump ethnical periods?"[106]

Morgan emphasized that Indians must be dealt with as Indians, not as white men. To help them, he said, both patience and forbearance must be expended. As barbarians, they were at a "low stage of barbarism," far beneath the level of civilization. "They are incapable of acting in the modes of a civilized race, but they are neither devoid of intelligence nor incapable of appreciating the usual incentives to human action." They know little of the arts of civilized life. "Any system of management, therefore, must be adapted to their mental as well as physical condition if success is expected or desired."[107]

This prescription was most important to Morgan's scheme for Indian advancement. Both their mental development and environment must be assessed. Bringing Indians into a timber, jam, and handicraft business, as S.P. Church had done in Michigan, would hardly be possible on the plains. Indians should be encouraged to utilize their area's unique resources for their own advancement. The initiative to help the Indian rested with the government; much could still be done. "It will be possible to stimulate their industry and to lead them gradually into the practice of labor, and with it into an improved plan of life." Only through experience

[105] Morgan, "The Indian Question," p. 332. This did not contradict his earlier view of the value of miscegenation, which he believed more expedient than progress through experience.

[106] Ibid.

[107] Morgan, "Factory System," p. 58.

[108] Ibid. See also Morgan's account of the S. P. Church experiment at Sugar Island, Michigan. Morgan, Manuscript Journal VI, pp. 92–112, Morgan Papers, UR.

would their brains increase to the size of civilized man's. Until that happened, the government would have to exercise patience and tolerance.[108]

The government never adopted Morgan's ideas. The tide in favor of the allotment of Indian reservations was too strong; allotment made more political sense and, given the amount of land thrown open to American settlement through the allotment process, engendered more popular enthusiasm.[109] Morgan's suggestions perhaps were considered too unworkable or too abstract for government officials charged with creating Indian policy. Too, Morgan apparently had acquired a rather philosophical reputation and was presumed more concerned with the implications of ethnological theory than with pragmatic politics and current realities.

As one writer put it in a letter to Senator Roscoe Conkling in 1868, "Mr. Morgan has devoted his whole life to the exploration of Indian antiquities, and so far by habit of mind linked himself with the aboriginal race, as to render him utterly unconscious of the ordinary events of the prosaic life of the present. . . . No politician or citizen would ever dream of regarding the diction of Lewis H. Morgan on a political matter of slightest value."[110]

Such an assessment of Morgan's influence is harsh and unfair. True he probably had little influence in powerful government circles in the late nineteenth century and certainly not much with the Bureau of Indian Affairs. But he did command respect among a host of intellectuals, including Francis Parkman, Asa Gray, Henry Adams, William Garrison, Joseph Henry, Jeffries Wyman, and John Wesley Powell. Indeed, Powell considered *Ancient Society* so valuable that, as director of the Bureau of American Ethnology, he made it required reading for fieldworkers employed at the bureau.[111] Morgan also had several followers in the field of ethnology besides Powell, but none more devoted than

---

[109] Prucha, pp. 156–57.

[110] Lewis Selye to Roscoe Conkling, June 6, 1868, Selye Papers, Rochester Public Library, quoted in Resek, p. 112.

[111] Resek, p. 150.

Adolph Bandelier, one of the first major ethnological scholars of Mexico and New Mexico.

Although Morgan had little impact on Indian policy per se, his effect on late nineteenth-century American anthropology was tremendous. He believed that Indian society, arts, and architecture held the secrets of Indian history and that the investigaton of these areas ought to be the true goal of American anthropology. According to Morgan, further proof of Indian evolution from savagery to barbarism and the precise paths this evolution took could still be discovered, and he called for anthropology to direct its efforts to this end.[112]

Toward the end of his life Morgan considered architectural remains, especially in the Southwest, as vital to this better understanding of social and cultural evolution. He made his last trip west to examine the Pueblo ruins in the Southwest. In his record of this trip and in his last book, *Houses and House Life of the American Aborigines*, one can glimpse the excitement that Morgan believed this new approach held for the future of anthropology.[113]

When Morgan died in 1881 he left many in the science of anthropology with memories of him and his presence at Harvard and in the American Association for the Advancement of Science.[114] But he also left more. He left a paradigm for the study of the American Indian to a generation of anthropologists. Not living in New York City, Morgan never became a member of the New York Ethnological Society, nor was he enmeshed in its contentious and slow decline. The development of Morgan's scientific career coincided with the rise of the AAAS, the foremost science organization in the last half of the nineteenth century. Mor-

[112] Lewis H. Morgan to Charles E. Norton, Oct. 25, 1879, copy, Morgan Papers, UR.

[113] Leslie A. White, ed., "Lewis H. Morgan's Journal of a Trip to Southwest Colorado and New Mexico," *American Antiquity* 8 (1942): 1–26; Lewis H. Morgan, *Houses and House Life of the American Aborigines*.

[114] Morgan was elected president of the American Association for the Advancement of Science in 1879, the first anthropologist to be so honored. Resek, p. 150.

gan proved both a staunch advocate and a wholehearted participant in its rise, and his career and reputation benefited from the contacts he gained through his participation in the organization and through the exposure the AAAS gave to him and his ideas.

Morgan also won acceptance for his ideas from directors of important institutions. As mentioned, Powell of the Bureau of American Ethnology was an enthusiastic supporter, as were Frederick Ward Putnam at Harvard's Peabody Museum and E. L. Hewitt of the School of American Research and the Museum of New Mexico. Such acceptance, and, to a degree, the institutionalization of Morgan's theory, did much to disseminate his ideas in an age when graduate work in anthropology had not yet assumed this function. Morgan's evolutionary ideas were accepted also because they seemed to mesh with Spencerian theory and the "survival of the fittest" notions prominent in a period of confidence in the superiority of Western civilization's phenomenal economic growth.

Although Morgan proved to be in the vanguard of late nineteenth-century anthropology, his ideas were inextricably linked with early nineteenth-century ethnology. As an adopted Seneca, Morgan was given the name of One Lying Across. In bestowing this name the Senecas sought to signify Morgan's role as a bridge between two cultures. The name is also apropos to his role in anthropology. Morgan carried on the Enlightenment tradition of social progress, of man marching toward civilization, into late nineteenth-century anthropology. This concept, inherent in the ethnology of Albert Gallatin and E. G. Squier, was the touchstone of Morgan's anthropology. When he wrote, "The latest investigations respecting the early condition of the human race are tending to the conclusion that mankind commenced their career at the bottom of the scale and worked their way up from savagery to civilization through the slow accumulation of experimental knowledge . . . ,"[115] he was echoing, perhaps without realizing it, the words of the Scottish

[115] Morgan, *Ancient Society*, p. 3.

historian William Robertson one hundred years earlier. Wrote Robertson, "In every part of the earth, the progress of man hath been nearly the same; and we can trace him in his career from the rude simplicity of savage life, until he attains the industry, the arts, and the elegance of polished society."[116] Juxtaposing Robertson in 1777 with Morgan in 1877 reveals how much Morgan's anthropology lay across the century and upheld the evolutionary tradition. In nineteenth-century anthropology Morgan was what the Senecas called a Ho-nun-de-ont, a keeper of the faith, a person "appointed . . . to take charge of their religious festivals." Morgan was a keeper of the faith, a keeper of the Enlightenment's faith in man.

[116] William Robertson, *The History of America*, 1: 294.

7

Conclusion

DURING THE LAST thirty years anthropologists seeking to reestablish evolutionary anthropology and searching for its theoretical roots trace them back to Lewis Henry Morgan and sometimes to late-eighteenth-century thought.[1] Of course, Morgan's evolutionary anthropology differs markedly from that of today or even from that espoused earlier. Yet Morgan is respected for reintroducing Enlightenment ideas of social progress and translating them into evolutionary stages of social structure, government, and invention. In their veneration for Morgan and Enlightenment ideas on progress, anthropologists interested in their discipline's past press quickly, and perhaps a bit embarrassing, over the ethnology of early-nineteenth-century America, denying its validity and deploring its claims to scientific ethnology. Indeed, it is a period generally ignored.[2] Yet it is this period's ethnology, suffused with environmentalism and evolutionary theory, that nourished Morgan and sustained his evolutionary thinking.

Historians of anthropology who see the early nineteenth century as barren of ethnological insight are a bit hasty in

[1] See for example Emmanuel Terray, "Morgan and Contemporary Anthropology," in Emmanuel Terray, *Marxism and "Primitive" Societies*, trans. Mary Klopper, pp. 5–92. For an excellent discussion of two anthropologists—Julian Steward and Leslie White—who sought as neo-evolutionists to resurrect Morgan's reputation, see Elvin Hatch, *Theories of Man and Culture*, pp. 112–61.

[2] Some of these histories are: Marvin Harris, *The Rise of Anthropological Theory: A History of Theories of Culture*; Robert H. Lowie, *The History of Ethnological Theory*; Annemarie de Waal Malefijt, *Images of Man: A History of Anthropological Thought*; Fred W. Voget, *A History of Ethnology*; Murray J. Leaf, *Man, Mind, and Science: A History of Anthropology*.

their assessment. Although this period did not produce sweeping new theories to dominate ethnology, it did, in the larger context of governmental attempts to reshape Indian policy and the public debate over slavery, serve to modify older ideas and theories. Eighteenth-century assumptions were changed. Certainly destroyed was the naïveté that characterized environmental thinking. Likewise, the facile theories regarding Indian progress were modified when it was discovered that "civilization" was not quickly achieved. Neither Indian "cultures" nor physical characteristics were ever again seen as so completely malleable as the sanguine thinkers of the eighteenth century had interpreted them to be. Although a teleological view of history enshrining progress still prevailed, a literal interpretation of the Bible began to crumble even before geology, biology, and archaeology so drastically undermined Biblical chronology.

American Indians played a significant role in this whole reinterpretation process. Questions were asked about their cultural, archaeological, and physical remains that in turn led to the reshaping of ethnological theory. These questions were prompted by a certain sense of urgency. The changing life-styles in many Indian tribes and the decline in Indian population resulted in cultural disintegration and raised the spectre of a whole race disappearing before its history was discovered. Efforts were made to record their languages, to gather their stories, to collect their pictorial representations and sign languages, to explore their archaeological remains, and to note their customs and cultural artifacts. These efforts were generally undertaken not out of any intrinsic appreciation for American Indian cultures but out of the belief that these data contained clues to Indian history and its connection with the history of the rest of mankind. Although some ethnologists expressed sadness at the passing of the Indians and the disappearance of aspects of their cultures, these were by and large romantic expressions and momentary lapses. Most ethnologists were committed to Indian "progress" and to the obliteration of the Indian way of life. As in the eighteenth century, nineteenth-century ethnologists viewed Indians as savages and barbarians living under social conditions that were the product of environmental influence and amenable to change. Such assumptions underscored the continuation of environmentalism and evolutionary concepts.

These concepts reached full force in the post-Civil War ethnology of Lewis Henry Morgan, whose evolutionary anthropology received extensive support not only among anthropologists but also from such thinkers as Henry Adams and Charles Eliot Norton. This was partly the result of the well-crafted nature of Morgan's theory and the wealth of data he mustered to support it, and partly the result of the increasing acceptance of Darwinian evolution in the United States. More important for the popularity and spread of Morgan's ideas, however, was their institutionalization.

What the development of the science of ethnology meant to American Indians or to the development of government Indian policy is difficult to assess. Nearly all of the ethnologists here examined couched the importance of their work in terms of its value to government Indian policy or to the "civilization" of Indians in general. Convinced of this fact, several sought funds from the government to further their research goals. The contributions of ethnographic research to government Indian policy and to missionary endeavors were, however, indirect and minimal. Most probably both government and church policy would have remained the same in the absence of a science of ethnology. It is true that in the late nineteenth century, ethnologists such as Alice Fletcher defended the allotment program with arguments derived from ethnology, but she was merely advocating support for a government policy already in operation among some tribes.[3] Although some ethnologists proved sensitive to the Indians' plight and consequent

[3]Robert F. Berkhofer, Jr., *The White Man's Indian: Images of the American Indian from Columbus to the Present*, p. 174. For Alice Fletcher, see Nancy Oestreich Lurie, "Women in Early Anthropology," in *Pioneers of American Anthropology*, ed. June Helm, pp. 43–54; Nancy Oestreich Lurie, "The Lady from Boston and the Omaha Indians," *American West* 3 (Fall, 1966): 31–33, 80–85; Joan Mark, *Four Anthropologists: An American Science in its Early Years*, pp. 62–95.

hardships and at times defended tribal resistance to government and public measures, ethnologists did not delude themselves into thinking that Indians as "savage Indians" could retain a position in American society. The answer always seemed clear: "civilization" or death.

Far more pervasive was the effect of the Indians' presence on the development of American anthropology. Both Jefferson and Morgan were quite right when they spoke of American ethnology showing European ethnology the way. Innumerable contacts with American Indians and their cultures produced an ethnology that was quite different from European ethnology in the nineteenth century. Benefiting from repeated contacts with Indians, American ethnologists were able to test their theories against the hard edges of data. That these data were perceived as facts then and are now perceived as opinion or bias does not alter the point that in their methodology Americans tried to be empirical in their approach and make their conclusions agree with the facts as they understood them.

Then, too, there was a certain romantic element in American anthropology, an identification with the Indian. Schoolcraft's view of himself as an Ojibwa chief, Morgan's pride in his adoption into the Seneca Nation, and Squier's joining—if only in his novel—the war against modernization, have their parallels in late nineteenth-century anthropology in Frank Hamilton Cushing's Zuni priesthood or among twentieth-century anthropologists who are card-carrying members of the Native American Church.[4]

After Morgan's death in 1881, the heyday of evolutionary anthropology soon collapsed. The eugenics movement and the new cultural anthropology of Franz Boas would contemptuously dismiss evolutionary anthropology as crude and unscientific. The achievements of the older ethnology that were useful to the new anthropology would be absorbed, generally without a trace of recognition; the rest

---

[4]An excellent study of Frank Hamilton Cushing can be found in Mark, *Four Anthropologists*, pp. 96–130. On the Native American Church, see Alice Marriott and Carol K. Rachlin, *Peyote*, p. 108, where they identify anthropologist Omer Stewart as a "card-carrying" member of the church.

were left to withstand the jibes of ridicule and scorn. Those who continued to write in the old evolutionary mode suffered a similar fate.[5]

This book about the schools of thought in early nineteenth-century ethnology and some of their more popular advocates seeks neither to disparage nor applaud their accomplishments. Although it does not condone early ethnological views of American Indians, it seeks to understand in the larger social and intellectual context why some of the views were held. Its emphasis has been to examine a period little noted in the history of American anthropology, to cast greater light on the totality of the period's ethnological achievements, and to underscore how American Indians and their cultures buttressed the early development of American ethnology.

[5] Elvin Hatch, *Culture and Morality: The Relativity of Values in Anthropology*, pp. 42–43; Hatch, *Theories of Man*, p. 43; Mark, *Four Anthropologists*, p. 48. The best accounts of Boas's role in American anthropology are found in several chapters in George W. Stocking, Jr., *Race, Culture, and Evolution: Essays in the History of Anthropology* and in George W. Stocking, Jr., ed., *The Shaping of American Anthropology 1883–1911: A Franz Boas Reader*.

Bibliography

MANUSCRIPT COLLECTIONS

In relating the history of early American ethnology and its encounter with native Indians, this study benefited from manuscript collections in several libraries, listed below. In those instances in which a library holds only a few manuscript pieces useful to this study, generally not in a specific collection, only the library is listed.

Edinburgh, Scotland
    National Library of Scotland. George Combe Papers.
Washington, D.C.
    National Archives. Records of the Bureau of Indian Affairs (Record Group 75).
    Library of Congress. Henry Rowe Schoolcraft Papers.
    ———. Ephraim George Squier Papers.
    Smithsonian Institution Archives. Joseph Henry Papers.
Philadelphia, Pa.
    American Philosophical Society. Stephen Du Ponceau Papers.
    ———. Benjamin Smith Barton Papers.
    ———. Samuel G. Morton Papers.
    Library Company of Philadelphia. Samuel G. Morton Papers.
New York City
    New York Historical Society. Albert Gallatin Papers.
    ———. Ephraim George Squier Papers.
Rochester, N.Y.
    University of Rochester Library. Lewis Henry Morgan Papers.
    ———. Ely S. Parker Papers.
An Arbor, Mich.
    William Clement Library. Lewis Cass Papers.
    ———. Peter Force Papers.
    ———. Lucius Lyon Papers.
    Burton Historical Collection, Detroit Public Library. Henry Rowe Schoolcraft Papers.

————. George Johnston Papers.

————. Lewis Cass Papers.

Providence, R.I.

John Carter Brown Library, Brown University. John Russell Bartlett Papers.

San Marino, Calif.

Henry E. Huntington Library and Art Gallery. Ephraim George Squier Papers.

————. Henry Rowe Schoolcraft Papers.

————. Ely S. Parker Papers.

Chicago, Ill.

Newberry Library. John Howard Payne Papers.

Chicago Historical Society. Jeremiah Porter Papers.

Boston, Mass.

Massachusetts Historical Society. Houghton Library, Harvard University.

Albany, N.Y.

New York State Library.

Indianapolis, Ind.

Indiana State Library. Dunihue Collection.

Ithaca, N.Y.

DeWitt Historical Society of Tompkins County, New York. Lewis H. Morgan Papers.

BOOKS

Ackerknecht, Erwin H. *Medicine at the Paris Hospital: 1794–1848*. Baltimore, Md.: Johns Hopkins University Press, 1967.

————, and Henri V. Vallois. *Franz Joseph Gall: Inventor of Phrenology and His Collection*, Wisconsin Studies in Medical History, vol. 1. Madison: Department of History of Medicine, University of Wisconsin, 1956.

Adair, John. *The History of the American Indians* [1775]. Edited by Samuel Cole Williams. Johnson City, Tenn.: Watauga Press, 1930.

Adams, Henry. *The Life of Albert Gallatin*. Philadelphia: J. B. Lippincott, 1880.

Allen, Don Cameron. *The Legend of Noah: Renaissance Rationalism in Art, Science, and Letters*. Urbana: University of Illinois Press, 1963.

Allen, John Logan. *Passage Through the Garden: Lewis and Clark and the Image of the American Northwest*. Urbana: University of Illinois Press, 1975.

Armstrong, William. *Warrior in Two Camps: Ely S. Parker Union General and Seneca Chief.* Syracuse, N.Y.: Syracuse University Press, 1978.

Atwater, Caleb. *Remarks Made on a Tour To Prairie du Chien; Thence to Washington City, in 1829.* Columbus, Mo.: Isaac N. Whiting, 1831.

Bachofen, J. J. *Das Mutterrecht.* Stuttgart: N.p., 1861.

Balinsky, Alexander. *Albert Gallatin: Fiscal Theories and Policies.* New Brunswick, N.J.: Rutgers University Press, 1958.

Bancroft, George. *History of the United States, from the Discovery of the American Continent.* 12th ed. 1840. Reprint, Boston: Charles C. Little and James Brown, 1846.

Bard, Sam [E. G. Squier]. *Waikna; or, Adventures on the Mosquito Shore.* New York: Harper and Brothers, 1855.

Bartlett, John Russell. *The Progress of Ethnology, an account of recent Archaeological, Philological and Geographical Researches . . . . Tending to elucidate The Physical History of Man.* 2d ed. New York: N.p., 1847.

Barnett, Louise K. *Ignoble Savage: American Literary Racism, 1790–1890.* Westport, Conn.: Greenwood Press, 1975.

Bartram, William. *Travels of William Bartram* [1791]. Edited by Mark Van Doran. New York: Dover, 1928.

Barton, Benjamin Smith. *New Views of the Origin of the Tribes and Nations of America.* Philadelphia: N.p., 1797. 2d ed., 1798.

Barzun, Jacques. *Race: A Study in Superstition.* New York: Harper & Row, 1965.

Baudet, Henri. *Paradise on Earth: Some Thoughts on European Images of Non-European Man.* Translated by Elizabeth Wentholt. New Haven, Conn.: Yale University Press, 1965.

Beatty, Charles. *The Journal of a Two Month Tour; With A View of Promoting Religion Among the Frontier Inhabitants of Pennsylvania, and of Introducing Christianity Among the Indians to the Westward of the Alegh-geny Mountains.* London: Davenhill, 1768.

Beaver, R. Pierce, ed. *To Advance the Gospel: Selections From the Writings of Rufus Anderson.* Grand Rapids, Mich.: William B. Eerdmans Publishing Co., 1967.

———. *Church, State and the American Indian: Two and a Half Centuries of Partnership in Missions Between Protestant Churches and Government.* St. Louis: Concordia Publishing House, 1966.

Berkhofer, Robert F., Jr. *Salvation and the Savage: An Analysis of Protestant Missions and American Indian Response, 1787–1862.* Lexington: University of Kentucky Press, 1965.

———. *The White Man's Indian: Images of the American Indian from Columbus to the Present.* New York: Alfred A. Knopf, 1978.

Bernheimer, Richard. *Wild Men in the Middle Ages: A Study in Art, Sentiment, and Demonology.* Cambridge: Harvard University Press, 1952.

Billington, Ray Allen. *Land of Savagery, Land of Promise: The European Image of the American Frontier.* New York: W. W. Norton, 1981; reprint, Norman: University of Oklahoma Press, 1985.

Boas, Franz. *The Ethnography of Franz Boas: Letters and Diaries of Franz Boas Written on the Northwest Coast from 1886–1931.* Edited by Ronald P. Rohner. Chicago: University of Chicago Press, 1969.

Bode, Carl. *Antebellum Culture.* Carbondale: Southern Illinois University Press, 1970.

Boorstin, Daniel J. *The Lost World of Thomas Jefferson.* Boston: Beacon Press, 1948.

Boudinot, Elias C. *A Star in the West; or a Humble Attempt to Discover the Long Lost Ten Tribes of Israel, Preparatory to their Return to their Beloved City, Jerusalem.* Trenton, N.J.: Fenton, Hutchinson & Durham, 1816.

Bradford, Alexander W. *American Antiquities and Researches into the Origin and History of the Red Race.* New York: Dayton and Saxton, 1841.

Breckenridge, Henry Marie. *Views of Louisiana; Containing Geographical, Statistical and Historical Notices of that Vast and Important Portion of America.* Baltimore, Md.: Schaeffer & Mannd, 1817.

Brew, J. O., ed. *One Hundred Years of Anthropology.* Cambridge: Harvard University Press, 1968.

Bryson, Gladys. *Man and Society: The Scottish Inquiry of the Eighteenth Century.* Princeton, N.J.: Princeton University Press, 1945.

Buffon, Count de. *Natural History, General and Particular.* Translated by William Smellie. London: A. Straham & T. Cadell, 1791.

Bury, John. *The Idea of Progress.* 1920. Reprint. New York: Dover, 1955.

A Cabinet of Curiosities. Charlottesville: University of Virginia Press, 1967.

Campbell, John. *Negro-Mania: Being an Examination of the Falsely Assumed Equality of the Various Races of Men.* Philadelphia: Campbell and Power, 1851.

Carter, Clarence Edwin, ed. *The Territorial Papers of the United States. The Territory of Michigan 1820–1829.* Washington, D.C.: Government Printing Office, 1943.

Carver, Jonathan. *Three Years' Travels Throughout the Interior Parts of North America.* Walpole, N.H.: Isaiah Thomas, 1813.

Cass, Lewis. *Additional Inquiries respecting the Indian Language.* Boston: Athenaeum, N.d.

————. *Inquiries, Respecting the History, Traditions, Languages, Manners, Customs, Religion, etc. of the Indians Living within the United States.* Detroit: Sheldon and Reed, 1823.

Cassedy, James H. *American Medicine and Statistical Thinking, 1800–1860.* Cambridge: Harvard University Press, 1984.

Cassirer, Ernst. *The Philosophy of the Enlightenment.* Translated by Fritz C. A. Koelln and James P. Pettegrove. Princeton, N.J.: Princeton University Press, 1951.

Catlin, George. *Letters and Notes on the Manners, Customs, and Condition of the North American Indians.* 1844. Reprint. New York: Dover, 1973.

————. *The Manners, Customs, and Condition of the North American Indians.* 2 vols. New York: Wiley & Putnam, 1841.

Chiappelli, Fredi, Michael J. B. Allen and Robert L. Benson, eds. *First Images of America: The Impact of the New World on the Old.* 2 vols. Berkeley: University of California Press, 1976.

Child, Lydia Marie. *Letters from New York.* New York: C. S. Francis & Co., 1843.

Clark, Harry Hayden, ed. *Transitions in American Literary History.* Durham, N.C.: Duke University Press, 1953.

Clinton, DeWitt. *An Introductory Discourse Delivered Before the Literary and Philosophical Society of New York on the Fourth of May, 1814.* New York: David Longworth, 1815.

————. *Memoir on the Antiquities of the Western Parts of the State of New York.* Albany: E. E. Hosford, 1820.

Cohen, William B. *The French Encounter with Africans: White Response to Blacks, 1530–1880.* Bloomington: Indiana University Press, 1980.

Coleman, William. *Biology in the Nineteenth Century.* New York: John Wiley, 1971.

Colfax, Richard. *Evidence Against the Views of the Abolitionists, Consisting of Physical and Moral Proofs, of the Natural Inferiority of the Negroes.* New York: James T. M. Bleakley, 1833.

Collyer, R. H. *Manual of Phrenology, or the Physiology of the Human Brain.* Dayton, Ohio: B. F. Ells, 1842.

Combe, George. *Notes on the United States of North America During a Phrenological Visit in 1838–9–40.* Philadelphia: Carey & Hart, 1841.

———. *A System of Phrenology.* 3d ed. from 3d Edinburgh ed. Boston: Caper & Lyon, 1835.

Crawford, Charles. *An Essay on the Propagation of the Gospel . . . to prove that . . . the Indians in America are descendants from the Ten Tribes.* Philadelphia: N.p., 1801.

Curtin, Philip D. *The Image of Africa: British Ideas and Actions, 1780–1850.* 2 vols. Madison: University of Wisconsin Press, 1964.

Cusick, David. *Sketches of ancient history of the Six Nations.* Lewiston, N.Y.: for the author, 1827.

Danziger, Edmund Jefferson, Jr. *Indians and Bureaucrats: Administering the Reservation Policy During the Civil War.* Urbana: University of Illinois Press, 1974.

Darnell, Regna. *Readings in the History of Anthropology.* New York: Harper & Row, 1974.

Davies, John D. *Phrenology: Fad and Science: A 19th-Century American Crusade.* New Haven: Yale University Press, 1955.

De Giustino, David. *Conquest of Mind: Phrenology and Victorian Social Thought.* London: Croom Helm Publisher, 1975.

Delafield, John. *An Inquiry into the Origin of the Antiquities of America.* New York: Colt, Burgess and Co., 1839.

Deuel, Leo. *Conquistadores Without Swords: Archaeologists in the Americas.* New York: St. Martin's Press, 1967.

Dippie, Brian W. *The Non-Vanishing American: White Attitudes and U.S. Indian Policy.* Middletown, Conn.: Wesleyan University Press, 1982.

Documents and Proceedings Relating to the Formation and Progress of a Board in the City of New York for the Emigration, Preservation, and Improvement, of the Aborigines of America, July 22, 1829. New York: Vanderpool, 1829.

Dole, G. E. and R. L. Caneiro, eds. *Essays in the Science of Culture in Honor of Leslie A. White.* New York: Crowell, 1960.

Drake, Daniel. *Natural and Statistical View, or Picture of Cincinnati and the Miami Country.* Cincinnati: Locher & Walker, 1815.

Dudley, Edward and Maximillian E. Novak, eds. *The Wild Man Within: An Image in Western Thought from the Renaissance to Romanticism.* Pittsburgh: University of Pittsburgh Press, 1972.

Dunbar, Willis E. *Lewis Cass*. Grand Rapids, Mich.: W. B. Eerdmans Publisher, 1970.

Dupree, A. Hunter. *Asa Gray: 1810–1888*. Cambridge: Harvard University Press, 1959.

Eggan, Fred. *The American Indian: Perspectives for the Study of Social Change*. Chicago: Aldine, 1966.

————, ed. *Social Anthropology of North American Tribes*. Chicago: University of Chicago Press, 1955.

Eighth Annual Report of the Board of Regents of the Smithsonian Institution. Washington: A.O.P. Nicholson, 1854.

Erickson, Paul. *Phrenology and Physical Anthropology: The George Combe Connection*, Occasional Papers in Anthropology no. 6. Halifax: Department of Anthropology, Saint Mary's University, 1979.

Fairchild, Hoxie Neale. *The Noble Savage: A Study in Romantic Naturalism*. New York: Columbia University Press, 1928.

The First Annual Report of the American Society for the Promoting the Civilization and General Improvement of the Indian Tribes in the United States. New Haven, Conn.: N.p., 1824.

Flint, Timothy. *Recollections of the Last Ten Years in the Valley of the Mississippi*. Edited by George R. Brooks. 1826. Reprint. Carbondale: Southern Illinois University Press, 1964.

Fortes, Meyer. *Kinship in the Social Order: The Legacy of Lewis Henry Morgan*. Chicago: Aldine, 1969.

Frederickson, George M. *The Black Image in the White Mind: The Debate on Afro-American Character and Destiny 1817–1914*. New York: Harper & Row, 1971.

Freidman, John Block. *The Monstrous Races in Medieval Art and Thought*. Cambridge: Harvard University Press, 1963.

Gallatin, Albert. *Selected Writings of Albert Gallatin*. Edited by E. James Ferguson. Indianapolis: Bobbs-Merrill Co., 1967.

————. *A Table of Indian Languages of the United States, East of the Stony Mountains, arranged according to languages and dialects*. N.p.: N.p., 1826.

————. *The Writings of Albert Gallatin*. 3 vols. Edited by Henry Adams. Philadelphia: J. B. Lippincott & Co., 1879.

Gallatin, James. *The Diary of James Gallatin, Secretary to Albert Gallatin A Great Peace Maker 1813–1827*. Edited by Count Gallatin. New York: Charles Scribner's Sons, 1916.

Gerbi, Antonello. *The Dispute of the New World: The History of a Polemic, 1750–1900*. Edited and translated by Jeremy Moyle. Pittsburgh: University of Pittsburgh Press, 1973.

Glacken, Clarence J. *Traces on the Rhodian Shore: Nature and Culture in Western Thought from Ancient Times to the End of the Eighteenth Century.* Berkeley: University of California Press, 1967.

Glass, Bentley, Owsei Temkin, and William L. Strauss, eds. *Forerunners of Darwin: 1745–1859.* Baltimore, Md.: Johns Hopkins University, 1968.

Godelier, Maurice. *Horizon: Trajets marxistes en anthropologie.* Paris: F. Maspero, 1973.

Gossett, Thomas F. *Race: The History of an Idea in America.* New York: Schocken Books, 1963.

Gould, Stephen Jay. *The Mismeasure of Man.* New York: W. W. Norton, 1981.

Greene, John C. *The Death of Adam: Evolution and Its Impact on Western Thought.* Ames: Iowa State University Press, 1959.

Gross, Samuel D., ed. *Lives of Eminent American Physicians and Surgeons of the Nineteenth Century.* Philadelphia: Lindsay & Blackiston, 1861.

Gruber, Jacob W., ed. *The Philadelphia Anthropological Society.* New York: Temple University Press, 1967.

Guizot, François. *François Guizot: Historical Essays and Lectures.* Edited by Stanley Mellon. Chicago: University of Chicago Press, 1972.

———. *General History of Civilization in Europe.* Rev. ed. New York: N.p., 1881.

Hagan, William T. *American Indians.* Chicago: University of Chicago Press, 1961.

Haller, John S., Jr. *Outcasts from Evolution: Scientific Attitudes of Racial Inferiority, 1859–1900.* Urbana: University of Illinois Press, 1971.

Halpin, Marjorie. *Catlin's Indian Gallery: The George Catlin Paintings in the United States National Museum.* Washington: Smithsonian Institution Press, 1965.

Hanke, Lewis. *Aristotle and the American Indians: A Study in Race Prejudice in the Modern World.* Bloomington: Indiana University Press, 1959.

———. *The Spanish Struggle for Justice in the Conquest of America.* Boston: Little & Brown, 1965.

Harris, Marvin. *The Rise of Anthropological Theory.* New York: Thomas Y. Crowell, 1968.

Harris, N. *Journal of a Tour in the Indian Territory in the Spring of 1844.* New York: Daniel Dana, 1844.

Harris, Thaddeus Mason. *The Journal of a Tour into the Ter-

ritory Northwest of the Alleghany Mountains; Made in the Spring of the Year 1803. Boston: Manning & Loring, 1805.

Hatch, Elvin. *Culture and Morality: The Relativity of Values in Anthropology.* New York: Columbia University Press, 1983.

———. *Theories of Man and Culture.* New York: Columbia University Press, 1973.

Haven, Samuel F. *Archaeology of the United States,* Smithsonian Contributions to Knowledge 8. Washington D.C.: Government Printing Office, 1856.

Haywood, John. *The Natural and Aboriginal History of Tennessee, Up to the First Settlements Therein by the White People in the Year 1768.* Nashville: Geo. Wilson, 1823.

Heckewelder, John. *History, Manners, and Customs of the Indian Nations Who Once Inhabited Pennsylvania and the Neighboring States.* 1819. Reprint. New York: Arno Press and the New York Times, 1971.

Helm, June, ed. *Pioneers in American Anthropology.* Seattle: University of Washington Press, 1966.

Henle, Mary, Julian Jayness, and John J. Sullivan, eds. *Historical Conceptions of Psychology.* New York: Springer, 1973.

Henry, Joseph. *The Papers of Joseph Henry.* Edited by Nathan Reingold, et al. Washington D.C.: Smithsonian Institution Press, 1981.

Hindle, Brooke, ed. *Early American Science.* New York: Science History Publications, 1976.

Hinsley, Curtis M., Jr. *Savages and Scientists: The Smithsonian Institution and the Development of American Anthropology, 1846–1910.* Washington D.C.: Smithsonian Institution Press, 1981.

Hodgen, Margaret T. *The Doctrine of Survivals: A Chapter in the History of Scientific Method in the Study of Man.* London: Allenson & Co., 1936.

———. *Early Anthropology in the Sixteenth and Seventeenth Centuries.* Philadelphia: University of Pennsylvania Press, 1964.

Horsman, Reginald. *Race and Manifest Destiny.* Cambridge: Harvard University Press, 1981.

Huddleston, Lee Eldridge. *Origins of the American Indian: European Concepts, 1492–1729.* Austin: University of Texas Press, 1967.

Ives, Joseph C. *Report Upon the Colorado River of the West (1857–58).* 36th Cong., 1st sess., 1861, Sen. Exec. doc. 90.

Jaenen, Cornelius J. *Friend and Foe: Aspects of French-Amerindian*

Cultural Contact in the Sixteenth and Seventeenth Centuries. New York: Columbia University Press, 1976.

Jameson, Anna B. *Winter Studies and Summer Rambles in Canada.* London: Saunders & Otley, 1838.

Jefferson, Thomas. *Notes on the State of Virginia.* 1861. Reprint. New York: Harper & Row, 1964.

———. *The Papers of Thomas Jefferson.* Edited by Julian P. Boyd. Princeton: Princeton University Press, 1954.

Jones, Howard Mumford. *O Strange New World. American Culture: The Formative Years.* New York: Viking Press, 1964.

Jordan, Winthrop D. *White Over Black: American Attitudes Toward the Negro 1550–1812.* Chapel Hill: University of North Carolina Press, 1968.

Jordy, William H. *Henry Adams: Scientific Historian.* New Haven: Yale University Press, 1952.

Keen, Benjamin. *The Aztec Image in Western Thought.* New Brunswick: Rutgers University Press, 1971.

Lafitau, Joseph François. *Customs of the American Indians Compared with the Customs of Primitive Times.* 2 vols. Edited and translated by William N. Fenton and Elizabeth L. Moore. Toronto: The Champlain Society, 1974.

Lanteri-Laura, George. *Histoire de la Phrenologie.* Paris: Presses Universitaires de France, 1970.

Leaf, Murray. *Man, Mind, and Science: A History of Anthropology.* New York: Columbia University Press, 1979.

Levin, David. *History as Romantic Art.* New York: Harper & Row, 1959.

Lovejoy, Arthur O. *The Great Chain of Being: A Study of the History of an Idea.* Cambridge: Harvard University Press, 1936.

Lowie, Robert. *History of Ethnological Theory.* New York: Holt, Rinehart & Winston, 1937.

Lurie, Edward. *Louis Agassiz: A Life in Science.* Chicago: University of Chicago Press, 1960.

McCoy, Isaac. *History of Baptist Missions: Embracing Remarks on the Former and Present Condition of Aboriginal Tribes, and Their Settlement within the Indian Territory, and their Future Prospects.* 1840. Reprint. New York: Johnson Reprint Corporation, 1970.

———. *Remarks on the Practicability of Indian Reform, Embracing Their Colonization, with an Appendix.* 2 ed. New York: Gray and Bunce, 1829.

McCracken, Harold. *George Catlin and the Old Frontier.* New York: The Dial Press, 1959.

McCulloh, James H. *Researches on America: Being an Attempt to Settle Some Points Relative to the Aborigines of America, etc.* Baltimore: Joseph Robinson, 1817.

————. *Researches, Philosophical and Antiquarian, Concerning the Aboriginal History of America.* Baltimore: Fielding Lucas, 1829.

McIlvaine, Josiah Hall. *The Life and Work of Lewis Henry Morgan: An Address at His Funeral.* Rochester: N.p., 1882.

McLennan, J. F. *Primitive Marriage.* London: Macmillian, 1865.

Maine, Henry. *Ancient Law.* London: Murray, 1861.

Malefijt, Annemarie de Waal. *Images of Man: A History of Anthropological Thought.* New York: Alfred A. Knopf, 1974.

Mandelbaum, Maurice. *History, Man, & Reason: A Study in Nineteenth-Century Thought.* Baltimore: Johns Hopkins University Press, 1971.

Manuel, Frank E. *The Eighteenth Century Confronts the Gods.* Cambridge: Harvard University Press, 1959.

Mardock, Robert Winston. *The Reformers and the American Indian.* Columbia: University of Missouri Press, 1971.

Mark, Joan. *Four Anthropologists: An American Science in its Early Years.* New York: Science Publications, 1980.

Marriott, Alice and Carol K. Rachlin. *Peyote.* New York: New American Library, 1971.

Marshall, H. *The History of Kentucky.* Frankfort: Geo. S. Robinson, 1824.

Mason, Philip P., ed. *Schoolcraft's Expedition to Lake Itasca. The Discovery of the Source of the Mississippi.* East Lansing: Michigan State University, 1958.

Meek, Ronald L. *Social Science and the Ignoble Savage.* Cambridge: Cambridge University Press, 1976.

Meggers, Betty, ed. *Evolution and Anthropology: A Centennial Appraisal.* Washington D.C.: Anthropological Society of Washington, 1959.

Meigs, Charles D. *A Memoir of Samuel George Morton, M.D., Late President of the Academy of Natural Sciences of Philadelphia.* Philadelphia: T. K. & P. G. Collins, 1851.

Miller, Robert L. *The Linguistic Relativity Principle and Humboldtian Ethnolinguistics.* The Hague & Paris: Mouton, 1968.

Morgan, Lewis H. *The American Beaver and His Works.* Philadelphia: J. B. Lippincott & Co., 1868.

————. *Ancient Society, or Researches in the Lines of Human Progress from Savagery through Barbarism to Civilization.* Edited by Eleanor Burke Leacock. 1877. Reprint. Cleveland: Meridian Books, 1963.

————. *Circular Letter in Regard to the Possibility of Identifying the System of Consanguinity of the North American Indians with That of Certain Peoples of Asia.* Rochester: Privately printed, 1859.

————. *Houses and House-Life of the American Aborigines.* 1881. Reprint. Chicago: University of Chicago Press, 1965.

————. *League of the Iroquois.* 1851. Reprint. New York: Corinth, 1962.

————. *Lewis Henry Morgan: The Indian Journals, 1859–62.* Edited by Leslie A. White. Ann Arbor: University of Michigan Press, 1959.

————. *Systems of Consanguinity and Affinity of the Human Family*, Smithsonian Contribution to Knowledge 17. Washington D.C.: Smithsonian Institution, 1871.

Morse, Jedidiah. *A Report to the Secretary of War of the United States, on Indian Affairs.* New Haven, Conn.: Converse, 1822.

Morton, Samuel G. *Brief Remarks on the Diversities of the Human Species, and on Some Kindred Subjects.* Philadelphia: Merrihew & Thompson, 1842.

————. *Crania Aegyptica; or, Observations on Egyptian Ethnography, Derived from Anatomy, History, and the Monuments.* Philadelphia: John Penington, 1844.

————. *Crania Americana; or, A Comparative View of the Skulls of Various Aboriginal Nations of North and South America, to which is Prefixed an Essay on the Varieties of the Human Species.* Philadelphia: N.p., 1839.

————. *An Inquiry into the Distinctive Characteristics of the Aboriginal Race of America.* Boston: Tuttle & Dennett, 1842.

————. *A Letter to Rev. John Bachman, D.D., on the Question of Hybridity in Animals, Considered in Reference to the Unity of the Human Species.* Charleston, S.C.: Steam Power Press of Walker and James, 1850.

Moulton, Joseph W., and J. V. N. Yates. *History of the State of New York including its Aboriginal and Colonial Annals.* New York: Goodrich, 1824.

Mühlmann, Wilhelm E. *Geschichte der Anthropologie.* Wiesbaden: AULA, 1984.

Murra, John V., ed. *American Anthropology: The Early Years, 1974 Proceedings of the American Ethnological Society.* St.

Paul: West Publishing Co., 1976.

Nash, Roderick. *Wilderness and the American Mind*. New Haven: Yale University Press, 1962.

Nott, J. C. *Two Lectures on the Connection Between the Biblical and Physical History of Man*. 1849. Reprint. New York: Negro Press, N.d.

Nott, J. C. and George R. Gliddon. *Types of Mankind: or Ethnological Researches, Based upon the Ancient Monuments, Paintings, Sculptures, and Crania of Races, and upon their Natural, Geographical, Philological, and Biblical History*. Philadelphia: J. B. Lippincott, 1854.

Nye, Russel. *Society and Culture in America, 1830–1860*. New York: Harper & Row, 1974.

Osborn, Chase S. and Stellanova Osborn. *Schoolcraft-Longfellow-Hiawatha*. Lancaster, Pa.: Jacques Cattell Press, 1942.

Pagden, Anthony. *The Fall of Natural Man: The American Indian and the Origins of Comparative Ethnology*. Cambridge: Cambridge University Press, 1982.

Pagliaro, Harold, ed. *Racism in the Eighteenth Century: Studies in Eighteenth-Century Culture*. Cleveland: Case Western Reserve University, 1973.

Pauw, Cornelius de. *Selections from M. Pauw, with additions by Daniel Webb*. Bath: R. Cruttwell, 1795.

Pearce, Roy Harvey. *Savagism and Civilization: A Study of the Indian and the American Mind*. Rev. ed. Baltimore: Johns Hopkins University Press, 1967.

Pickering, John. *An Essay on a Uniform Orthography for the Indian Languages of North America*. Cambridge: Cambridge University Press, 1820.

Poliakov, Léon. *The Aryan Myth: A History of Racist and Nationalist Ideas in Europe*. New York: Basic Books, 1974.

Prichard, James Cowles. *Researches into the Physical History of Man*. Edited by George W. Stocking, Jr. Chicago: University of Chicago Press, 1973.

Priest, Josiah. *American Antiquities and Discoveries in the West*. Albany, N.Y.: Hoffman and White, 1834.

Priest, Loring Benson. *Uncle Sam's Stepchildren: The Reformation of United States Indian Policy, 1865–1887*. New Brunswick, N.J.: Rutgers University Press, 1942.

Prucha, Francis Paul. *American Indian Policy in Crisis: Christian Reformers and the Indian, 1865–1900*. Norman: University of Oklahoma Press, 1976.

———. *American Indian Policy in the Formative Years: The In-*

dian Trade and Intercourse Acts, 1790–1834. Cambridge: Harvard University Press, 1962.

———. *Lewis Cass and American Indian Policy.* Detroit: Wayne State University Press, 1967.

Reining, Priscilla, ed. *Kinship Studies in the Morgan Centennial Year.* Washington D.C.: The Anthropological Society of Washington, 1972.

Resek, Carl. *Lewis Henry Morgan: American Scholar.* Chicago: University of Chicago Press, 1960.

Robertson, William. *The History of the Discovery and Settlement of America,* 2 vols. 1777. Reprint. Edinburgh: J. Robinson, 1785.

Romans, Bernard. *Concise Natural History of East and West Florida.* 1775. Reprint. Gainesville: University of Florida Press, 1962.

Rosenberg, Charles. *No Other Gods: On Science and American Social Thought.* Baltimore, Md.: Johns Hopkins University Press, 1976.

Rush, Benjamin. *An Inquiry into the Natural History of Medicine Among the Indians of North America: and A Comparative View of Their Diseases and Remedies With Those of Civilized Nations.* N.p.: N.p., 1774.

Satz, Ronald N. *American Indian Policy in the Jacksonian Era.* Lincoln: University of Nebraska Press, 1975.

Schiller, Francis. *Paul Broca: Founder of French Anthropology, Explorer of the Brain.* Berkeley: University of California Press, 1979.

Schneider, Louis, ed. *The Scottish Moralists On Human Nature and Society.* Chicago: University of Chicago Press, 1967.

Schoolcraft, Henry R. *An Address Delivered Before the Was-ah-Ho-de-no-son-ne, or New Confederacy of the Iroquois, August 14, 1846.* Rochester, N.Y.: Jerome & Bros., 1846.

———. *Algic Researches, Comprising Inquiries Respecting the Mental Characteristics of the North American Indians.* 2 vols. New York: Harper and Row, 1839.

———. *Constitution of the Algic Society, Instituted March 28, 1832.* Detroit: Cleland and Sawyer, 1833.

———. *A Discourse Delivered on the Anniversary of the Historical Society of Michigan.* Detroit: Geo. L. Whitney, 1830.

———. *Historical and Statistical Information respecting the History, Condition and Prospects of the Indian tribes of the United States,* 6 vols. Philadelphia: Lippincott, Grambo & Co., 1851–1857.

————. *Incentives to the Study of the Ancient Period of American History.* New York: Press of the Historical Society, 1847.

————. *The Literary Voyager or Muzzeniegun.* Edited by Philip P. Mason. East Lansing: Michigan State University Press, 1962.

————. *Narrative of an Expedition through the Upper Mississippi to Itasca Lake.* New York: Harper Brothers, 1834.

————. *Notes on the Iroquois.* Albany, N.Y.: Erastus H. Pease & Co., 1847.

————. *Oneota, or Characteristics of the Red Race of America. From Original Notes and Manuscripts.* New York: Wiley & Putnam, 1845.

————. *Oneota, or Characteristics of the Red Race of America. Their History, Traditions, Customs, Poetry, Picture-Writing . . . .* 8 nos. New York: Burgess, Stringer & Co., 1844–45.

————. *Personal Memoirs of a Residence of Thirty Years with the Indian Tribes on the American Frontiers.* Philadelphia: Lippincott & Grambo, 1851.

————. *Plan for the Investigation of American Ethnology.* New York: Edward O. Jenkins, 1846.

————. *The Red Race of America.* New York: W. H. Graham, 1847.

————. *Suggestions for Travellers Visiting the Ancient Sites of Indian Occupancy in America.* Washington D.C.: N.p., N.d.

————. *Travels in the Central Portions of the Mississippi Valley.* New York: Collins & Hannay, 1825.

————. *A View of the Lead Mines of Missouri.* New York: Charles Wiley, 1819.

Schoolcraft, Mary H. *The Black Gauntlet.* Philadelphia: Lippincott, 1860.

Seaver, J. E., ed. *Life of Mary Jeminson: Deh-he-wa-mis.* New York: Miller, 1856.

Seitz, Don C., ed. *Letters from Francis Parkman to E. G. Squier.* Cedar Rapids, Iowa: The Torch Press, 1911.

Sheehan, Bernard. *Savagism and Civility: Indians and Englishmen in Colonial Virginia.* New York: Oxford University Press, 1980.

Sheehan, Bernard. *Seeds of Extinction: Jeffersonian Philanthropy and the American Indian.* Chapel Hill: University of North Carolina Press, 1973.

Shryock, Richard Harrison. *The Development of Modern Medicine: An Interpretation of the Social and Scientific Factors Involved.* Philadelphia: University of Pennsylvania Press, 1936.

————. *Medicine and Society in America: 1660–1860.* Ithaca, N.Y.: Cornell University Press, 1960.

Silverberg, Robert. *Mound Builders of Ancient America: The Archaeology of a Myth.* Greenwich, Conn.: New York Graphic Society, 1968.

Slotkin, J. S. *Readings in Early Anthropology.* New York: Werner-Gren Foundation, 1965.

Smith, Ethan. *Views of the Hebrews; Exhibiting the Destruction of Jerusalem; the Certain Restoration of Judah and Israel; The Present State of Judah and Israel; and An Address of the Prophet Isaiah Relative to Their Restoration.* Poultney, Vt.: Smith & Shute, 1823.

Smith, James Morton, ed. *17th-Century America: Essays in Colonial History.* Chapel Hill: University of North Carolina Press, 1959.

Smith, Samuel Stanhope. *An Essay on the Causes of the Variety of Complexion and Figure in the Human Species.* Philadelphia: N.p., 1787.

———. *An Essay on the Causes of the Variety of Complexion and Figure in the Human Species.* Edited by Winthrop Jordan. Cambridge: Harvard University Press, 1965.

Spiro, Medford E., ed. *Context and Meaning in Cultural Anthropology.* New York: The Free Press, 1965.

Squier, Ephraim G. *Lecture on the Condition and True Interest of the Laboring Class of America, The Working Man's Miscellany.* Albany: New York State Mechanic and Cultivator, 1843.

———. *Nicaragua: Its People, Scenery, Monuments, and the Proposed Interoceanic Canal.* 2 vols. London: Longman, Brown, Green & Longman, 1852.

———. *Peru: Incidents of Travel and Exploration in the Land of the Incas.* New York: Harper & Brothers, 1877.

———. *The Serpent Symbol, and the Worship of the Reciprocal Principles of Nature in America,* American Archaeological Researches 1. New York: G. P. Putnam, 1851.

———. *Ancient Monuments of the Mississippi Valley.* Smithsonian Contribution to Knowledge 1. Washington D.C.: Smithsonian Institution, 1848.

Stanton, William. *The Leopard's Spots: Scientific Attitudes Toward Race in America 1815–59.* Chicago: University of Chicago Press, 1960.

Stepan, Nancy. *The Idea of Race in Science: Great Britain 1800–1900.* Hamden, Conn.: Archon Books, 1982.

Stern, Bernard. *Lewis Henry Morgan: Social Evolutionist.* Chicago: University of Chicago Press, 1931.

Stern, Madelein B. *Heads and Headlines: The Phrenological Fowlers.* Norman: University of Oklahoma Press, 1971.

Stevens, John Austin. *Albert Gallatin.* Boston: Houghton Mifflin Co., 1883.

Stocking, George W. Jr. *Race, Culture, and Evolution: Essays in the History of Anthropology.* New York: The Free Press, 1968.

————. *The Shaping of American Anthropology 1883–1911: A Franz Boas Reader.* New York: Basic Books, 1974.

Stoddard, Amos. *Sketches, Historical and Descriptive, of Louisiana.* Philadelphia: Mathew Carey, 1812.

Stone, William L. *The Life and Times of Red Jacket, or Sa-Go-Ye-Wat-Ha; Being the Sequel to the History of the Six Nations.* New York: Wiley & Putnam, 1841.

————. *Life of Joseph Brant-Thayendanegea,* 2 vols. New York: A. V. Blake, G. Dearborn, 1838.

Teggart, Frederick J. *Theory of History.* New Haven: Yale University Press, 1925.

Terray, Emmanuel. *Marxism and "Primitive" Societies.* Translated by Mary Klopper. New York: Monthly Review Press, 1972.

Thoresen, Timothy, ed. *Toward a Science of Man: Essays in the History of Anthropology.* The Hague: Mouton, 1975.

Thornbrough, Gayle, ed. *The Correspondence of John Badollet and Albert Gallatin 1804–1836,* Indiana Historical Society Publication 22. Indianapolis: Indiana Historical Society, 1963.

Tolles, Frederick B. *Meeting House and Counting House: The Quaker Merchants of Colonial Philadelphia 1682–1763.* New York: W. W. Norton, 1948.

Turner, James. *Reckoning with the Beast: Animals, Pain, and Humanity in the Victorian Mind.* Baltimore: Johns Hopkins University Press, 1980.

Van Amringe, William Frederick. *An Investigation of the Theories of the Natural History of Man, by Lawrence, Prichard, and Others. Founded upon Animal Analogies and an Outline of a New Natural History of Man, Founded upon History, Anatomy, Physiology, and Human Analogies.* New York: Baker & Scribner, 1848.

Viola, Herman J. *Thomas L. McKenney: Architect of America's Early Indian Policy 1816–1830.* Chicago: Swallow Press, 1974.

Voget, Fred W. *A History of Ethnology.* New York: Holt, Rinehart & Winston, 1975.

Volney, C. F. *View of the Climate and Soil of the United States of America: to which are annexed Some Accounts of Florida, The*

French Colony on the Scioto, Certain Canadian Colonies, and the Savages or Natives. London: C. Mercier, 1804.

Walters, Raymond, Jr. *Albert Gallatin: Jeffersonian Financier and Diplomat.* New York: Macmillan, 1957.

Walters, Ronald G. *American Reformers, 1815–1860.* New York: Hill & Wang, 1978.

———. *Primers for Prudery.* Englewood Cliffs: Prentice Hall, 1974.

Washburn, Wilcomb E. *The Indian in America.* New York: Harper & Row, 1975.

———. *Red Man's Land White Man's Law: A Study of the Past and Present Status of the American Indian.* New York: Charles Scribner's Sons, 1971.

Wauchope, Robert. *Lost Tribes and Sunken Continents: Myth and Method in the Study of American Indians.* Chicago: University of Chicago Press, 1962.

Weiner, Philip P. and Aaron Noland, eds. *Roots of Scientific Thought: A Cultural Perspective.* New York: Basic Books, 1957.

White, Charles. *An Account of the Regular Gradation in Man, and in Different Animals and Vegetables; and from the Former to the Latter.* London: C. Dilly, 1799.

White, Leslie A., ed. *Pioneers in American Anthropology: The Bandelier-Morgan Letters 1873–1883,* 2 vols. Albuquerque: University of New Mexico Press, 1940.

Willey, Gordon and Jeremy Sabloff. *A History of American Archaeology.* San Francisco: W. H. Freeman & Co., 1974.

Williams, Roger. *A Key into the Language of America.* Edited by John Teunissen and Evelyn J. Hinz. 1643. Reprint. Detroit: Wayne State University Press, 1973.

Williams, Samuel. *The Natural and Civil History of Vermont.* Walpole, N.H.: I. Thomas & D. Carlish, 1794.

Williamson, Hugh. *Observations on the Climate in Different Parts of America, Compared with the Climate in Corresponding Parts of the Other Continent, to which are added, Remarks on the Different Complexions of the Human Race; with some account of the Aborigines of America.* New York: T. &. J. Swords, 1811.

Woodford, Frank B. *Lewis Cass: The Last Jeffersonian.* New Brunswick, N.J.: Rutgers University Press, 1950.

Yard, Robert Sterling. *Our Federal Lands: A Romance of American Development.* New York: Charles Scribner's Sons, 1928.

Young, Robert M. *Mind, Brain, and Adaptation in the Nineteenth*

Century: Cerebral Localization and Its Biological Context from Gall to Ferrier. Oxford: Clarendon Press, 1970.

ARTICLES

A. B. "To the Editor." *North American Review* 1 (1815): 21–22.

Ackerknecht, Erwin H. "Elisha Bartlett and the Philosophy of the Paris Clinical School." *Bulletin of the History of Medicine* 24 (1950): 43–60.

———. "George Forster, Alexander von Humboldt, and Ethnology." *Isis* 46 (1955): 83–95.

Adams, Ann. "Early Days at Red River Settlement, and Fort Snelling: Reminiscences of Mrs. Ann Adams." Edited by William J. Fletcher. *Collections of the Minnesota Historical Society* 6 (1894): 75–115.

"Administration of Indian Affairs." *Democratic Review* 18 (1846): 333–36.

"Albert Gallatin." *Cyclopedia of American Literature.* Edited by Evart A. Duyckinck and L. George. New York: Scribner, 1866. 1:492–95.

"Albert Gallatin: Autobiography, 1798." *Collections of the Maine Historical Society* 6 (1859): 93–103.

[Review of] *American Antiquities, and Researches into the Origin and History of the Red Race.* In *New-York Review* 10 (January 1842): 88, 91–92.

Atwater, Caleb. "Description of the Antiquities Discovered in the State of Ohio and Other Western States." *American Antiquarian Society Transactions and Collections* 1 (1820): 105–299.

Barnes, J. A. "Anthropology in Britain Before and After Darwin." *Mankind* 5 (July 1960): 369–85.

Barton, Benjamin Smith. "Essay Toward a Natural History of the North American Indian." *Dissertations of the Royal Medical Society of Edinburgh* 23 (1788–89): 1–17.

———. "Observations and Conjectures concerning certain Articles which were taken out of an ancient Tumulus, or Grave, at Cincinnati, in the County of Hamilton, and Territory of the United-States, North-West of the River Ohio: in a letter from Benjamin Smith Barton to the Reverend Joseph Priestly, LLD FR etc." *Transactions of the American Philosophical Society* 4 (1799): 181–215.

Beaver, R. Pierce. "Church, State and the Indians: Indian Missions in the New Nation." *Journal of Church and State* 4 (May 1962): 11–30.

Bieder, Robert E. "The Grand Order of the Iroquois: Influences on Lewis Henry Morgan's Ethnology." *Ethnohistory* 27 (Fall 1980): 349–61.

———. "Scientific Attitudes Towards Mixed-Bloods in Early Nineteenth-Century America." *Journal of Ethnic Studies* 8 (Summer 1980): 17–30.

Bowdin, James. "A Philosophical Discourse Publickly Addressed to the American Academy of Arts and Sciences." *Memoirs of the American Academy of Arts and Sciences* 1 (1785): 1–20.

[Bowen, Francis]. Review of *Historical and Statistical Information respecting the History, Condition, and Prospects of the Indian Tribes of the United States . . . .* In *North American Review* 77 (July 1853): 243–62.

Bremer, Richard G. "Henry Rowe Schoolcraft: Explorer in the Mississippi Valley, 1818–1832." *Wisconsin Magazine of History* 66 (Autumn 1982): 40–59.

[Burke, Luther]. "Progress of Ethnology in the United States." *The Literary World* 3 (September 23, 1848): 663.

Carpenter, Edmund S. "The Role of Archaeology in the 19th Century Controversy between Developmentalism and Degeneration." *Pennsylvania Archaeologist* 20 (1950): 5–18.

[Cass, Lewis]. Review of *Documents and Proceedings relating to the Formation and Progress of a Board in the City of New York, for the Emigration, Preservation, and Improvement of the Aborigines of America.* In *North American Review* 30 (1830): 62–121.

———. Review of *Indian Treaties, and Laws and Regulations relating to Indian Affairs; to which is added an Appendix, containing the Proceedings of the Old Congress, and Other important State Papers in relation to Indian Affairs. Compiled and published under the Orders of the Department of War.* In *North American Review* 24 (1827): 365–442.

———. Review of *Manners and Customs of several Indian Tribes, located west of the Mississippi, including some Account of the Soil, Climate and Vegetable Productions; and the Indian Materia Medica; to which is prefixed the History of the Author's Life, during a Residence of several Years among them.* By John Hunter. *Historical Notes respecting the Indians of North America, with Remarks on Attempts made to convert and civilise them.* By John H. Halkett, Esq. In *North American Review* 22 (1826): 53–119.

————. Review of *A Narrative of the Captivity and Adventures of John Tanner (United States' Interpreter at the Sault Ste. Marie) during thirty years residence among the Indians, in the interior of North America*. In *American Quarterly Review* 8 (1830): 108–34.

————. Review of *Travels in the Central Portions of the Mississippi Valley; comprising Observations on its Mineral Geography, Internal Resources, and Aboriginal Population*. By Henry R. Schoolcraft. *A Vindication of the Rev. Mr. Heckewelder's History of the Indian Nations*. By William Rawle. In *North American Review* 26 (1828): 357–403.

Chinard, Gilbert. "Eighteenth Century Theories on America as a Human Habitat." *Proceedings of the American Philosophical Society* 91 (1947): 27–55.

————. "Jefferson and the American Philosophical Society." *Proceedings of the American Philosophical Society* 87 (1943): 263–76.

Clinton, DeWitt. "A Discourse Delivered Before the New-York Historical Society, 6 December 1811." *Collections of the New-York Historical Society* 2 (1814): 37–116.

Coates, B. H. "Annual Discourse, Delivered Before the Historical Society of Pennsylvania . . . On the Origin of the Indian Population of America." *Memoirs of the Pennsylvania Historical Society* 3 (1836): 3–63.

Cole, Richard G. "Sixteenth-Century Travel Books as a Source of European Attitudes Toward Non-White and Non-Western Culture." *Proceedings of the American Philosophical Society*, 116 (1972): 59–67.

Coleman, Michael C. "Not Race, but Grace: Presbyterian Missionaries and American Indians, 1837–1893." *Journal of American History* 67 (June 1980): 41–60.

Combe, George. Review of *Crania Americana . . . .* In *The American Journal of Science and Arts* 38 (1840): 341–75.

Count, Earl W. "The Evolution of the Race Idea in Modern Western Culture during the Period of the Pre-Darwinian Nineteenth Century." *Transactions of the New York Academy of Sciences* 8, n.s. (1946): 139–65.

[Review of] *Crania Americana*. In *American Phrenological Journal and Miscellany* 2 (1839): 143–44.

[Review of] *Crania Americana*. In *North American Review* 51 (1840): 173–86.

Du Ponceau, Peter S. "Correspondence between Mr. Heckewelder and Mr. Du Ponceau, on the Language of the American

Indian." *Transactions of the American Philosophical Society* 1 (1819): 351–448.

Edgerton, Franklin. "Notes on Early American Work in Linguistics." *Proceedings of the American Philosophical Society* 87 (1943): 25–34.

Erickson, Paul. "Phrenology and Physical Anthropology: The George Combe Connection." *Current Anthropology* 18 (1977): 92–93.

Fenton, William N. "Answers to Governor Cass's Questions by Jacob Jameson, A Seneca [ca. 1821–1825]." *Ethnohistory* 16 (Spring 1969): 113–39.

Fortes, Meyer. "Kinship and the Social Order: The Legacy of L. H. Morgan." *Current Anthropology*, 13 (1972): 285–96.

Freeman, John F. "The Indian Convert: Theme and Variation." *Ethnohistory*, 12 (1965): 113–128.

————. "Religion and Personality in the Anthropology of Henry Schoolcraft." *Journal of the History of the Behavioral Sciences*, 1 (1965): 301–312.

Gallatin, Albert. "Introduction to Hale's Indians of North-west America, and Vocabularies of North America." *Transactions of the American Ethnological Society* 2 (1848): xxiii–clxxxviii.

————. "Notes on the Semi-civilized Nations of Mexico, Yucatan, and Central America." *Transactions of the American Ethnological Society* 1 (1845): 1–352.

————. "A Synopsis of the Indian Tribes of North America." *Transactions and Collections of the American Antiquarian Society* 2 (1836): 1–422.

————. [Review of] George Catlin's *Letters and Notes on the Manners, Customs and Conditions of the North American Indians*. Alexander W. Bradford's *American Antiquities and Researches* . . . . In *New York Review* 10 (April 1842): 419–48.

George, Katherine. "The Civilized West Looks at Primitive Africa 1400–1800." *Isis* 49 (1958): 62–72.

Gibson, Charles. "Lewis Henry Morgan and the Aztec 'Monarchy.'" *Southwestern Journal of Anthropology* 35 (1947): 78–84.

Gilbert, Mrs. Thomas D. "Memoirs of the Soo." *Michigan Pioneer and Historical Collections* 30 (1903): 623–33.

Goddard, Pliny Earle. "The Present Condition of Our Knowledge of North American Languages." *American Anthropologist* 16, n.s. (1914): 555–601.

Goetzmann, William H. "The West and the American Age of Exploration." *Arizona and the West* 2 (Autumn 1960): 265–78.

Gould, Stephen Jay. "Morton's Ranking of Races by Cranial Capacity: Unconscious manipulations of data may be a scientific norm." *Science* 200 (May 5, 1978): 503–509.

———. "Nasty Little Facts." *Natural History* 94 (February 1985): 14–25.

Gray, Philip Howard. "The Early Animal Behaviorists: Prolegomenon to Ethnology." *Isis* 59 (Winter 1968): 372–83.

Greene, John C. "Some Early Speculations on the Origin of Human Races." *American Anthropologist* 56 (1954): 31–41.

Haas, Mary R. "Grammar or Lexicon? The American Indian Side of the Question from Du Ponceau to Powell." *International Journal of American Linguistics* 35 (July 1969): 239–55.

[Hale, Edward E.] "Memoirs of the Life of Gallatin." *Proceedings of the American Antiquarian Society* (1850): 16–31.

Harrison, William Henry. "A Discourse on the Aborigines of the Valley of the Ohio." *Transactions of the Historical and Philosophical Society of Ohio* 1 (1839): 219–67.

Hoebel, E. Adamson. "William Robertson: An 18th Century Anthropologist-Historian." *American Anthropologist* 62 (1960): 648–55.

Horsman, Reginald. "Scientific Racism and the American Indian in the Mid-Nineteenth Century." *American Quarterly* 27 (1975): 152–68.

Hoyme, Lucile E. "Physical Anthropology and Its Instruments: An Historical Study." *Southwestern Journal of Anthropology* 9 (1953): 408–30.

Hrdlicka, Ales. "Contribution to the History of Physical Anthropology in the United States of America: With Special Reference to Philadelphia." *Proceedings of the American Philosophical Society* 87 (1943): 61–64.

Hudson, Charles. "James Adair as Anthropologist." *Ethnohistory* 24 (Fall 1977): 311–28.

Joyce, William L. "Antiquarians and Archaeologists: The American Antiquarian Society, 1812–1912." *Proceedings of the American Antiquarian Society* 91 (1982): 306–307.

Kerber, Linda K. "The Abolitionist Perception of the Indian." *Journal of American History* 62 (1975): 271–95.

Lurie, Edward. "Louis Agassiz and the Races of Man." *Isis* 45 (1954): 227–42.

Lurie, Nancy Oestreich. "The Lady from Boston and the Omaha Indians." *American West* 3 (Fall 1966): 31–33, 80–85.

McIlvaine, Josiah Hall. "The Life and Work of Lewis Henry Morgan: An Address at His Funeral." *Rochester Historical Society Publications* 2 (1923): 47–60.

Madison, James. "A Letter on the supposed Fortifications of the Western Country, from Bishop Madison of Virginia to Doctor Barton." *Transactions of the American Philosophical Society 6*, pt. 1 (1804): 132–42.

Marsden, Michael T. "Henry Rowe Schoolcraft: A Reappraisal." *The Old Northwest: A Journal of Regional Life and Letters* 2 (1976): 153–82.

Mitchell, Samuel L. "Communications from Dr. Samuel L. Mitchell." *Transactions and Collections of the American Antiquarian Society* 1 (1820): 313–54.

Molella, Arthur P. and Nathan Reingold. "Theorists and Ingenious Mechanics: Joseph Henry Defines Science." *Science Studies* 3 (1973): 323–51.

Monette, J. W. "Indian Mounds; or, American Monuments, in the South-West." *South-Western Journal: A Magazine of Science, Literature and Miscellany* 1 (1838): 228–31.

Morgan, Lewis H. "Architecture of the American Aborigines." *Johnson's New Universal Cyclopedia* 1 (New York: A. J. Johnson & Son, 1875): 217–29.

———. "Athenian Democracy." *The New-York Quarterly* 2 (1853): 341–67.

———. "Factory System for the Indians." *The Nation* 23 (July 27, 1876): 58–59.

———. "The Hue and Cry Against the Indians." *The Nation* 23 (July 20, 1876): 40–41.

———. "The Indian Question in 1878." *The Nation* 27 (November 28, 1878): 332–333.

———. [Review of] *Instinct: Its Office in the Animal Kingdom . . . .* In *The Nation* 14 (May 2, 1872): 291–92.

———. "Laws of Descent of the Iroquois." *Proceedings of the American Association for the Advancement of Science* 11 (1858): 132–48.

———. "Letters on the Iroquois Addressed to Gallatin." *American Whig Review* 5 (1847): 177–90, 242–57, 447–61; 6 (1848): 477–90, 626–33.

———. "Montezuma's Dinner." *North American Review* 122 (1876): 265–308.

———. "On the Ruins of a Stone Pueblo on the Animas River, in New Mexico; with a Ground Plan." *Peabody Museum of American Archaeology and Ethnology, Twelfth Annual Report* 2 (1880): 536–56.

————. "The 'Seven Cities of Cibola.'" *North American Review* 108 (1869): 457–98.

————. "A Study of the Houses of the American Aborigines with suggestions for the exploration of the ruins in New Mexico, Arizona, the Valley of the San Juan, and in Yucatan and Central America under the auspices of the Archaeological Institute." *Archaeological Institute of America. Annual Report* 1 (1879–80): 27–80.

————. "Vision of Kar-is-ta-gi-a, a Sachem of the Cayuga." *Knickerbocker* 24 (1844): 238–45.

Morton, Samuel G. "Account of A Craniological Collection; with Remarks on the Classification of Some Families of the Human Race." *Transactions of the American Ethnological Society* 2 (1842): 217–22.

————. "Analysis of Tabular Spar, from Bucks County, Penna." *Journal of the Academy of Natural Sciences of Philadelphia* 6 (1829): 46–49.

————. "Description of a new fossil species of Ostrea." *Journal of the Academy of Natural Sciences of Philadelphia* 6 (1829): 50–51.

————. "Description of the Fossil Shells which characterize the Atlantic Secondary Formation of New Jersey and Delaware." *Journal of the Academy of Natural Sciences of Philadelphia* 6 (1829): 72–100.

————. "Description of two new species of Shells of the genera Scaphites and Crepidula; with some observations on the Ferruginous Sand, Plastic Clay, and Upper Marine formations of the United States." *Journal of the Academy of Natural Sciences of Philadelphia* 6 (1829): 107–19.

————. "Note: containing a notice of some Fossils recently discovered in New Jersey." *Journal of the Academy of Natural Sciences of Philadelphia* 6 (1829): 120–28.

————. "Study of Ancient Crania," *The Boston Medical and Surgical Journal* 31 (1844): 422–23.

Muzzey, David S. "Gallatin, Abraham Alfonse Albert." *Dictionary of American Biography* 4 (1960): 103–10.

Nash, Gary. "The Image of the Indian in the Southern Colonial Mind." *William & Mary Quarterly* 29 (April 1972): 197–230.

Nott, J. C. "Unity of the Human Race." *Southern Quarterly Review* 9 (1846): 1–56.

Odom, Herbert H. "Generalizations on Race in Nineteenth-Century Physical Anthropology." *Isis* 58 (1967): 5–18.

"On the Aborigines of the Western Country." *The Port Folio* 1

(June 1816): 457–63.

Parkman, Francis. Review of *The Serpent Symbol and the Worship of the Reciprocal Principles of Nature in America.* By E. G. Squier. *Christian Examiner* 51 (1851): 140–41.

Parssinen, T. M. "Popular Science and Society: The Phrenology Movement in Early Victorian Britain." *Journal of Social History* 8 (1974): 1–20.

Pickering, John. "Remarks on the Indian Languages of North America." *Encyclopedia Americana* 6 (1831): 581–600.

Piggott, Stuart. "Prehistory and the Romantic Movement." *Antiquity* 11 (1937): 31–38.

Powell, John W. "Indian Linguistic Families of America North of Mexico." *Seventh Annual Report of the Bureau of American Ethnology* (1885–86): 1–142.

———. "Sketch of Lewis H. Morgan." *Popular Science Monthly* 18 (December 1880): 114–21.

Prucha, Francis Paul. "Andrew Jackson's Indian Policy: A Reassessment." *Journal of American History* 56 (1969): 527–39.

Prucha, Francis Paul and Donald F. Carmony, eds. "A Memorandum of Lewis Cass: Concerning a System for the Regulation of Indian Affairs." *Wisconsin Magazine of History* 52 (1968): 35–50.

Putnam, Frederick Ward. "Sketch of Hon. Lewis H. Morgan." *Proceedings of the American Academy of Arts and Sciences* 9 (1882): 429–36.

Reed, Eugene E. "The Ignoble Savage." *The Modern Language Review* 59 (1964): 53–64.

"Reports of Societies." *Literary World* 8 (1851): 371–74.

[Review of] *A Report to the Secretary of War of the U.S. on Indian Affairs. . . .* By Rev. Jedidiah Morse in *North American Review* 16 (1823): 30–45.

Ryding, James N. "Alternatives in Nineteenth-Century German Ethnology: A Case Study in the Sociology of Science." *Sociologus* 25 (1975): 1–28.

[Schoolcraft, Henry R.] Review of *Archaeologia Americana: Transactions and Collections of the American Antiquarian Society* 2; *Inquiries respecting the History, Traditions, Languages, within the United States.* By Lewis Cass. In *North American Review* 45 (1837): 34–59.

———. Review of *La Découverte des Sources du Mississippi et de la Rivière Sanglante . . . .* By J. C. Beltrami. In *North American Review* 27 (1828): 89–114.

———. "Ethnological Sketch of the North American Indians." *American Quarterly Register and Magazine* 1 (1848): 169–77.

———. Review of *Letters and Notes on the Manners, Customs, and Condition of the North American Indians.* By George Catlin. *American Antiquities and Researches into the Origin and History of the Red Race.* By Alexander W. Bradford. In *North American Review* 54 (1842): 283–99.

———. "Memoir of John Johnston." Edited by J. Sharpless Fox. *Collections of the Michigan Pioneer and Historical Society* 36 (1908): 53–94.

———. "Mythology, Superstitions and Languages of the North American Indians." *Literary and Theological Review* 2 (1835): 96–121.

———. "Observations Respecting the Grave Creek Mound in Western Virginia." *Transactions of the American Ethnological Society* 1 (1845): 366–420.

———. "Our Indian Policy." *Democratic Review* 14 (1844): 169–84.

———. "Plan for the Investigation of American Ethnology . . . ." *Annual Report of the Board of Regents of the Smithsonian Institution, July 1885* (1886): 907–14.

———. Review of *Proceedings and Fourteenth Annual Report of the Board of Managers of the Baptist General Convention, at the Meetings held in New York, April 1828; A Discourse on the Occasion of Forming the African Mission School Society, delivered in Christ Church in Hartford, Conn. on Sunday Evening, August 10, 1828.* In *North American Review* 28 (1829): 354–68.

Semenov, I. I. "The Doctrine of Morgan, Marxism and Contemporary Ethnography." *Soviet Anthropology and Archaeology* 4 (1965): 3–15.

Service, Elman R. "The Mind of Lewis H. Morgan." *Current Anthropology* 22 (1981): 25–43.

Shryock, Richard H. "The Advent of Modern Medicine in Philadelphia, 1800–1850." *Yale Journal of Biology and Medicine* 13 (1941): 715–38.

———. "Trends in American Medical Research During the Nineteenth Century." *Proceedings of the American Philosophical Society* 91 (1947): 58–63.

Smith, Raoul N. "The Interest in Language and Languages in Colonial and Federal America." *Proceedings of the American Philosophical Society* 123 (1979): 29–46.

Squier, E. G. "American Ethnology: Being a Summary of Some of the Results Which Have Followed the Investigation of this Subject." *American Review* 3, n.s. (1849): 385–98.

———. "Historical and Mythological Traditions of the Algonquins." *American Review* 3, n.s. (1849): 273–93.

———. "Manabozho and the Great Serpent." *American Review: A Whig Journal* 8 (1848): 392–98.

———. "Ne-She-Kay-Be-Nais, or the 'Lone Bird.'" *American Review: A Whig Journal* 8 (1848): 255–59.

———. "New Mexico and California." *American Review* 2, n.s. (1848): 503–28.

———. "Observations on the Aboriginal Monuments of the Mississippi Valley." *Transactions of the American Ethnological Society* 2 (1848): 131–207.

———. "Observations on the Archaeology and Ethnology of Nicaragua." *Transactions of the American Ethnological Society* 3 (1853): 85–158.

———. "Observations on the Uses of the Mounds of the West With an Attempt at their Classification." *American Journal of Science and Arts.* 3, n.s. (1847): 237–49.

———. "Proceedings Preliminary to the Organization of the Anthropological Institution of New-York." *Journal of the Anthropological Institute of New-York* 1 (1871–72): 14–20.

Stewart, T. D. and Marshall T. Newman. "An Historical Résumé of the Concept of Difference in Indian Types." *American Anthropologist* 53 (1951): 19–36.

"Study of Ancient Crania." *The Boston Medical and Surgical Journal* 31 (1844): 422–23.

Sturtevant, William C., ed. "John Ridge on Cherokee Civilization in 1826." *Journal of Cherokee Studies* 6 (Fall 1981): 79–91.

Temkin, Owsei. "Gall and the Phrenological Movement." *Bulletin of the History of Medicine* 21 (May–June 1947): 275–321.

Thomas, Cyrus. "Report on the Mound Explorations of the Bureau of Ethnology." *Twelfth Annual Report of the Bureau of American Ethnology for the Years 1890–1891* (1894).

Tolstoy, P. "Morgan and Soviet Anthropological Thought." *American Anthropologist* 54, n.s. (1952): 8–17.

Tooker, Elisabeth. "Isaac N. Hurd's Ethnographic Studies of the Iroquois: Their Significance and Ethnographic Value." *Ethnohistory* 27 (Fall 1980): 363–69.

Trigger, Bruce J. "Sir Daniel Wilson: Canada's First Anthropologist." *Anthropologica* 8 (1966): 14–17.

U.S. Congress. "Message from the President of the United States to the Two Houses of Congress . . . December 7, 1830." 21st Cong., 2d Sess., 1830.

"Unity of the Human Race." *American Whig Review* 12 (1850): 567–86.

Walters, Raymond, Jr. "The Making of a Financier: Albert Gallatin in the Pennsylvania Assembly." *Pennsylvania Magazine of History and Biography* 70 (1946): 258–69.

Washburn, Wilcomb E. "Indian Removal Policy: Administrative, Historical and Moral Criteria for Judging Its Success or Failure." *Ethnohistory* 12 (Summer 1965): 274–78.

Weber, Gay. "Science and Society in Nineteenth Century Anthropology." *History of Science* 12 (1974): 260–83.

Weisenburger, Francis P. "Caleb Atwater: Pioneer Politician and Historian." *Ohio Historical Quarterly* 68 (1959): 18–37.

Welter, Rush. "The Idea of Progress in America." *Journal of the History of Ideas* 14 (1955): 401–15.

White, Leslie A. "The Correspondence Between Lewis Henry Morgan and Joseph Henry." *University of Rochester Library Bulletin* 12 (Winter 1957): 17–22.

———. "How Morgan Came to Write Systems of Consanguinity and Affinity," *Papers of the Michigan Academy of Science, Arts and Letters* 42 (1957): 261–62.

———, ed. "Lewis H. Morgan's Journal of a Trip to Southwest Colorado and New Mexico." *American Antiquity* 8 (1942): 1–26.

White, Richard. "The Winning of the West: The Expansion of the Western Sioux in the Eighteenth and Nineteenth Centuries." *Journal of American History* 65 (1978): 319–43.

Wilson, Daniel. "Physical Anthropology." *Annual Report of the Board of Regents of the Smithsonian Institution for 1862* (1863): 240–302.

Zirkle, Conway. "Father Adam and the Races of Man: Some Notes on Medieval Anthropology." *Journal of Heredity* 45 (1954): 29–34.

DISSERTATIONS

Erickson, Paul Alfred. "The Origins of Physical Anthropology." Ph.D. diss., University of Connecticut, Storrs, 1974.

Freeman, John F. "Henry Rowe Schoolcraft." Ph.D. diss., Harvard University, Cambridge, 1960.

Hildebrandt, Hans-Jürgen. "Der Evolutionismus in der Familienforschung des 19. Jahrhunderts. Ansätze einer allgemeinen, historisch orientierten Theorie der Familie bei Johann Jakob Bachofen, John Ferguson McLennan und Lewis Henry Morgan." Ph.D. diss., Johannes Gutenberg-Universität, Mainz, 1981.

Tax, Thomas G. "The Development of North American Archeology 1800–1879." Ph.D. diss., University of Chicago, Chicago, 1973.

Index